THE "NOCTURNAL SIDE OF SCIENCE"
IN DAVID FRIEDRICH STRAUSS'S *LIFE
OF JESUS CRITICALLY EXAMINED*

Society of Biblical Literature

Emory Studies in Early Christianity

Vernon K. Robbins, General Editor
David B. Gowler, General Editor
Bart B. Bruehler, Associate Editor
Robert H. von Thaden Jr., Associate Editor
Richard S. Ascough
Juan Hernández Jr.
Susan E. Hylen
Brigitte Kahl
Mikeal C. Parsons
Christopher C. Rowland
Russell B. Sisson
Elaine M. Wainwright

Number 17

THE "NOCTURNAL SIDE OF SCIENCE" IN DAVID FRIEDRICH STRAUSS'S *LIFE OF JESUS CRITICALLY EXAMINED*

Thomas Fabisiak

SBL Press
Atlanta

Copyright © 2015 by SBL Press

Publication of this volume was made possible by the generous support of the Pierce Program in Religion of Oxford College of Emory University.

The editors of this volume express their sincere gratitude to David E. Orton and Deo Publishing for publication of this series 2009–2013.

All rights reserved. No part of this work may be reproduced or transmitted in any form or by any means, electronic or mechanical, including photocopying and recording, or by means of any information storage or retrieval system, except as may be expressly permitted by the 1976 Copyright Act or in writing from the publisher. Requests for permission should be addressed in writing to the Rights and Permissions Office, SBL Press, 825 Houston Mill Road, Atlanta, GA 30329 USA.

Library of Congress Cataloging-in-Publication Data

Fabisiak, Thomas.
  The "nocturnal side of science" in David Friedrich Strauss's Life of Jesus critically examined / By Thomas Fabisiak.
      p. cm. — (Society of Biblical Literature Emory studies in early Christianity ; 17)
  Originally presented as the author's thesis (doctoral)—Emory University, 2014.
  Includes bibliographical references and index.
  ISBN 978-1-62837-108-6 (paper binding : alk. paper) — ISBN 978-1-62837-110-9 (electronic format) — ISBN 978-1-62837-109-3 (hardcover binding : alk. paper)
  1. Strauss, David Friedrich, 1808–1874. Das leben Jesu. 2. Jesus Christ—Biography. I. Title.
  BT301.S73F33 2015
  230.092—dc23   2015005710

Cover design is an adaptation by Bernard Madden of Rick A. Robbins, Mixed Media (19" x 24" pen and ink on paper, 1981). Online: http://home.comcast.net/~rick1216/Archive/1981penink.htm. Cover design used by permission of Deo Publishing.

Printed on acid-free, recycled paper conforming to
ANSI/NISO Z39.48-1992 (R1997) and ISO 9706:1994
standards for paper permanence.

Contents

Acknowledgments vii
Abbreviations ix

Introduction 1

1. Strauss on the Science of the Nocturnal Side of Nature 23

2. The Nocturnal Side of Strauss's Historical Critique of
   Miracle Stories 69

3. Strauss on Myth and the Nocturnal Side of Nature 103

4. The Nocturnal Side of Christian and Modern Origins 141

Conclusion: Strauss's Visions of Modernity and Historical Science 177

Works Cited 199

Biblical Index 211
Modern Primary Sources Index 213
Modern Authors Index 217

Acknowledgements

I wish first to thank my Ph.D. dissertation committee, in whom I was unusually fortunate, for the environment where this manuscript originated. Professor Geoffrey Bennington and Professor Tina Pippin's comments and questions were crucial to the development of the manuscript. I am grateful for the time that they dedicated to reading and discussing my work, especially as my focus changed. I owe thanks above all to my co-chairs, Professor Jill Robbins and Professor Vernon Robbins. Jill Robbins has done more than anyone, through her teaching, her mentorship, and the example of her own work, to raise the standards to which I strive in thinking and writing. In my first semester at Emory, Vernon Robbins introduced me to the then unfamiliar landscape of eighteenth- and early nineteenth-century biblical criticism. Since then, his support, encouragement, and scholarly example have been invaluable to me. Vernon Robbins and Jill Robbins also deserve special thanks for the time that they dedicated to meeting with me during the final stages of the writing of the manuscript. I benefited from their knowledge and insight in these meetings, and I enjoyed our conversations. They trusted me to pursue the wayward course of my research and helped me draw it back within the realm of legibility. I am also highly grateful for the generous support of the Pierce program in Religion of Oxford College of Emory University, which made possible the publication of this volume.

I am deeply indebted to Professor Elisabeth Schüssler Fiorenza, who taught me to think critically about the discipline of biblical studies and encouraged me to imagine what it might be. For their guidance, example, and encouragement, I must also thank Professors Kim Haines-Eitzen, Nancy Bouzrara, Eric Reinders, Elizabeth Bounds, Deborah Ayer, Carol Newsom, and Carl Holladay. Conversations with Professors Yvonne Sherwood, Steven Kraftchick, and Sander Gilman also influenced the course of my research.

The students, teachers, and staff of the Candler Certificate in Theological Studies Program at Lee Arrendale Correctional Facility; the administration, graduate fellows, and undergraduate staff of the Emory Writing Center; the staff of the Emory Writing Program; and the staff of the Graduate Writing Support Service at Woodruff Library have all contributed to my intellectual and writerly development. My work in these contexts contributed to a number of the driving questions behind the manuscript.

Many friends deserve thanks for their important roles in my life and work as I completed this project. Conversations with Joseph Laycock and Catherine Morgan had a significant impact on the manuscript. Tiffany Hodge, Anne Dalphin, and George Dalphin provided essential moral support and intellectual inspiration. Christopher Keister, Regan Eldridge, Justin Roig, Susannah Laramee-Kidd, Joshua Laramee-Kidd, Leah Rosenberg, Jean-Paul Cauvin, David Morgen, Sarah Feuquay, and Steven Alvarez have been invaluable conversation partners and have generally been a blast to be around over the last few years. I have benefited as well from conversations and friendships with Samira Mehta, Cayenne Claassen-Luttner, Ingrid Lilly, Yoshimi Azuma, Janelle Peters, Letitia Campbell, Barry Sawicki, Christina Conroy, Cathy Zappa, Galen Richmond, Meggie Dant, Emily Brennan, Manuela Ceballos, Kelly Murphy, George Branch-Trevathan, Elizabeth Venell, Carl Hughes, Moira Diaz-French, Kate Wilkinson, Nate Hofer, Kazumi Hasegawa, Diana Louis, and Camila Restrepo. For her incredible support in the final stages of the project, I wish to thank Christy Bradley.

Lastly, I wish to thank my family, Kathleen Fox, Stan Fox, Susie Fox, and Seann Colgan, along with my best friend, Tyson Black. You deserve more gratitude than I can express. I am grateful for your support, of course, and patience, but also because I can see the influence of each of you in this work, which have been a consolation and an encouragement throughout the process.

I dedicate this book to my uncle and godfather, Raymond Fabisiak.

Abbreviations

ARA	*Annual Review of Anthropology*
CH	*Church History*
HLQ	*Huntington Library Quarterly*
JR	*Journal of Religion*
JWK	*Jahrbücher für wissenschaftliche Kritik*
LJ 1835	Strauss, David Friedrich. *Das Leben Jesu: Kritisch bearbeitet.* Vol. 1. Tübingen: Osiander, 1835.
LJ 1836	Strauss, David Friedrich. *Das Leben Jesu: Kritisch bearbeitet.* Vol. 2. Tübingen: Osiander, 1836.
LJ 1840	Strauss, David Friedrich. *Das Leben Jesu: Kritisch bearbeitet.* Vol. 2. Tübingen: Osiander, 1840.
LJ 1892	Strauss, David Friedrich. *The Life of Jesus Critically Examined.* Translated by George Eliot. New York: Macmillan, 1892. Translation of *Das Leben Jesu: Kritisch bearbeitet.* 2 vols. 4th rev. ed. Tübingen: Osiander, 1839–1840.
NLJ 1865	Strauss, David Friedrich. *A New Life of Jesus.* London: Williams & Norgate, 1865. Translation of *Das Leben Jesu: Für das deutsche Volk bearbeitet.* Leipzig: Brockhaus, 1864.
NTM	*Zeitschrift für Geschichte und Ethik der Naturwissenschaften, Techik, und Medizin*
NTS	*New Testament Studies*
OFN 1872	Strauss, David Friedrich. *The Old Faith and the New: A Confession.* Translated by Mathilde Blind. 2 vols. New York: Holt, 1873. Translation of *Der alte und der neue Glaube: Ein Bekentniss.* 6th edition. Leipzig: Hirzel, 1872.
OFN 1873	Strauss, David Friedrich. *Der alte und der neue Glaube: Ein Bekentniss.* 6th ed. Leipzig: Hirzel, 1872.
RH 19	*Revue d'histoire du XIXe siècle*

Streitschriften	Strauss, David Friedrich. *Die Evangelische Kirchenzeitung, die Jahrbücher für wissenschaftliche Kritik und die theologischen Studien und Kritiken in ihrer Stellung zu meiner kritischen Bearbeitbung des Lebens Jesu.* Vol. 3 of *Streitschriften zur Vertheidigung meiner Schrift über das Leben Jesu und zur Charakteristik der gegenwärtigen Theologie.* 3 vols. Tübingen: Osiander, 1837.

Introduction

Disenchantment and Exorcism in Early Nineteenth-Century Germany

In his 1869 autobiography, the German Reformed theologian Friedrich Wilhelm Krummacher relates an anecdote that he heard many years earlier from the romantic poet and physician, Justinus Kerner. The story concerns Frederike Hauffe née Wanner, who came under Kerner's care in 1826. Hauffe suffered from epileptic seizures and died young at the age of twenty-eight; she claimed she was attacked by demons and entered into ecstatic trances in which she diagnosed her ailments and communicated with the dead. In 1829, Kerner published an account of her illness and clairvoyant revelations, *The Seeress of Prevorst*,[1] in which he claimed that Hauffe's experiences offered scientific evidence of a rich pneumatic realm concealed in the natural order. The work was immensely popular. While some contemporaries regarded Kerner and Hauffe with disdain, many welcomed his research. Krummacher was one of a number of important figures at the time—Friedrich Wilhelm Joseph von Schelling, for example, Friedrich Schleiermacher, and David Friedrich Strauss—who visited Kerner in his home in Weinsberg. It was during this visit that Kerner described to him the following incident:

> A short time before, he allowed a celebrated theologian to accompany him to the sick-bed of the Seeress of Prevorst. There he granted him permission to try exorcism upon her in his own way. Approaching her bed in a ceremonial posture, [the theologian] began his demystification [*Entzauberung*] with this strange formula: "In the name of Reason, to which power is given over all specters; in the name of Science [*Wis-*

---

1. Justinus Kerner, *Die Seherin von Prevorst: Eröffnungen über das innere Leben des Menschen und über das Hereinragen einer Geisterwelt in die Unsere* (Stuttgart: Cotta, 1829).

senschaft] before whose light all deceptive images vanish; in the name of Christianity, which has purified the air of all evil spirits, I command you, demon who does not exist, depart from this sick woman!" She suddenly interrupted this solemn address and, in her crude Swabian dialect, she dealt the learned necromancer a flood of abuse, which included the delicate exclamation, "You human ass, you think I'm afraid of your filthy talk? Get out of here unless you want what's coming to you!" The noble exorcist hurried sheepishly away.[2]

In his 1834 *Accounts of the Modern Possessed*, Kerner records an incident that may have been the basis for the story. He describes how a "respected scholar" sought to rid a possessed woman under his care, an Anna U, of her demon. He declared the invader a "delusion" and a "non-entity" and ordered it to come out. The demon replied with a barrage of insults and complained that it was "an evil thing, that he should be called a delusion and a non-entity."[3]

If the story had some basis in fact, however, the telling is comical[4] and draws on an ancient narrative type whose roots can be traced to the Bible. In Acts 19, Luke narrates a similar incident in which the sons of the Jewish chief priest Sceva attempt to cast out a demon by appealing to "the name of Jesus in whom Paul preaches." The demon refuses to be exorcised and responds, "Jesus I know and Paul I know, but who are you?" (Acts 19:13-16).[5] It then compels its host to attack the would-be exorcists and chase them away. This tale became a *locus classicus* by which Christian writers in later centuries defined illegitimate religious practices as "magic."[6]

---

2. Friedrich Wilhelm Krummacher, *An Autobiography*, trans. M. G. Easton (New York: Carter & Brothers, 1869), 208–9 (translation modified); trans. of *Eine Selbstbiographie* (Berlin: Wiegandt & Grieben, 1869), 166.

3. Justinus Kerner with Carl August von Eschenmayer, *Geschichten Besessener neuerer Zeit: Beobachtungen aus dem Gebiete kakodaemonisch-magnetischer Erscheinungen nebst Reflexionen über Bessessenseyn und Zauber* (Stuttgart: Wachendorf, 1834), 100.

4. Krummacher adds that the incident "offered many an occasion for laughter, which repeated itself among us when Kerner narrated it in his drastic fashion" (*Autobiography*, 209).

5. This story drew in turn on older traditions about competing ritual specialists. In the story of the Exodus, for example, Moses and Aaron's miracles outstrip those of Pharaoh's magicians.

6. The story helped to define "magic" against "faith" or "religion" by distinguishing legitimate, faithful propitiation of Christ from attempts to coerce divine and pneu-

Kerner's story, like Luke's, defines his religious opponents as illegitimate representatives of a shared tradition. But he adapts this trope to his modern polemical aims. Kerner, a romantic, and Krummacher, a conservative preacher, objected to demystifying critics who rejected orthodox religious views. They opposed arguments against the truth of biblical miracles, for example, or the reality of demon possession. Krummacher plays on the valences of *Entzauberung* ("demystification" or "disenchantment") and caricatures demystifying assaults on religious belief as illegitimate versions of exorcism, failed attempts to dis-spell (*ent-zaubern*) a religious spirit. Kerner's scientific theologian must endure a rebuke, ironically, from a demon whose existence he denies. His story takes an old polemic against false religion and turns it against the critics who might have seen his own work as superstitious or magical.

We generally associate the rise of the modern, secular era with the "disenchantment of the world," the "*Entzauberung der Welt*," to use Max Weber's famous phrase.[7] Between the sixteenth and nineteenth centuries in the West, beliefs that rested on miracle and mystery were eclipsed by the conviction that nature could be subjected to rational control and calculation. Many traditional religious views faded under scientific scrutiny.[8] This rationalization and demystification was not a straightforward process, however. The relationship between science and faith or secularity and religion remained complex and tangled throughout the period. Kerner's anecdote illustrates this complexity. We might object to his insinuation that demystifying critique is a derivative form of esoteric religious practices. But the story points to the fact that distinctions between religion, science, reason, and superstition at the time were flexible. The very notion of "disenchantment" was contested.

---

matic beings or to appeal to their bare names. Christians associated the latter polemically with Jewish and pagan magical practices. Nevertheless such practices have their own rich history in Christian tradition. Luke's story in Acts 19 suggests as much—these practices may have occurred among followers of Jesus whom Luke did not count as members of his community.

7. "The fate of our times is characterized above all by rationalization and intellectualization and, above all, by the 'disenchantment of the world'" (Weber, "Science as Vocation," in *From Max Weber: Essays in Sociology*, trans. and ed. Hans Heinrich Gerth and C. Wright Mills [New York: Oxford, 1946], 155). Gerth and Mills add the quotation marks around "disenchantment of the world."

8. Thus in Weber's view, a modern scientist's integrity stands opposed to "pure religious devotion" (ibid.).

In nineteenth-century Germany, "science" (*Wissenschaft*) encompassed a wide range of disciplines—natural science, historical criticism of the Bible, and speculative philosophy, for example. These disciplines had in common the aim of analyzing their subject matter in a systematic, repeatable, and transparent fashion. But scientific disciplines did not spring forth fully-formed, nor did they univocally oppose "superstition" and religious mystification. On the contrary, they often took shape in the crucible of arcane religious controversies. Debates about demon possession offer a case in point. Fifty years before Kerner published the *Seeress of Prevorst*, the Catholic Priest Johann Joseph Gassner became famous throughout Germany by performing well-attended public exorcisms.[9] Gassner could appeal to hard, empirical evidence to justify his reputation. Even his most dedicated critics acknowledged the solid testimony that his successes as a healer presented. He faced his most significant challenge when Franz Anton Mesmer produced similar results without any mention of demons or devils. The medical historian Henri Ellenberger has claimed that this confrontation between Mesmer and Gassner represented the "fateful turning point from exorcism to dynamic psychotherapy."[10] But Mesmer's own theory of "animal magnetism"—the idea of an ethereal fluid that permeates the cosmos and bodies of living creatures and that could be manipulated by a physician—would soon come under scrutiny in its own right; ironically, it would eventually serve as the foundation for Kerner and others' defenses of the old ideas about demons and exorcism.

Kerner's writings on possession exemplify this enduring complexity in the early nineteenth century. Kerner, like Gassner, claimed that demons were real and appealed to empirical evidence. His 1834 *Accounts of the Modern Possessed* included a series of case studies of modern "demonomaniacs" with supplemental theoretical reflections by the philosopher and physician Carl August von Eschenmayer.[11] Although skeptics rejected

---

9. H. C. Erik Midelfort has considered Gassner's history as evidence for the significance of esoteric religious debates in the Enlightenment in *Exorcism and Enlightenment: Johann Joseph Gassner and the Demons of Eighteenth-Century Germany* (New Haven: Yale University Press, 2005).

10. Henri Ellenberger, *The Discovery of the Unconscious: The History and Evolution of Dynamic Psychotherapy* (New York: Basic Books, 1970), 57.

11. He includes two case studies of women he observed personally (Kerner and Eschenmayer, *Geschichten Besessener neuerer Zeit*, 20–103), along with supplemental

Kerner and Eschenmayer's conclusions, many admired his careful observations of human psychology and physiology. Ellenberger and other historians of psychiatry still credit him with helping to found the discipline.[12] Even a romantic and traditionalist in religious matters like Kerner could claim the mantle of science. Nor was he an isolated example. Kerner stood among an array of notable contemporaries who drew on Schelling's natural philosophy, Mesmer's theory of magnetism, or Etienne Esquirol's writings on "demonomania" to offer scientific justifications for esoteric and miraculous religious phenomena.

Kerner's anecdote also captures the fact that struggles between science and faith were struggles over spiritual authority, religious legitimacy, and the legacy of Christianity. Demystifying critics vied with orthodox theologians and folk preachers to show who could best mediate the truths of religion. Just as Kerner could claim to represent "science," it would not have been unusual for a critic of religion in his day to claim the mantle of "Christianity." Theologians and philosophers who undermined Christian doctrines regularly asserted that they were its most faithful representatives. "Criticism"—biblical, philosophical, or historical—outlined legitimate foundations for belief as much as it proscribed its illegitimate expressions. When Johann Semler argued that much of the biblical canon was not meant for modern believers, for example, he did so to demonstrate that it still contained a core of inspired, universal moral truth.[13] When Immanuel Kant set limits on what people could reasonably claim about God, he sought to protect personal faith from the incursions of rationalist analysis. When Georg Wilhelm Friedrich Hegel argued that philosophers, not theologians, were best prepared to grasp religious concepts, he explained that philosophy was the culmination of Christianity's core principles. In the dominant strains of eighteenth- and early nineteenth-century German philosophy, it was commonly believed that

---

notes by a Pastor Gerber, followed by summaries of four other modern cases of possession from 1559–1829 (pp. 104–23). Eschenmayer's reflections make up the bulk of the rest of the work.

12. Ellenberger writes, "In spite of their shortcomings, Kerner's investigations of the seeress were a milestone in the history of dynamic psychiatry" (*Discovery of the Unconscious*, 79).

13. Johannes Salomo Semler, *D. Joh. Salomo Semlers Abhandlung von freier Untersuchung des Canon*, 4 vols. (Halle: Hemmerde, 1771–1775).

modern, secular, or scientific disciplines and forms of life evolved out of the heart of Christianity.

Such arguments reflected a widespread belief that the European Enlightenment had manifested Christianity's own illuminating and disenchanting principles. When Kerner has his exorcist appeal to Christianity as a force "which has purified the air of all evil spirits," for example, he echoes the actual rhetoric of his contemporaries. In the forward to the 1830 edition of his *Encyclopedia of Philosophical Sciences*, Hegel presents precisely this image of demystification and exorcism. He complains that orthodox and Pietist Christians had sought to keep philosophy from laying any claim on Christian truths. But the very individuals who would excommunicate philosophers from the circle of legitimate Christians "have not carried their faith so far as to cast out devils"; he explains: "Instead, many of them, like those who have faith in the medium of Prevorst, are inclined to congratulate themselves about being on good terms with a mob of ghosts, of whom they stand in awe, instead of driving out and banishing these lies that belong to a servile and anti-Christian superstition."[14] Hegel, like Kerner, plays on the valences of "demystification," but to the opposite effect. The orthodox and Pietists in his day appeal to superstitious ideas about clairvoyants, ghosts, and exorcisms, but Christianity's real miracles are that it "drives out" and "banishes" these illusions. In his view, Christianity is from its inception and at its core a demystifying religion. When orthodox Christians refuse to think philosophically about God and divine things, they turn aside from the underlying principle of the religion that they claim: they "deliberately and scornfully disdain the elaboration of doctrine that is the foundation of the faith of the Christian church."[15] Like Luke's sons of Sceva or Kerner's exorcist, such Christians could appeal only to the bare "*name of the Lord Christ.*"[16] Thus the struggle between "philosophy" and "theology" is also a struggle about what Christianity is in its essence—and how it will define and be defined by a modern, secular, or rational age.

---

14. Georg Wilhelm Friedrich Hegel, *The Encyclopaedia Logic, with the Zusätze*, vol. 1 of *The Encyclopaedia of Philosophical Sciences with the Zusätze*, trans. Theodore F. Geraets, W. A. Suchting, and H. S. Harris (Indianapolis: Hackett, 1991), 19–20.
15. Ibid., 20.
16. Ibid., 19.

Strauss and the *Life of Jesus Critically Examined*

If Krummacher had been pressed to name an individual as the prototype for Kerner's rationalist exorcist, he would not likely have named Hegel, however, but one of his students, Strauss. Strauss was and remains best known for the two volumes of his *Life of Jesus Critically Examined* (1835–1836),[17] a pathbreaking piece of critical biblical scholarship and Hegelian philosophy. In this work, Strauss gathers together the most significant results of historical critical research on the Gospels over the preceding hundred-and-fifty years. He argues that the stories are "mythical" compositions with only a scanty basis in fact: the evangelists crafted narratives about Jesus long after his death from a well of ancient religious ideas. He undermines the dominant Enlightenment image of Jesus as a proto-modern, rational, and ethical teacher. His historical Jesus belongs to the milieu of first-century messianic Judaism—he is a deluded apocalyptic prophet who awaits God's imminent, dramatic intervention in the world. For Strauss as for his contemporaries, modern faith could not be based on such an alien, ancient figure. In the conclusion to the work, he argues consequently that the truth of the Gospels is not to be found in the person of Jesus, but in the ideas behind the narrative, which were primitive expressions of humanist philosophy. The Christian idea that God and humanity are reconciled is true, for Strauss, but this reconciliation did not occur in an individual person: it takes place in the totality of the human species over the course of its development. Humanity does not produce any supernatural miracles, but it demonstrates its "divine" quality in the great, historical wonders of science, industry, and culture.

The *Life of Jesus* generated a storm of controversy and had enormous literary success. Strauss intended the work only for trained theologians, but it soon became notorious among the broad sweep of educated Germans. Its readership surpassed that of contemporary works by Hegel and even Schleiermacher, for example. The work also had a significant influence on modern historical science. It shaped the historical critical study of the Gospels from Ernst Renan to Albert Schweitzer. Strauss showed that Hegelianism could be used in support of humanism and historical criti-

---

17. David Friedrich Strauss, *Das Leben Jesu: kritisch bearbeitet*, 2 vols. (Tübingen: Osiander, 1835–1836), cited hereafter as *LJ* 1835 and *LJ* 1836; idem, *The Life of Jesus Critically Examined*, trans. George Eliot (New York: Macmillan, 1892), cited hereafter as *LJ* 1892.

cism; the work stood alongside contemporary writings by Ludwig Feuerbach and Bruno Bauer,[18] for example, that influenced Karl Marx, Friedrich Nietzsche, and other critical readers of Hegel. His later works continued to be widely read, and he came to identify himself as a representative of the bourgeois reading public.[19] But it was the *Life of Jesus* that had defined him as a demystifying theologian *par excellence*. Krummacher was among those who made Strauss's name synonymous with the philosophical drift toward atheism.

The *Life of Jesus* models perfectly the confluence of "science" and "Christianity" that Kerner and Krummacher caricatured. On the one hand, it is expressly scientific. In the preface to the first edition, Strauss declares his commitment to the "seriousness of science" in opposition to the "frivolity" and "fanaticism" that he sees in contemporary studies of the Bible.[20] He claims that he is best prepared to investigate the Gospels, because he had experienced an "internal liberation of the feelings and intellect from certain religious and dogmatical presuppositions" through his study of the philosophy of Hegel. He then adds, "If theologians regard this absence of presupposition from his work, as unchristian: he regards the believing presuppositions of theirs as unscientific."[21] Nevertheless, he assures his readers that his findings by no mean oppose Christian faith. On the contrary, he claims to have saved these truths by liberating them from their entanglement with the mere facts of history: "The supernatural birth of Christ, his miracles, his resurrection and ascension, remain eternal truths, whatever doubts may be cast on their reality as historical facts."[22] Strauss believed he had protected Christianity from the negative tendencies of the Enlightenment by translating it into a philosophical, humanist form.

---

18. Especially Ludwig Feuerbach's 1840 *The Essence of Christianity*, trans. George Eliot (New York: Harper, 1957), and Bruno Bauer's *Kritik der Evangelischen Geschichte der Synoptiker*, 3 vols. (Leipzig: Wigand, 1841–1842).

19. He does so most notably in David Friedrich Strauss, *A New Life of Jesus* (London: Williams & Norgate, 1865); trans. of *Das Leben Jesu: Für das deutsche Volk bearbeitet* (Leipzig: Brockhaus, 1864); and in idem, *The Old Faith and the New: A Confession*, trans. Mathilde Blind, 2 vols. (New York: Holt, 1873); trans. of *Der alte und der neue Glaube: Ein Bekentniss*, 6th ed. (Leipzig: Hirzel, 1872). Hereafter cited as *NLJ* 1865, *OFN* 1872, and *OFN* 1873, respectively.

20. *LJ* 1835, 1:vi–vii; *LJ* 1892, xxx.

21. *LJ* 1835, 1:vi; *LJ* 1892, xxx.

22. *LJ* 1835, 1:vii; *LJ* 1892, xxx.

Strauss also knew Kerner personally and wrote about his life and work. He visited Kerner and Hauffe for the first time in 1827, while he was studying theology at the Tübingen seminary. He witnessed one of Hauffe's trances, during which she told him he would never know unbelief. He later teased Kerner with this recollection, but he wrote of Hauffe with admiration and remained friends with Kerner until his death in 1854. Soon afterward, he wrote an appreciative essay, which remains an important account of the physician's life and character.[23] During the 1830s, he also composed a number of short critical pieces in response to Kerner's studies of clairvoyance, ghost seeing, animal magnetism, and possession.[24] His first publication, in 1830, was a critical review of recent explanations of the "Seeress's" otherworldly powers. In these writings, Strauss praises Kerner's research but rejects his religious conclusions. In a response to Kerner's 1834 *Accounts of the Modern Possessed*, for example, he argues that although Kerner's writings are exacting as empirical studies, they fail to theorize rigorously the events in question.[25] Kerner neglected to follow out his own principles of psychological and physiological analysis. Strauss took these instead as the grounds for a remarkably materialist psychophysical approach: the demoniacs' illnesses did not have to do with spiritual activity in the outside world, but with the disordered state of their own brains, nerves, and "ganglionic systems."

Strauss later gathered together these writings under the heading "On the Science of the Nocturnal Side of Nature" ("*Zur Wissenschaft der Nachtseite der Natur*"). The phrase originated with the romantic physician Gotthilf Heinrich Schubert, to whom Kerner dedicated the *Seeress of Prevorst*. It refers to what we now think of as "occult" or "paranormal" matters. Schubert intended it to describe observed empirical phenomena that stand beyond the horizon of our quotidian, "everyday" or "enlightened," rational understanding of the world. These phenomena would

---

23. David Friedrich Strauss, "Justinus Kerner," in *Kleine Schriften* (Berlin: Duncker, 1866), 298–332. See also idem, "Justinus Kerner," in *Zwei Friedliche Blätter* (Altona: Hammerich, 1839), 1–57.

24. Strauss collected and republished these in 1839 under the heading "Zur Wissenschaft der Nachtseite der Natur" in his *Charakteristiken und Kritiken: Eine Sammlung zerstreuter Aufsätze aus den Gebieten der Theologie, Anthropologie und Aesthetik* (Leipzig: Wigand, 1839).

25. David Friedrich Strauss, "Kerner, Geschichten Besessener neuerer Zeit," in *Charakteristiken und Kritiken*, 301–27.

include the clairvoyant powers of people who enter into somnambulic trances, dreams, and marvelous healings effected through obscure magnetic forces. For Kerner and Strauss, it also included demonomania.

Strauss's works on the nocturnal side of nature are striking for a number of reasons—because Strauss, who became infamous as a skeptic, earnestly engages people's beliefs in ghosts and demons, for example, and because they presage insights in the modern study of neurology and behavioral psychology. Also remarkable is the extent to which their concerns resemble those of his better-known writings on early Christianity. Strauss's personal familiarity with cases of possession and other paranormal phenomena in the German countryside shaped his analysis of Jesus's miracle-working activity in the Gospels—beginning, of course, with the various stories about demons and exorcisms.[26] But Strauss's writings on psychology also engage questions that stand at the heart of the *Life of Jesus*—questions about the conditions for objective knowledge, for example, about the limits and intersections of souls and bodies and about the nature of divine action in the world.

The *Life of Jesus* and the Scientific Study of the New Testament

The *Life of Jesus* stands at the apex of a long history of Enlightenment biblical criticism. From the fifteenth and sixteenth centuries onward, scholars brought tremendous critical, philological, philosophical, and historical resources to bear on analyzing the texts of the Hebrew Bible and New Testament. They did a great deal in the process to undermine Scripture's status as an authoritative, inspired account of revelation and sacred history. By the early nineteenth century, critics had shown that much of this "history" was unhistorical; the stories were riddled with contradictions and their texts had been cobbled together from a mass of earlier manuscripts. The miracle stories were simply impossible, the Gospels were not altogether trustworthy as eye-witness accounts of Jesus, and the books of the Pentateuch were not authored by Moses. In addition, the Bible reflected the morals and rarefied concerns of a distant, ancient world. Some stories were unethical; others were irrational. English deists and

---

26. In a 1982 monograph on Strauss, Jean-Marie Paul knowingly writes that "one gets the impression in reading the critical treatment of the demon possessions [in the *Life of Jesus*] that Strauss could speak of demoniacs in familiar terms" (*D. F. Strauss et son époque* [Paris: Les Belles Lettres, 1982], 144).

French *philosophes* in the seventeenth and eighteenth centuries sought to turn their contemporaries away from this primitive collection of texts altogether. Many argued it had been crafted by an ancient priestly caste to bring people into submission.[27]

Nevertheless, in Germany in particular, the historical critical study of the Bible also helped to preserve and augment its authority, albeit in new idioms. To transplant oneself imaginatively onto the theater of ancient history could appear as an act of piety, for example; to cull the sacred history's husk of supernatural or parochial elements was to expose its universal, rational core. Critical interpretation also had an irenic function: when critics called into question the authoritative, revealed status of Scripture, they kept the Bible safe from the divisive, sectarian controversies that began in the Reformation and wars of religion.[28] Furthermore, they redefined it as a new kind of historical and cultural authority. The Bible offered a unique set of poetic, literary, and political resources for reflecting on human history and culture and on the life of the modern state.[29] Thus scholars transformed the Bible from a sacred Scripture into a uniquely privileged cultural text. Their work defined the university, in the place of the church, as the proper sphere in which to understand religion and Scripture; it helped to shore up civil authority against religious insurrections and to shape the secular state.

In the late eighteenth and early nineteenth centuries, German biblical criticism stood at the center of debates about the relation between science [*Wissenschaft*] and faith [*Glaube*]. The Bible was an important testing ground for modern scientific methods. An empirical or philosophical

---

27. In the introduction to the *Life of Jesus*, Strauss credits attacks by "deists and naturalists" on Christianity and the Bible with setting the stage for early nineteenth-century German biblical criticism and for his work in particular. He mentions the English writers John Toland, Henry St. John Bolingbroke, Thomas Morgan, Thomas Chubb, and Thomas Woolston (*LJ* 1835, 1:12–14; *LJ* 1892, 45–46) as well as the German deist Hermann Samuel Reimarus (*LJ* 1835, 1:14–15; *LJ* 1892, 46). Strauss later wrote an appreciative piece on Reimarus (*Hermann Samuel Reimarus und seine Schutzschrift für die vernünftigen Verehrer Gottes* (Leipzig: Brockhaus, 1862) in which he also credited Baruch Spinoza's *Tractatus Theologico-Politicus* (1677) and Pierre Bayle's *Dictionnaire historique et critique* (1697) as important precedents for his work.

28. Michael Legaspi, *The Death of Scripture and the Rise of Biblical Studies* (Oxford: Oxford University Press, 2010).

29. Jonathan Sheehan, *The Enlightenment Bible: Translation, Scholarship, Culture* (Princeton: Princeton University Press, 2005).

critic could demonstrate scientific neutrality by overcoming the temptation to treat a biblical text as an immediate, inspired authority. At the same time, historical criticism defined specific problems for belief. In the older religious view, the historical truth of the sacred history was part and parcel with its religious truth. But early modern critics questioned the historical truth of Scripture in its own right. David Hume famously argued, for example, that miracle stories could never be credible.[30] The numerous deist writings that were translated into German in the eighteenth century raised the question of whether faith should depend on the historical content of the texts. In 1774, Gotthold Ephraim Lessing began publishing a series of pieces from a work by Hermann Samuel Reimarus, although he did not identify the author, in which Reimarus claimed among other things that Jesus was a failed political messianic enthusiast and that Moses was an impostor.[31] For Lessing, this proved that Christian truth should stand apart from scientific, historical investigation.[32] Kant echoed these claims and argued that the real truth of the Bible could not be the object of historical investigation.[33]

Others tried to reconcile faith and historical science. Many German theologians reinterpreted the Gospels on strictly natural and historical terrain, for example, in order to present Jesus as a unique, great personality. One could argue that the supernatural and otherwise disturbing elements of the text were only the time-conditioned way in which ancient people conceived of him. In Strauss's day, Schleiermacher and many of those who embraced his theology maintained that although the results of faith and historical science were distinct, they led to the same conclusions.[34] Hegel

---

30. David Hume, "On Miracles," in *An Enquiry Concerning Human Understanding and Other Writings*, ed. Stephen Buckle (Cambridge: Cambridge University Press, 2007), 96–116. Originally published in 1748.

31. *Fragmente des Wolfenbüttelschen Ungennanten* (1774–1778). The fragments were from Reimarus's *Apologie oder Schutzschrift für die vernünftigen Verehrer Gottes*. Lessing claimed to have discovered them in the Herzog-August-Bibliothek in *Wolfenbüttel* in order to avoid censorship.

32. He famously wrote, "Accidental truths of history can never become the proof of necessary truths of reason" (Gotthold Lessing, *Lessing's Theological Writings*, trans. Henry Chadwick [Stanford: Stanford University Press, 1957], 53).

33. Immanuel Kant, "Religion within the Limits of Mere Reason," in *Religion and Rational Theology*, trans. and ed. Allen Wood and George di Giovanni (Cambridge: Cambridge University Press, 1996), 39–216.

34. Friedrich Schleiermacher, *The Christian Faith*, trans. and ed. H. R. Mackin-

argued that both could come under the auspices of speculative philosophy.[35] Strauss was inspired by Schleiermacher's commitment to historical science and took up Hegel's philosophy, but he rejected the mediating tendency of their approaches to theology. In the *Life of Jesus*, he argued that faith could not depend on the results of scientific or historical investigation, on the one hand, and that it should be replaced entirely by the concepts of philosophy, on the other. This argument liberated the ruthless historical critique that constituted the bulk of the work, as well as its final philosophical and theological conclusion on the humanist significance of Christian dogma.

The Ghosts and Demons of the *Life of Jesus*

One could analyze Strauss's scientific contribution by juxtaposing it to any number of influences. In the introduction to the *Life of Jesus*, he acknowledges his debt to a range of historical-critical interpreters, from contemporaries like Schleiermacher, Heinrich Paulus, and W. M. L. de Wette, to neologians[36] and deists in earlier centuries. He studied at Tübingen

---

tosh and James A. Stewart (Edinburgh: T&T Clark, 1928); trans. of *Der christliche Glaube nach den Grundsäzen der evangelischen Kirche im Zusammehange dargestellt*, 2nd ed., 2 vols. (Berlin: Reimer, 1830–1831).

35. Hegel's mediating view appears in his earlier work—in, for example, the sections on religion in the *Phenomenology of Spirit*—but takes its most apologetic religious form in his later works, especially the 1821–1831 *Lectures on the Philosophy of Religion*. In Strauss's day, the major interpreters of Hegel often appealed to his work in defense of the eternal truth of orthodox religion. See the third volume of David Friedrich Strauss's *Streitschriften zur Vertheidigung meiner Schrift über das Leben Jesu und zur Charakteristik der gegenwärtigen Theologie*, 3 vols. (Tübingen: Osiander, 1837); translated by Marilyn Massey as *In Defense of My Life of Jesus against the Hegelians* (Hamden, CT: Archon, 1983).

36. "Neologians" (*Neologien*) were German theologians who attempted to articulate Christian faith in a modern, rational idiom in the middle of the eighteenth century. They believed that rational inquiry could serve to identify and clarify revealed religious truth. Neologian biblical critics developed novel historical and philological methods to defend the historicity of revelation, in contrast to both orthodox interpreters who rejected these methods and deists who argued that the truths of religion did not lie in the realm of history. Michaelis and Johannes Semler are often identified as the most prominent neologians, although neither adopted the label for himself. Semler's canonical criticism exemplifies the general orientation of neologism. In his four-volume *Abhandlung von freier Untersuchung des Canon* (1771–1775), he identi-

with Ferdinand Baur, who introduced him to Schleiermacher's scientific approach to theology and history, which was shaped in turn by Baruch Spinoza's immanent theology.[37] He also engages seriously the arguments of contemporary "supernaturalists"—apologists who defended the veracity of the Gospel miracle reports—like Hermann Olshausen. De Wette's application of "mythical interpretation" to the Hebrew Bible modeled for Strauss the analytical rubric that he would apply to the Gospels. This mode of interpretation was developed in turn by romantic theories of myth in the works of Schelling and Johann Gottfried Herder.[38] Kant's writings on the Bible were important for Strauss, because they separated religious truth from historical content. Finally, Strauss claimed the philosophy of Hegel had laid the basic foundation for his studies.[39] Hegel's notion that reli-

---

fies parts of the Bible that reflect the concerns of ancient people and no longer apply to the world of modern Christians. He attempts thereby to liberate the kernel of eternal, universal truth in the text from its time-conditioned chaff.

37. Dietz Lange, *Historischer Jesus oder mythischer Christus: Untersuchungen zu dem Gegensatz zwischen Friedrich Schleiermacher und David Friedrich Strauss* (Gütersloh: Gütersloher Verlaghaus, 1975) frames Schleiermacher as Strauss's primary point of reference. Hans Frei, "David Friedrich Strauss," in *Nineteenth Century Religious Thought in the West*, ed. Ninian Smart et al., 3 vols. (Cambridge: Cambridge University Press, 1985), 1:215–60, nuances this view and argues that Schleiermacher replaces Hegel as a key reference point for Strauss only after 1837.

38. Christian Hartlich and Walter Sachs, *Der Ursprung des Mythosbegriffes in der modernen Bibelwissenschaft* (Tübingen: Mohr Siebeck, 1952); George Williamson, *The Longing for Myth in Germany: Religion and Aesthetic Culture from Romanticism to Nietzsche* (Chicago: University of Chicago Press, 2004).

39. Debates over the extent to which Strauss should be read as a Hegelian have dominated much of the commentary on his work. These began soon after he published the first edition of the *Life of Jesus* (Strauss, *In Defense of My Life of Jesus*, 7–8). In the twentieth century, Gotthold Müller, *Identität und Immanenz: Zur Genese der Theologie von David Friedrich Strauss, eine theologie- und philosophiegeschichtliche Studie mit einem bibliographischen Anhang zur Apokatastasis-Frage* (Zürich: EVZ-Verlag, 1968) has argued that Strauss's youthful immersion in the world of Swabian Pietism and mysticism led to a flawed, too-monistic, and one-sided reading of Hegel. A more balanced assessment of Strauss's engagement with Hegel appears in Jörg F. Sandberger, *David Friedrich Strauss als theologischer Hegelianer* (Göttingen: Vandenhoeck & Ruprecht, 1972) and Hans Frei, "David Friedrich Strauss." Marilyn Massey, "David Friedrich Strauss and His Hegelian Critics," *JR* 57 (1977): 341–62, defends his status as a Hegelian. As in Müller's work, much of the discussion has centered on the value of his contribution to critical thought in philosophy, theology, or history. Where for Müller Strauss was not legitimately Hegelian, however, others have asked how his

gious "representations" (*Vorstellungen*) and philosophical "concepts" (*Begriffen*) captured the same truth enabled Strauss to argue that the Christian dogmas anticipated humanist philosophical ideas and that nothing was lost as modern culture transitioned from one mode to the other.

The writings on psychology add a crucial supplement to these influences. Commentators have often treated Strauss's acquaintance with Hauffe and Kerner as a reflection of his early flirtation with romantic and mystical ideas. This passing interest serves in turn to explain Strauss's choice, in the third edition of the *Life of Jesus*, to place some of Jesus's miracles in a new category "unusual powers of nature," that he compared to somnambulism, animal magnetism, and clairvoyance.[40] Few, however, have considered in

---

Hegelianism might affect his contributions to history or theology (Robert Morgan, "A Straussian Question to New Testament Theology," *NTS* 23 [1977]: 243–65; Van A. Harvey, "D. F. Strauss's Life of Jesus Revisited," *CH* 30 [1961]: 191–211). There are in addition a number of studies that emphasize specific elements of Strauss's engagement with Hegel (e.g., his attempt to set historical criticism at the avant-garde of secular modernity, Ward Blanton, *Displacing Christian Origins: Philosophy, Secularity, and the New Testament* [Chicago: University of Chicago Press, 2007], 25–66; his contribution to the scientific study of history and theology, Johannes Zachhuber, *Theology as Science in Nineteenth-Century Germany: From F. C. Baur to Ernst Troeltsch* [Oxford: Oxford University Press, 2013], 73–95). Others situate Strauss within a broader field of critical theologians, literary authors, and philosophers in the German *Vormärz*, many of whom were grappling with Hegel's philosophy in particular. His *Life of Jesus* regularly appears among works by "Young Hegelians," for example, such as Arnold Ruge, Ludwig Feuerbach, Bauer, Max Stirner, and the young Marx, who interpreted, critiqued, and altered Hegel's philosophy in a religiously or politically radical fashion (William Brazill, *The Young Hegelians* [New Haven: Yale University Press, 1970], 95–132). John Edward Toews (*Hegelianism: The Path toward Dialectical Humanism, 1805-1841* [Cambridge: Cambridge University Press, 1985]) and Warren Breckman (*Marx, the Young Hegelians, and the Origins of Radical Social Theory: Dethroning the Self* [Cambridge: Cambridge University Press, 1999]) establish his important position among these critical readers of Hegel as well as alongside other "fellow travelers" such as Friedrich Richter, August Cieszkowski, and Heinrich Heine who were critical of the *Vormärz* era Prussian state and church. Marilyn Massey (*Christ Unmasked: The Meaning of the Life of Jesus in German Politics* [Chapel Hill: University of North Carolina Press, 1983]) offers a thorough portrait of Strauss's work in its social and historical context. She considers his work and his Hegelianism in the light of the contemporary literature of Young Germany. Her introduction to the *In Defense of My Life of Jesus* summarizes clearly Strauss's own position on the question as of 1837.

40. For example, Theobald Ziegler, *David Friedrich Strauss* (Strassburg: Trübner, 1908); Peter Hodgson's introduction to *The Life of Jesus: Critically Examined*, by

detail the intersections between his work on the nocturnal side of nature and the Gospels.[41] Admittedly, Kerner's name does not appear in the *Life of Jesus*. Strauss only mentions his own psychological writings once, in a footnote to the section on demon possession that he added to the 1840 edition of the *Life of Jesus*.[42] But this single footnote rests on a network of threads that connect his writings on and encounters with possessed people in the German countryside to central, defining features of his vision of critical science and his *Life of Jesus*.

To begin with, the psychological works reflect Strauss's early and ongoing fascination with the margins of Christian belief. His image of Jesus as an apocalyptic prophet in the *Life of Jesus* and his writings on demon possession both focus on elements of Christianity—apocalypticism and exorcism—that mainstream theologians disdained, although they remained popular among the broad sweep of German Christians. Commentators have long recognized that eschatology was a driving obsession throughout Strauss's career.[43] He began writing on the kingdom of God, resurrection of the dead, and immortality of the soul as early as an 1828 essay on the "Resurrection of the Flesh" and returned to the subject in his 1830 dissertation on the doctrine of the "Restoration of all Things." Strauss did not hold any expressly eschatological beliefs himself; on the contrary, by 1830 he explicitly rejected ideas about the immortal soul and future resurrection of the dead. Nevertheless, just as he earnestly took up Kerner's work on demon possession, he took very seriously the importance of apocalypticism in the history of ancient and modern Christian faith. If eschatology

---

David Friedrich Strauss, ed. Peter Hodgson, trans. George Eliot (Philadelphia: Fortress, 1972).

41. Paul, as an exception, focuses on their relevance for understanding the passages on miracles and exorcisms in the earlier and fourth editions. In *Identität und Immanenz*, Müller considers his later work in light of his early interest in mysticism and romanticism, but argues that these elements of Strauss's thought invalidate his contribution to a truly scientific theology. They prove that he was a bad or one-sided reader of Hegel who neglected the latter's insights into "history." Müller neglects as such to consider the specific, critical ways in which Strauss engages and alters the beliefs and ideas that he encountered in his youth.

42. Strauss, *Das Leben Jesu: kritisch bearbeitet*, 4th ed., 2 vols. (Tübingen: Osiander, 1840), 2:18 n. 34, cited hereafter as *LJ* 1840.

43. Hodgson writes, for example, "The great offense of the faith of Christianity was for Strauss its futuristic eschatology, yet his fascination with eschatology and his struggle against it continued to the end of his career" (introduction, xvi.).

was a problem for faith, it was a central, crucial problem. He set eschatological ideas at the heart of his Christology, dogmatics, and image of Jesus and his earliest followers. This engagement stood in marked contrast with the work of liberal theologians and rationalists, who marginalized these beliefs at each corresponding point. It brought Strauss into a strange proximity with Pietism.

In addition, Strauss's interest in eschatology converged with his interest in exorcism in that both concerned the operation of "spirit" and "spirits" in nature and history. Strauss's theory of mind was bound up with his theory of revelation. The claim that bodies and souls were united and coextensive stood behind his analysis of exorcisms in the Gospels and German countryside, but also his reflections on Jesus's resurrection, the immortality of the soul, and the future reconciliation of God and humanity. Even more, these concerns shaped his scientific, historical method. As in the history of psychological medicine, Strauss's secularizing approach to historical criticism formed in religious and theological debates that can only seem esoteric from our twenty-first century perspective. Strauss understood anachronistic views on Jesus and the Bible, for example, in terms of his immanent view of God's operation in the cosmos and spirit's movement in material bodies. People who read modern ideas into ancient texts had, in effect, a flawed, dualistic understanding of spirit and matter. Those liberal theologians and rationalists who treated Jesus as a protomodern, ethical rationalist for example, were little better than modern ghost seers or the ancient disciples who experienced visions of his return during the "resurrection event."

At the same time, Strauss sought to describe and understand the states of consciousness behind these deluded views of history and physiology. The limits that he set on the operation of spirit in nature opened onto the experience and state of mind of those who could imaginatively transgress them. The science of the nocturnal side of nature and the science of biblical criticism took distinct "mentalities" as their object. When Strauss acknowledges Hauffe and Kerner's sincerity in his writings on ghost seeing and possession, he follows a principle that also features in his "mythical interpretation" in the *Life of Jesus*: Stories about supernatural events do not result from the mendacity or credulity of eyewitnesses or storytellers. In the *Life of Jesus*, Strauss famously rejects the deist argument that the Gospels are intentional fictions, as well as the more moderate, "rationalist" argument that the disciples were duped when Jesus allowed them to believe he had worked miracles. One could explain the stories' extraordinary aspects by radicalizing the rationalists' main insight, that is, that they emerged out of a distinct, ancient mode of consciousness. Rationalists like Paulus believed that this mode of thought colored the eyewitnesses' understanding of events; under their mythical shell, however, the narratives still contained a baseline of historical truth. Strauss held, on the contrary, that the events themselves, including their historical frame, were only the expression of the mentality that crafted them. There was no universally accessible, objective field underneath their confused reports. Like possessed people speaking of demons or ghosts, the authors of the narratives represented their symbolic world in the terms that were ready to hand. Jesus's followers in the first century thought the appearance of a messianic figure could only be accompanied by dramatic, miraculous signs and events. Whether or not eyewitnesses reported events accurately was beside the point; the accounts turned on the religious categories people used to express their ideas.

Ancient religion resembled modern mental illness, then, in that both were equally incommensurate with educated philosophical and historical reason. In his reflections on Hauffe and the ancient followers of Jesus, Strauss constructed mental illness and mythical consciousness as two distinct antitheses to the modern, rational mind. Scholars in a number of fields have shown that Enlightenment discourses on delusion and unreason helped to define modern notions of subjectivity, autonomy, and rationality. Foucault famously argued in *Madness and Civilization* that the "age of reason" could only take shape by defining "madness" as its other—and separating and confining "mad" people in the process.[44] Discourses on "religion" and religious mentalities also played an essential role in this process. Registers of patients in the first asylums in Germany abound with diagnoses of religious disorders, including demonomania.[45] At the same time, notions of religious "enthusiasm" and "fanaticism" were key topoi in the rhetoric of modernity from John Locke and Martin Luther to Kant, Voltaire, and Strauss.[46] In Germany, this rhetoric took shape in Protestant

---

44. Michel Foucault, *Madness and Civilization: A History of Insanity in the Age of Reason* (New York: Pantheon, 1965).

45. Ann Goldberg, *Sex, Religion, and the Making of Modern Madness: The Eberbach Asylum and German Society, 1815–1849* (Oxford: Oxford University Press, 1999), 37.

46. Anthony La Vopa, "The Philosopher and the 'Schwärmer': On the Career of a German Epithet from Luther to Kant," *HLQ* 60 (1997): 85–115; Peter Fenves, "The

polemics against *Schwärmerei* ("fanaticism"), for example. Luther popularized this term as a means to caricature rival spiritual leaders and movements, whom he claimed suffered from demonic influence.[47] It later came to feature in late eighteenth-century debates about the medical sources of illegitimate religious and philosophical ideas; it could be used in particular to denote forms of religious intolerance. Apocalyptic beliefs were a primary object of both demonological and psychopathological versions of this discourse on *Schwärmerei*. In the *Life of Jesus*, Strauss identifies other writings on the New Testament as results of both *Fanatismus* and "intolerance toward heresies" (*Ketzereifer*),[48] but also takes up the question of whether Jesus, who believed that he would soon be taken by angels to the right hand of God where he would judge the living and the dead, was a *Schwärmer*. In the process, he distinguishes religious from fanatical mentalities even as he defines both over and against modern reason.

We can see a similar dynamic at work in the history of discourses on "fanaticism" and of those on "possession" between the sixteenth and nineteenth centuries. Strauss and others who wrote on philosophy, theology, and psychology gradually put aside old religious ideas about moral contamination, demonic influence, and supernatural evil. They focused instead on the psychological and physical health of the individual "fanatic" or "demoniac." Nevertheless, they carried on certain features of religious polemics against false belief. As Kerner suggested in his anecdote, demystifying discourses took over the older forms of spiritual authority with which they also stood in competition. Strauss's writings fell within a series of Enlightenment analyses of demon possession, which claimed to represent both scientific truth and correct theological belief. Fifty years

---

Scale of Enthusiasm," *HLQ* 60 (1997): 117–52; Jon Mee, *Romanticism, Enthusiasm, and Regulation: Poetics and the Policing of Culture in the Romantic Period* (Oxford: Oxford University Press, 2005); Alberto Toscano, *Fanaticism: On the Uses of an Idea* (London: Verso, 2010); Jordana Rosenberg, *Critical Enthusiasm: Capital Accumulation and the Transformation of Religious Passion* (Oxford: Oxford University Press, 2011).

47. Luther's various polemics against competing reform movements and ideas in the early 1520s formed the early modern use of the term in Germany. Thomas Müntzer and the peasant rebellion qualified as *Schwärmern*, for example, as did Ulrich Zwingli for his views of the Eucharist. See Martin Brecht, *Martin Luther: Shaping and Defining the Reformation, 1521–1523*, trans. James Schaaf (Minneapolis: Fortress, 1990), 137–95; John S. Oyer, *Lutheran Reformers against Anabaptists* (The Hague: Martinus Nijhoff, 1964).

48. *LJ* 1835, 1: vii; *LJ* 1892, xxx, translation modified.

earlier, the biblical critic Semler took up medical explanations of possession in explicit defense of orthodox Christianity in writings on Gassner and other exorcists and possessed people. As medical explanations displaced their religious competitors, they defined specific forms of cultural practice, training, and education as the requisites for any discourse on spiritual health. Strauss's writings on apocalyptic belief can be analyzed in a similar light. They consolidated the spiritual authority of a modern culture and modern critical methods. And they defined "religion" in a distinctly modern way. Strauss ultimately defines a hierarchy of culture and spiritual authority, which underwrites in turn the ethos and rhetoric of critical science.

The "Nocturnal Side" of the Scientific Criticism of Religion and History

Strauss's early writings on psychology and Christianity present an opportunity to trace the relation between modern scientific disciplines and the regions of esoteric religious thought in and against which these disciplines defined themselves. In the fields of history, religion, and psychology, Strauss's approach was ahead of its time. His work in the 1830s presents a strikingly modern blend of methodological agnosticism and openness to foreign, unsettling phenomena.

It presages a wide field of social and psychological research as well as major aspects of the twentieth- and twenty-first-century study of religion. In particular, Strauss sets the tone for later scholarship by refusing to reject strange beliefs outright; on the contrary, he takes them utterly seriously and struggles to understand them on their own terms. And he does so within a materialist cosmology that he has defined in advance. Nevertheless, this cosmology and approach only become possible for Strauss by way of romantic medicine and natural philosophy. He places exorcistic rituals and apocalyptic beliefs in a close, explicit relation to demystifying science. Strauss repeats throughout his writings of the 1830s and early 1840s that the progress of modern culture and education, *Bildung*, only occurs as we pass in full self-awareness through the fields of nonmodern religious mentalities. Practices of scientific critique mirror and secure this passage. As he carves out a disenchanting path to a modern age, Strauss must wander into strange territories. His work reflects a painstaking awareness of the difficulties involved in announcing the advent of modernity and completing the labor of disenchantment. To return to his work is to recall those difficulties.

In the following four chapters, I consider how Strauss engaged esoteric religious themes in his scientific and critical writings on religion and history in the 1830s. In the first chapter, I consider his lesser-known writings on the nocturnal side of natural science and discuss his early ventures into the German countryside, including his early meetings with Kerner and Hauffe. This chapter establishes Strauss's complex affinity for esoteric and mystical beliefs and practices that pervaded early nineteenth-century Germany. The succeeding chapters examine the ways in which his engagement with these beliefs and practices shaped his better-known work on the New Testament Gospels. In chapters two, three, and four, I focus on three major, well-known critical and scientific contributions of the *Life of Jesus*: Strauss's historical critique of the Gospel miracle stories; his adaptation of "mythical interpretation"; and his image of the historical Jesus and Christian origins, respectively. In each of these three areas, I explore the role played by romantic cosmology and medicine. I emphasize in particular those moments at which his studies of the nocturnal side of natural science had an impact on his conclusions and methods. In the third and fourth chapters, I demonstrate how they helped him to define categories that continue to play a central role in the modern secular discourse of disenchantment and criticism: "religion" and "fanaticism."

In the conclusion, I consider the significance of this analysis as a contribution to a genealogy of modern scientific criticism. When dealing with modern notions of "religion," "fanaticism," and "mental illness," the imperative to undertake genealogical analysis stems from the formative influence that these concepts have had on social and political realities in the modern era. The rise of secular science from the Enlightenment to the present is bound up with the troubled lives of modern institutions—the state, the university, the asylum, and capitalism. Strauss undertook his early work out of sincere religious and scientific interests, and, in the context of *Vormärz*-era Germany (ca. 1830–1848), the *Life of Jesus* includes certain subversive elements.[49] Furthermore, it influenced

---

49. A number of recent studies have emphasized the radical implications which Strauss's work would have had for his contemporaries. The standard term for the period in which he wrote, the *Vormärz*, or "pre-march," suggests the fragile political situation leading up to the March revolution of 1848. Massey focuses in *Christ Unmasked* on elements of Strauss's image of Jesus that would have appeared subversively democratic in this context. She highlights points of continuity between his approach to the Gospel narratives and the modes of critical irony that had developed

important contributions to the fields of social and historical theory in the succeeding centuries. Nevertheless, his systematic worldview and attendant practices of scientific critique contributed to defining the divergent, unhealthy subjects of a modern age—and to obscuring the challenges that they might pose to it. Esotericism and fanaticism have provided recurring foils for modern, rational religion and science.[50] In return, I wish to recall how the spiritual claims and experiences of demoniacs and clairvoyants in the German countryside, figures like Hauffe, shaped the fields of scientific and religious discourse that developed in the writings of Strauss.

---

in the literature of Young Germany. Like the Young German writers, Strauss struck out against the ideological foundations of the restoration state, but did so in the field of theology. In *Origins of Radical Social Theory*, Breckman argues that Strauss's humanistic conception of the incarnation formed part of a wide-ranging attack on the concept of "personality," a theopolitical notion that served during the restoration era to legitimate monarch, property owner, and personal God. Toews's *Hegelianism* highlights the connections between theological and political themes in Strauss's writings. At the same time, Massey, Toews, and Blanton emphasize areas in which Strauss presses back against the democratic implications of his own work. Blanton takes his cue in part from Nietzsche's critique, in the first of his *Untimely Meditations*, of Strauss's later posturing as a modern, "scientific man" (*David Friedrich Strauss, the Confessor and the Writer*, vol. 1 of *Untimely Meditations*, ed. Daniel Breazeale, trans. R. J. Hollingdale [Cambridge: Cambridge University Press, 1997]; trans. of *David Friedrich Strauss, der Bekenner und Schriftsteller*, vol. 1 of *Unzeitgemässe Betrachtungen, erstes Stück* [Leipzig: Fritzsch, 1873]). I revisit Nietzsche's critique in the conclusion.

50. Wouter J. Hanegraaff, *Esotericism and the Academy: Rejected Knowledge in Western Culture* (Cambridge: Cambridge University Press, 2012).

1
Strauss on the Science of the Nocturnal Side of Nature

Strauss composed a series of essays on clairvoyance, demon possession, and ghost seeing between 1830 and 1839.[1] He developed a demystifying, scientific approach to these matters, which appears in especially clear relief in an 1836 response to Kerner and Eschenmayer's 1834 *Accounts of the Modern Possessed*. In the *Accounts*, Kerner and Eschenmayer had presented case studies of modern demoniacs, including two women whom Kerner had observed personally. Kerner described how these women entered into "demonic paroxysms" in which their minds were displaced by alien, malevolent souls who also controlled their bodies. They leered and convulsed and blasphemed against the Bible. At times they spoke in different voices and described experiences that were manifestly not their own. The women were also visited by good, tutelary spirits who protected them from the attacks. Kerner saw their conditions as both religious and medical. He treated them with medicine, "magnetic healing," prayers, and exorcism. He and Eschenmayer claimed that they offered concrete evidence of a cosmic struggle between good and evil forces; the women bore witness to actual troubled, dead souls as they strived toward unity with God. When an exorcist compelled one of the possessing spirits to confess its sins, for example, Kerner inferred that this repentant act loosened the demon's hold on its host—it brought the demon out of its base materiality and closer to the divine.[2]

In his response, Strauss offers an alternative, "inverted image"[3] of the demonic condition; that is, he inverts the priority that Kerner and the

---

1. Strauss, *Charakteristiken und Kritiken*, 301–406.
2. Kerner and Echenmayer, *Geschichten Besessener neuerer Zeit*, 20–103.
3. Strauss, *Characteristiken und Kritiken*, 304.

possessed women grant to objective, empirical phenomena over the subjects who experience them. Strauss affirms that the women's experiences of possession were authentic, but he traces the origins of these experiences to their own psychological and physiological states: the spirits whom they encounter are projections of internal derangements and inversions in the normal, healthy order of their bodies and minds.[4] Their strange memories and behavior can be explained from their inner lives and personal histories. Strauss maintains that the women fabricated the life stories of the demonic souls unconsciously out of buried memories, hearsay, and imagination. He agrees with Kerner that exorcistic confessions are effective, but not because the "demons" repent of their "sins"; rather, the exorcist enters into the possessed woman's *idées fixes*, whose conflicted internal presuppositions these "confessions" open up and resolve. Strauss prefers to call such ostensible exorcisms "the psychological dissolution of the sick person's demonic delusion."[5]

At a glance, this inverted image appears to set a modern psychological view of illness against an outdated religious alternative. But the distinction between the two is less straightforward than it appears at first glance. Strauss makes his case on the basis of theories about magnetism and the

---

4. Strauss's use of this trope of inversion sets him within a certain lineage of modern critical discourse from Kant to Hegel and Marx. As we will see below, Strauss follows the lead of Kant in the preface to the first critique (*Critique of Pure Reason*) and refers to Copernicus's heliocentric theory as a precedent for his "inverted" turn to the grounds of subjective consciousness. At the same time, his adaptation of this theme presages works by Bauer and the young Marx, in which these authors take up Hegel's enigmatic notion of an "inverted world" (*Verkehrte Welt*) from the end of the first section of the *Phenomenology of Spirit* to describe social and religious alienation. For Bauer and Marx, modern religious representations project the internal disorders or derangement (*Verkehrung*) of modern institutions and collective life. Thus Bauer writes in 1842, for example, that Christian religion is the "expression, isolated appearance, and sanction of the incompleteness and sickness of existing relations. It is the universal essence of all human relations and strivings, but an inverted essence, an essence that is torn away from them and thus is also the disfigured expression of their inessentiality and derangement" (Bauer, "Die gute sache der Freiheit und meine eigene Angelgenheit," in *Feldzüge der Reinen Kritik* [Frankfurt: Suhrkamp, 1968], 134). A year later, Marx would famously write that religion is "the opium of the people," but also that "man is *the world of men, the* state, society" and that "this state and this society produce religion, which is an *inverted consciousness of the world*, because they are an *inverted world*" (Karl Marx, "Toward the Critique of Hegel's Philosophy of Law: Introduction," in *Writings of the Young Marx on Philosophy and Society*, trans. and ed. Loyd David Easton and Kurt H. Guddat [Indianapolis: Hackett, 1997], 250).

5. Strauss, *Charakteristiken und Kritiken*, 316.

organization of the body, mind, and soul that he had learned *from* Kerner. Although Kerner and Eschenmayer's most extravagant claims put them on the margins of mainstream theology, their ideas were anchored in respected scientific research and theory. Kerner was a trained physician and careful scientist; in the *Accounts*, he adheres to strict empirical observation and localizes demonic and magnetic phenomena in the sick bodies of his patients.

The *Accounts* and Strauss's response reflect the same context of early nineteenth-century romantic medicine and philosophy. Romantic physicians appealed to both intuitive and empirical knowledge and emphasized obscure natural forces such as electricity and magnetism. Little understood phenomena like "animal magnetism" and "somnambulic" trances offered them access to the obscure workings of the human and divine spirit in nature and history. Along with many contemporary philosophers and theologians, they rejected the disjunctive tendencies of previous Enlightenment rationalism and materialism. They sought to conceive nature, humanity, and God within a united and dynamic totality. The insights of medicine, they believed, could contribute along with religion, history, and philosophy to knowledge of universal truths. They valorized accordingly ancient and folk religious ideas alongside modern philosophical and medical notions of bodies, souls, and sickness. In the region of Württemberg where Strauss and Kerner grew up, these scholarly discourses converged with Swabian Pietism and popular beliefs about demon possession and ghosts. At the time when he began his career as a theologian, Strauss actively sought out folk healers, fortune tellers, and somnambulists in the countryside. It was here that he first encountered Kerner and Hauffe, the Seeress of Prevorst.

In the chapter that follows, I consider how Strauss's early encounters with romantic medicine and the esoteric regions of popular belief enabled him to develop a scientific, critical approach to religious belief and experience. I first overview how German romantic medicine and natural philosophy shaped the scientific study of phenomena like ghost seeing and clairvoyance, after which I turn to Strauss's account of his early experiences in the German countryside. I then consider a series of his writings on ghost seers and possessed people. I argue that in these writings Strauss takes up and radicalizes certain tendencies that he finds in studies of esoteric, "nocturnal" phenomena by Kerner and others. The interests that guide this effort are religious and scientific: he strives to give a coherent and systematic form to romantic visions of nature, spirit, and spiritual disorder. As he takes on these theories, however, he consolidates the Enlightenment vision of an autonomous, rational subject that Kerner and others had called into question. Strauss puts a materialist twist on romantic monism. He reduces the conditions and experiences of the sick and clairvoyant individuals to the material, embodied limits of mortal life. At the same time, he explains their experience in a new light: people's perceptions of demons and ghosts are real, even if what they perceive is not; distinct psychologies and cultural mentalities lead them to experience the world differently. For Strauss, culture, education, and gender shape the contours of subjective consciousness, as much as mental or physical illness.

In these psychological writings, Strauss models a distinctly modern approach to the study of religion and pathology. He *takes seriously* and seeks to *understand* uncultured and irrational beliefs, even those that other enlightened critics disdained as examples of superstition or fraud. He gives voice to divergent mentalities and grants them relative legitimacy within their own, respective cultural and psychological sphere. But he lets these uneducated or protorational mentalities speak only in the idiom of a materialist world whose limits he has defined in advance. This approach forms part of a social struggle, moreover, over competing forms of spiritual authority. Strauss undermines the legitimacy of local religious cultures more effectively than previous rationalism and materialism could hope to do. He uses his analysis to frame a hierarchy of culture, at the apex of which he sets modern critical and scientific thought.

The Nocturnal Side of Natural Science in Early Nineteenth-Century German Philosophy and Medicine

The project of a scientific study of nature's nocturnal side originated with Gotthilf Heinrich Schubert, a physician who had studied with Herder and Schelling, and to whom Kerner dedicated the *Seeress of Prevorst*. In 1808 Schubert delivered a series of widely-attended lectures with the title *Ansichten von den Nachtseite der Naturwissenschaft* (*Opinions on the Nocturnal Side of Natural Science*). In these lectures as in a wide sweep of Romantic art, poetry, and philosophy, the darkness and mystery of "the night" connoted new possibilities in human knowledge, as well as the limitations and blind spots of a too-confident Enlightenment. For Schubert, "nocturnal" meant something like "occult." On the one hand, these phenomena are obscure: little understood or rarely observed, they had also been neglected by scientific study. But they are more than curiosities. Properly conceived and studied, they offer a glimpse of deep, hidden truths about the ends, origins, and structure of the universe:

> The oldest relation of man to nature, the living harmony of the individual with the whole, the connection of a present existence with a future higher one, and how the seed of the new future life gradually unfolds in the midst of the present one, are therefore the chief subjects of this work of mine.[6]

Schubert frames his lectures around a romantic history of humanity and science—the *Ansichten* resemble in some respects his teacher Herder's *Ideas of a Philosophy of History*. He argues that at its origin the human species lived in a vital, intimate connection with God and the universe. This was the "nighttime" of humanity in the sense that human beings submitted reflexively and fatalistically to nature; they did not embrace individual autonomy or recognize nature as an object distinct from themselves. At the same time, it was a Golden Age in which peace prevailed and people could attain extraordinary, immediate knowledge about their world.[7] The great achievements of ancient astronomers, for example, show that the first humans were native natural scientists. They understood that all natural beings and events are united into a grand, evolving totality.

But this harmonious situation could not last. Just as children are weaned from their mothers, humanity dissociated itself from nature and so began our "daylight" world.[8] We came to take nature as an object, asked

---

6. Gotthilf Heinrich von Schubert, *Ansichten von der Nachtseite der Naturwissenschaft* (Dresden: Arnold, 1808). Discussions of Schubert and the development of German romantic medicine and theories of animal magnetism, somnambulism, etc. appear in Frederick Gregory, "Gotthilf Heinrich Schubert and the Dark Side of Natural Science," *NTM* 3 (1995): 255–69; Diethard Sawicki, *Leben mit den Toten : Geisterglauben und die Entstehung des Spiritismus in Deutschland 1770–1900* (München: Schöningh, 2002); Theodore Ziolkowski, *Clio the Romantic Muse: Historicizing the Faculties in Germany* (Ithaca, NY: Cornell University Press, 2004), 154–61; Matthew Bell, *The German Tradition of Psychology in Literature and Thought 1700–1840* (Cambridge: Cambridge University Press, 2005), 170–88; Karl Baier, *Meditation und Moderne: Zur Genese eines Kernbereichs moderner Spiritualität in der Wechselwirkung zwischen Westeuropa, Nordamerika und Asien*, 2 vols. (Könighausen & Neumann: Würzburg, 2009), 1:179–249; Luis Montiel, "Une révolution manquée: Le magnétisme animal dans la médicine du romantisme allemand," *RH 19* 38 (2009): 61–77; Hanegraaff, *Esotericism and the Academy*, 262–73.

7. Strauss, *Ansichten*, 7.
8. Ibid., 8.

after its principle, and attempted to dominate it. For Schubert, this turn to the subjective pursuit of knowledge constituted a veritable fall. Humanity left behind the paradisiacal age described in ancient myths.[9] It was at this point, moreover, that the tempo of our cultural development as a species diverged from that of natural science. The liberated gaze of individual subjects drowned out immediate natural knowledge of the old world, just as the dawn blots out the stars in the night sky.[10]

True natural science would consist accordingly in reestablishing our ancient conception of the unified totality in which we are embedded. This knowledge could no longer be immediate, however; it would have to come from the striving and research of autonomous beings. Examples of this new natural science appeared throughout history but they reached a new stage in the modern era, beginning with Renaissance art and astronomy. Raphael and Michelangelo, Copernicus and Kepler rediscovered "nature" when they conceived it in universal terms—"no longer the earth, but rather the universe, no longer the particular phenomenon, but rather the ideal."[11] Modern scientific discoveries in the disciplines of chemistry, plant and animal life, meteorology, and physics offered further evidence that nature is an interconnected totality. Scientific taxonomies of plants and animals, for example, show connections and analogies between the lowest and highest species. The surest proof, however, comes from observations of matters that once would have been classed as miracles: "animal magnetism, precognition, dreams, sympathy, and the like."[12] In these phenomena, individual consciousness dissolves back into its original unity with nature; it ranges throughout the whole cosmos, beyond the individual's limited mind and body. Such experiences prove that human beings still retain some buried traces of our ancient, nocturnal knowledge of the world. Our scientific observations of them give us insight into the totality of nature and the harmony of all individual beings;[13] they open as such a future in which humanity is reconciled again to nature.[14]

---

9. Ibid., 7.
10. Ibid., 9.
11. Ibid., 13–14.
12. Ibid., 22.
13. Ibid., 371.
14. Ibid., 22.

Schubert's account of humanity's fall and future redemption is manifestly romantic and religious. But it also demonstrates his emphatic commitment to the rigorous pursuit of *Naturwissenschaft*, the speculative study of nature informed by empirical observation and experimental method. Copernicus's heliocentric theory and recent findings in botany and chemistry foreshadow discoveries in animal magnetism and clairvoyant perception. He emphasizes that nocturnal phenomena are observed, empirical *facts* (*Thatsachen*). If naive people had used them as a basis for superstitious ideas or wild speculations, this did nothing to call their facticity into question. Schubert knew that early theories about the miraculous power of "galvinism," for example, had not diminished the reality and power of electricity. In addition, Schubert was a physician, and his romantic enthusiasm about the nocturnal side of nature was coupled with real concern for individuals whose souls were prone to ranging beyond their bodies and rational consciousness. He believed clairvoyance stood in an intimate connection with madness. In both cases the rational, diurnal mind releases its hold on our unconscious connection to the whole.

Schubert was a leading representative of psychological theory in his day. The *Ansichten*, along with his later *Symbolik des Traumes*, influenced figures from Schelling and E. T. A. Hoffman to Hegel and Sigmund Freud. The constellation of philosophical history, nocturnal phenomena, religious language, and romantic views of sickness, on the one hand, and scientific rigor, empiricism, and dedication to experimental method, on the other, appear in a number of contemporaneous writings in Germany. His work exemplifies the far-ranging, speculative ambitions of *Wissenschaft* at the turn of the nineteenth century: that it would not only illuminate particular phenomena, but would provide insight into the whole of nature and humanity's participation in it. Schubert drew, in particular, on Schelling's philosophy of nature (*Naturphilosophie*), which he helped to popularize. With the influence of Schubert and others, it came to serve as a basis for medical research and theory throughout the early decades of the nineteenth century. Schelling's works between 1797 and 1799 granted philosophical and theological legitimacy to attempts by romantic physicians to grapple with matters of primal and universal significance.[15] Their

---

15. F. W. J. von Schelling, *Ideen zu einer Philosphie der Natur* (Leipzig: Breitkopf & Härtel, 1797); idem, *Von der Weltseele: Eine Hypothese der höhern Physik zur Erklärung des allgemeinen Organismus* (Hamburg: Perthes, 1798); idem., *Erster Entwurf eines Systems der Naturphilosophie: Zum behuf seiner Vorlesungen* (Leipzig: Gabler, 1799). The *Ideen* and *Ent-*

research into the nocturnal world of spiritual phenomena would influence Schelling—along with Hegel, Strauss, and others—in turn.

Schelling stood among a number of contemporary philosophers, most notably Johann Gottlieb Fichte and Hegel, who sought to define a monistic "absolute," a dynamic totality in which the distinctions between subject and object, spirit and nature, or freedom and necessity could be reconciled to the union of the whole. This project reflected philosophical interests that were at once ideal and practical. It would provide a coherent and systematic ground for science, moral action, and the formation of ethical communities. But it also reflected a general dissatisfaction with the fragmenting tendencies of Enlightenment positivism and rationalism. Romantic philosophers and physicians sought a higher, unified, and meaningful account of the universe, one that could unite the various fields of human thought and experience.

Previous Enlightenment thinkers had tended to follow Descartes and to separate the rational, thinking subject from the empirical, objective world. The latter then became the object of science. At the same time, Newtonian physics presented a world governed by natural laws, and many enlightened thinkers consequently rejected miracles—interruptions in the natural chains of cause and effect. The distinction between the freedom of the subject and the fixed laws of nature posed certain problems, however. Where, for example, did the grounds of the subject's freedom lie if not in objective nature? How did it escape determination by the natural order? Furthermore, if subjective consciousness is in fact distinct from the world, how do we guarantee that it adequately grasps what exists? Kant defined the terms of this discussion in a decisive fashion. He claimed in the preface to his 1783 *Prolegomena to Any Future Metaphysics* that he first confronted the issue through the skepticism of Hume, who had suggested that even causality, a foundation of experimental methods, does not appear anywhere as a feature of the world itself apart from our cognition of it.[16] Kant accepted, with Hume, that human consciousness supplied forms

---

wurf have been translated into English as *Ideas for a Philosophy of Nature as Introduction to the Study of This Science*, trans. Errol E. Harris and Peter Heath (Cambridge: Cambridge University Press, 1988) and *First Outline of a System of the Philosophy of Nature*, trans. Keith R. Peterson (Albany: SUNY Press, 2004), cited hereafter as *Ideas* and *Outline*, respectively.

16. Immanuel Kant, *Prolegomena to Any Future Metaphysics that Will Be Able to Come Forward as Science with Selections from the Critique of Pure Reason*, trans. Gary Hatfield (Cambridge: Cambridge University Press, 1997), preface.

of causality and, therefore, natural law. He maintained that consciousness could only grasp the world as it appeared to our minds—it could access "phenomena" or appearances, but not "things-in-themselves." At the same time, he argued that in a different light this limit is also a condition of universality. The fact that our minds give shape to the objective world through the same categories—natural law, for example—means we have a substantial, shared, consistent ground for empirical science and moral action. He radicalized the position of the subject and inverted the conundrum he took from Hume into a solution. Rather than looking for an "empirical" ground in the objective world, he sought a "transcendental" ground in the way the mind organizes experience.

Schelling, Fichte, and Hegel believed, however, that if Kant had identified the problem, his solution had exacerbated it. He reinforced the separation between ideal consciousness and the actual world. Furthermore, he failed to identify any convincing unconditioned ground for his transcendental subject. His concepts of human freedom and the religious experience of things-in-themselves—God, in particular—felt accordingly thin. These figures consequently sought an alternative that would establish a more primary unity of subject and object, one that would in turn grant more certain and immediate access to the truths of religion and nature. Two distinct possibilities presented themselves. The first found expression in Fichte's writings in the 1790s. Fichte took Kant's transcendental turn a step further and conceived of the absolute "I," which posits the objective, natural world as its "not-I" as part of its evolution toward self-determination. The world could be derived as such from the starting point of the active, self-producing and unconditioned Ego.[17] The second drew from Spinoza's philosophical writings from the seventeenth century. Spinoza had presented a natural order in which God and human freedom were wholly immanent. Nature is God and vice versa: they constitute the "substance" that is the universal condition of all being. The divine was itself the laws of nature and continuous interactions of finite beings.[18]

Schelling's philosophy of nature united Spinozan "substance" with Fichte's emphasis on the dynamic movement of the self-intuiting Ego.

---

17. Johann Gottlieb Fichte, *The Science of Knowledge, with the First and Second Introductions*, trans. Peter Lauchlan Heath and John Lachs (Cambridge: Cambridge University Press, 1982).

18. Baruch Spinoza, *Ethics*, ed. Seymour Feldman, trans. Samuel Shirley (Indianapolis: Hackett, 1992).

Fichte supplied him with an active, productive conception of the absolute, by which he could inscribe the principle of freedom into the monist, immanent universe of Spinoza. Schelling, and later Hegel, conceived the absolute as a living unity in which distinctions between finite beings or subjects and objects are real, but form part of an ever-shifting organic infinity. The absolute is no longer an object to be grasped, in this view, but an active, evolving reality in which human consciousness, natural science, and collective life participate. Historically speaking, our ability to engage nature as an object of science, for example, reflects the fact that our subjective consciousness evolves out of and participates in it. As humans take account of "the world," objective spirit becomes self-conscious.

Schelling's 1797 *Ideas for a Philosophy of Nature* follows the lead of Kant's 1786 *Metaphysical Foundations of Natural Science*, in which Kant rejected the static, mechanistic view of matter and postulated that matter is made up of a dynamic arrangement of attractive and repulsive forces.[19] Kant and Schelling were both influenced by late eighteenth-century research on chemistry, mathematics, and physics, which drew attention to obscure electrical and magnetic forces, as well as to organic processes of metamorphosis—elements of nature did not always fit neatly into the Newtonian universe of mechanistic laws and atomistic objects. For Schelling, these elements offered insight into the nature of the absolute. He conceived the infinite totality of the universe as a series of ascending polar oppositions from unthinking matter to human consciousness. These polarities appeared in the human sexes as well as in the ends of magnets, for example.[20] Polarities are bound together and exert attractive and repulsive forces on one another, so that nature never remains static. Their incessant movement, in turn, Schelling posits as the true uniting ground and productive drive of all being. In his 1798 *On the World-Soul*, he identifies this drive with the "world-soul," the invisible spirit of life, growth, and transformation.[21] Schelling's world-soul is not an object like others. It is a principle, and it pervades and links together the entirety of nature, from animal and human spirit to inorganic matter. As reflective subjects we do not grasp this infinite productivity per se. We only see it in discrete beings and polar oppositions, the "products" that arise

---

19. Immanuel Kant, *Metaphysical Foundations of Natural Science*, trans. Michael Friedman (Cambridge: Cambridge University Press, 2004).
20. Schelling, *Outline*, 149.
21. Schelling, *Von der Weltseele*.

as eddies in the stream of its movement.[22] At the same time, scientific research enables the experimenter to participate in nature's productivity and to bring the universal concept of nature to light.[23] The inner worlds of human life and thought are bound up with the outer world of nature, and the knowledge of one opens onto the other.

For many romantic thinkers, these notions pointed to a secret, inner world in living nature as in human bodies and minds. If such forces could not be seen, they could be detected. Romantic natural scientists looked to the concrete evidence of electric, magnetic, and other subtle energies as a confirmation of the world-soul at work. Mesmer's theory of animal magnetism proved especially useful to that end. Mesmer had argued in the late eighteenth century that an ethereal fluid permeated the cosmos and the nervous systems of living creatures.[24] He distinguished the organic, "animal magnetism" in living bodies from mineral magnetism. Sicknesses could be traced to a blockage in magnetic fluids, which could be resolved in turn through magnetic provocation of a "crisis" in the patient. Mesmer came to believe that because magnetic forces circulated through human bodies, doctors could heal people through mere physical contact.[25] He engaged in "magnetic passes," in which the physician passed his or her hands over a patient to set magnetic forces in motion.[26] Animal magnetism later became linked to hypnotic or "somnambulic" trances in the clin-

---

22. Schelling, *Outline*, 139–40. In the later works on *Naturphilosophie*, including the *Outline*, Schelling grants this invisible productivity and self-organizing movement to nature itself.

23. Ibid., 196–99.

24. Franz Anton Mesmer, "Letter from M. Mesmer, Doctor of Medicine at Vienna, to A. M. Unzer, Doctor of Medicine, on the Medical Use of the Magnet," in *Mesmerism*, trans. and ed. George Bloch (Los Atlos, CA: Kaufmann, 1980), 25–29. See also *Mémoire sur la découverte du magnetisme animal* (Paris: P. Didot le jeune, 1779). This work appeared in German as *Abhandlung über die Entdeckung des thierischen Magnetismus: Aus dem Französischen übersetzt* (Carlsruhe: Macklot, 1781). Kerner wrote the first biography of Mesmer, *Franz Anton Mesmer aus Schwaben, Entdecker des thierischen Magnetismus: Erinnerungen an Denselben, nebst Nachrichten von den letzten Jahren seines Lebens zu Meersburg am Bodensee* (Frankfurt am Main: Literarische Anstalt, 1856). Other English translations of Mesmer's writings appear in Bloch's edition of *Mesmerism*.

25. "Letter from M. Mesmer," 27–28. On the significance of this innovation see Adam Crabtree, *From Mesmer to Freud: Magnetic Sleep and the Roots of Psychological Healing* (New Haven: Yale University Press, 1993), 6.

26. Crabtree, *From Mesmer to Freud*, 14.

ical practices of the Puységur brothers beginning in 1784.[27] They claimed that in the somnambulic state patients could achieve clairvoyance. The magnetized individuals could diagnose diseases and prescribe treatments for themselves and others.

German physicians in the early decades of the nineteenth century adapted theories of magnetism and somnambulism to romantic visions of the cosmos. Mesmer began his career as a Newtonian, Enlightenment thinker. But in the hands of German romantics, the subtle fluid of animal magnetism became a means for discrete, polarized entities to make contact with each other and the whole universe. These views came to be shaped in turn by Christian Reil's division of the human body into two systems, the brain system and the "ganglionic" system, located in the *Herzgrub*, the "epigastric" region or solar plexus.[28] This division formed one of the Schellingian polarities. The brain and nerves, as the rational organs, stood at the height of the natural order and dominated over all. Like many of the "lower" polarities, however, the epigastric organs retained a more immediate unity with the world-soul. Sensitive, sick, ancient, and non-Western people, especially women—all of whom were on the lower end of their respective polarities—had special access to it. Schubert argued that the magnetic state of somnambulic trance begins when the patient passes into this lower region, as does mental illness. As the brain relinquishes its dominance, the epigastric region takes flight. The fact that patients could diagnose their disorders in somnambulic states showed they could trespass the divide between the mind and body; this power was confirmed further in their precognitive dreams, ability to recover long-buried memories, and unity with the psyches of other individuals. For Schubert, the breakdown of the rational mind returns a person to the original state of unity with nature and can allow access to the future and afterlife.

Schubert and others' romantic image of sickness was not without ambivalence, however. He saw somnambulic trances as dangerous territory. Kerner and Hauffe believed likewise that her clairvoyant powers were

---

27. Ibid., 38; Ellenberger, *Discovery of the Unconscious*, 70–74.

28. Christian Reil, *Rhapsodieen über die Anwendung der psychischen Curmethode auf Geisteszerrüttungen* (Halle: Curt, 1803). Carl Alexander Ferdinand Kluge, *Versuch einer Darstellung des animalischen Magnetismus als Heilmittel* (Vienna: Franz Haas, 1815), and Schubert popularized the connection between Reil's theory and magnetism (Hanegraaff, *Esotericism and the Academy*, 262; Baier, *Meditation und Moderne*, 1:190).

bound up with her imperfect state of psychophysical health.[29] If the individual, rational, and healthy subject is an eddy in the stream of spirit, then death represents the most perfect unity with the totality. In Kerner's writings and letters, he struggles with whether access to her revelations would come at the cost of her health. He decided he could fully pursue the former only when he had assured himself that she would not live.[30]

The dynamic movement of polarities also shaped romantic views of history in the vein of Schubert. The world-soul presses nature to evolve constantly upward on the scene of cultural history. As in the shift from the epigastric to brain regions, this upward movement could involve both progress and a kind of fall. Romantic theorists, including Schelling, Herder, and others, had set the stage for Schubert when they countered the deist caricature of ancient religious myths as fables or deluded nonsense.[31] They had already argued that primitive people lacked rationality and civilization, but lived, like children, in a closer unity with the divine soil from which humans had sprung. Romantic physicians speculated therefore that the epigastric region dominated in archaic peoples. In his 1814 *Symbolik des Traumes*, Schubert argues that primeval, natural humans were ruled by the life of the *Herzgrub*.[32]

In the *Seeress of Prevorst* and other writings, Kerner takes up substantial portions of Schubert's vision of somnambulism, magnetism, and cultural history. He had been initiated into magnetic healing as a teenager, when Eberhard Gmelin used magnetic passes to heal his stomach disorder. He became, along with Eschenmayer and Johann Friedrich von Meyer, one of the most important popularizers of Schubert's ideas. Later, he would write the first biography of Mesmer. In Kerner's *Blätter aus Prevorst* and *Magikon*, he and Meyer offered a myriad of first-hand testimonies and case studies of somnambulic occurrences. It was the *Seeress of Prevorst*, however, that decisively shifted the landscape of nocturnal science and came to

---

29. Kerner, *Seherin von Prevorst*, 252.
30. Hanegraaff, "A Woman Alone," in *Women and Miracle Stories*, ed. Anne-Marie Korte (Leiden: Brill, 2001), 41.
31. Johann Gottfried Herder, *Vom Geist der Ebräischen Poesie: Eine Anleitung für die Liebhaber derselben, und der ältesten Geschichte des menschlichen Geistes*, 2 vols (Desau: Buchhandlung der Gelehrten, 1782–1783); Schelling, "Ueber Mythen, historische Sagen, und Philosopheme der ältesten Welt," in *Friedrich Wilhelm Joseph von Schellings Werke* (Stuttgart: Cotta, 1856) 1:43–83. See Williamson, *Longing for Myth in Germany*, 19–71.
32. Schubert, *Die Symbolik des Traumes*, ed. F. H. Ranke, 4th ed. (Leipzig: Brockhaus, 1862), 134.

serve as the "key text in the study of spirits in the second third of the nineteenth century."[33] At the same time, the *Seeress of Prevorst* and Kerner's other works turned the study of somnambulic and magnetic phenomena toward more occult regions still, to the world of dead souls. Many notable figures, including skeptics like Hegel and Strauss could accept elements of somnambulic prophecy or magnetic healing, for example; but few were willing to brook Kerner's ideas about ghosts and demons. These ideas fell rather into the world of popular superstition and folk belief. Strauss speaks of them as "popular opinions from which the culture of our century has recoiled in terror once and for all; opinions with which ... it was the pride of our fathers to have disposed, and which ... it is now the endeavor of all rational educators to expel from the youth."[34]

Württemberg—the home of Kerner, Eschenmayer, and Strauss—provided an especially rich soil for these marginal developments in the nocturnal side of natural science. The region was one privileged seat of Pietist belief and practice since the eighteenth century and abounded with local religious culture outside of the established theological mainstream. Millenarianism, miracle healing, and beliefs about ghosts and demons were prevalent in the countryside. At the same time, the combination of rigorous approaches to historical, natural, and theological science and speculative religious thought was typical of the late eighteenth- and early nineteenth-century Swabian Pietist context. Prominent figures like Friedrich Oetinger and Johann Jung-Stilling, disciples of the great textual scholar and millenarian Johann Albrecht Bengel, wrote meticulous theological tomes about the advent of the eschaton, alchemy, Jakob Böhme, and the worldly activities of dead souls.[35] Here and throughout Germany popular

---

33. Sawicki, *Leben mit dem Toten*, 162.

34. Strauss, *Charakteristiken und Kritiken*, 302.

35. A number of studies have demonstrated the importance of Swabian Pietist and theosophical traditions, including writings by Oetinger and Bengel, and reaching back to Böhme, for Schelling and Hegel's philosophy. See for example, Robert Schneider, *Schellings und Hegels Schwäbische Geistesahnen* (Würzburg-Aumühle: Triltsch, 1938); Ernst Benz, *The Mystical Sources of German Romantic Philosophy* (Allison Park, PA: Pickwick, 1983); Glenn Alexander Magee, *Hegel and the Hermetic Tradition* (Ithaca, NY: Cornell University Press, 2001). These studies offer valuable insight into the context of Swabian Pietism in which Schelling, Hegel, and later Strauss began their careers; they help to complicate any oversimple or triumphalist narrative of secular disenchantment. I do not wish, however, to reduce Strauss's work to any preexisting traditions. The interest of his work on the nocturnal side of nature lies in the ways that he takes on and alters religious traditions and models of science from that context.

and scholarly speculation combined religious, philosophical, and medical themes. Clairvoyant trances and ghost visions could seem to open the supernatural, heavenly realm, for example. They could also offer proof that the eschaton was near: one could appeal to the quotation of Joel's prophecy (Joel 2:28) in Acts 2:17, "In the last days it will be, God declares, that I will pour out my Spirit upon all flesh, and your sons and your daughters shall prophesy, and your young men shall see visions, and your old men shall dream dreams."[36]

Kerner rejected some of these beliefs, but he reworked others into a new and paradigmatic synthesis. He had taken to heart the organic and monistic worldview. His era had moved from the full-fledged eschatology of Bengel to the more mystical inclinations of his disciple Oetinger. Kerner dispensed with chiliastic speculation and notions of a wholly transcendent, supernatural order. Nevertheless, he affirmed the objective, tangible reality of an inner world of spirit. In the place of a transcendent future or heavenly realm of the immortalized dead, he substituted an immanent, intermediate realm. From this intermediate realm, dead souls who had not yet achieved unity with God could still contact and possess the living—especially magnetic individuals dominated by the *Herzgrub*. Furthermore, he offered Hauffe and others' revelations about this realm as the source of religious insight. Hauffe's encounters with the dead, for example, presented a distinct moral and spiritual hierarchy. She described how souls in states of relative illumination or darkness—and therefore proximity to God—were able to pass between or beyond the distinct spheres of the intermediate realm. Kerner treated such revealed knowledge with reverence, as confirmations of his deeply felt Christian pieties. Where they stood in contradiction, he took Hauffe's claims as more authoritative than the Bible.

Strauss's *Bildung* in Württemberg

Strauss was born and raised in the same town as Kerner. As a young student at the Blaubeurn seminary and Tübingen University in the late 1820s, he was an eager participant in the mystical, romantic atmosphere of Württemberg. "He learned more outside the classroom than within it," as Peter

---

36. Sawicki, *Leben mit den Toten*, 149–52.

Hodgson puts it.[37] He befriended the poet Eduard Mörike, studied Johann Ludwig Tieck and Novalis, and composed his own verses. At Blaubeurn, his romantic affinity for myths and folk tales deepened as he studied classical antiquity under Ferdinand Baur. At Tübingen, when he and his friends found the instruction wanting, they began to study Schelling in private: Kant's rational, methodical approach to mediated knowledge left them with a bitter taste, and Friedrich Heinrich Jacobi's philosophy was a little "sweeter," but Schelling's *Naturphilosophie* satisfied their longing for immediate, mystical knowledge of the cosmos.[38] Reports from his tutors (*Repetenten*) testify that Strauss dedicated most of his intellectual energy to the speculative aspects of *Naturphilosophie*.[39] In 1828, he composed a prize-winning essay in which he used Schelling's theories to defend the possibility of resurrection from the dead.

From there, Strauss ranged still further afield: after passing from "the steppes of Kant and his interpreters to the lush fields of [Schelling's] nature philosophy, I likewise strayed into the mysterious woods of Jacob Böhme."[40] If Schelling opened the possibility that an immediate intuition of the absolute was possible, Böhme's visionary, mystical writings confirmed this promise. The accounts by Kerner and others of somnambulists and ghosts, which Strauss discovered in short order, provided still further confirmation. In a piece that he wrote soon after Strauss's death, William Nast, his former roommate at Tübingen, recalls,

> Before we were advanced to the university, and still more during the metaphysical course there, Strauss manifested a strange inclination to seek out everything mysterious, with a strong desire to investigate the abnormal and exaggerated. He liked to read ghost stories, and hunted up the books of the Mystics, Paracelsus, and Jacob Böhme, and others, espe-

---

37. Hodgson, introduction, xx ("The chief influences on him at the time were romanticism, mysticism, and natural philosophy"). Numerous commentators have remarked on this early romantic inclination. See for example Müller, *Identität und Immanenz*, and Eduard Zeller, *David Friedrich Strauss in His Life and Writings* (London: Smith Elder, 1874), 15–21 who also rehearse many of the details of Strauss's autobiographical writings that follow.

38. Strauss, *Christian Märklin: Ein Lebens- und Charakterbild aus den Gegenwart* (Mannheim: Basserman, 1851), 33.

39. Müller, *Identität und Immanenz*, 42–43.

40. Strauss, *Zwei Friedlich Blätter*, 15.

cially the accounts of the sympathetic cures which were then practiced in Württemberg more than in any other part of Germany.[41]

Nor did Strauss rest content with reading about these matters. He and his friends sought out living examples. They visited clairvoyants and folk healers in the nearby countryside. During one of these journeys, a companion's hands became frostbitten, but he was miraculously healed by a shepherd with "mysterious powers." Strauss and some friends made their way eventually to Weinsberg to see Hauffe. Although many of Strauss's colleagues took part in these extracurricular adventures, his interest was noticeably deep and sincere. Nast describes how, when they visited a fortune teller, "an old peasant woman who told fortunes out of a coffee pot … it made no impression on any of us except Strauss. He seemed disturbed, but would not tell us what had been said to him."[42] His friend Friedrich Vischer[43] similarly recalled that when he happened to meet Strauss after his first trip to Weinsberg,

> It was as if he was electrified, a deep yearning after the poppy seed of the twilight of spirits passed through him; where he believed he noticed only the faintest trace of flat, enlightened rationalism in our discussion, he disagreed agitatedly, and called everyone heathens and turks who would not follow him into his moon-illuminated magic garden.[44]

Strauss's recollections of the period confirm the impressions of Vischer and Nast. In a piece that he wrote on Kerner in 1839, he presents the meeting with Hauffe ten years earlier as the last stage in a sort of mystical initiation. The moment he read Böhme, he felt he had a source of direct revelation, on par with the Bible: "he spoke as seer, as one to whom the sight is given, to glimpse the living powers in his own inner being and in

---

41. William Nast, "Recollections of David Friedrich Strauss," *The New Princeton Review* 4 (1887): 343–48 (345).

42. Ibid., 345.

43. Vischer, a close friend of Strauss's, became famous for his own critical adaptation of Hegel's philosophy in the field of aesthetics. His piece on Strauss, "Dr. Strauss und die Wirtemburger," in *Kritische Gänge*, 2 vols. (Tübingen: Fues, 1844), 1:3–130, emphasizes the confluence of rationalism and Württemberg Pietism in Strauss's intellectual development. He presents this confluence as the force that shaped Strauss into a leading representative of the *Zeitgeist*.

44. Ibid., 94.

nature 'as they dip and soar and hold their golden pails.'"[45] The experience evoked the kind of "supernaturalistic belief reserved only for the prophets and apostles" and engendered a longing for a "living visual intuition" (*lebendigen Anschauung*) of the world of spirit. When he read Kerner's "History of Two Somnambulists," he said it cast a further "rosy sheen over my impressionable young soul." But even with these works in hand, Strauss still wished to pass beyond the mere "unliving medium, dead writing" and encounter the spirit realm in a living, present form.[46] The trip to see Hauffe would satisfy this desire. The time of his departure was, he writes, "a solemn moment.... I had the feeling that ... I was approaching a most mysterious and horrifying consecration, that I was entering into a connection with the invisible world that until then I had only longed for in vain."[47] When he met Hauffe, she entered into a somnambulic trance and predicted that he would "never know unbelief." For Strauss, the experience was "incomparable": "I remember no similar moment in my life." He describes how her face underwent a "heavenly transfiguration" and how she spoke in the "most pure German"; when he gave her his hand, he felt as if his "entire mind and being lay open to her" and the floor fell out from under him.[48] Strauss did not doubt that he was in the presence of a genuine seeress, one who trafficked with a higher world. For some time afterward, he lived surrounded by a sense of enchantment: "The miracle was no longer a distant thing which we sought. It became a living presence."[49]

Nevertheless, Strauss's mystical inclinations did not last. His feeling of enchantment soon dissipated. During a later visit to Weinsberg, Hauffe, in her declining health, failed to recognize him. His interest in his extracurricular pursuits waned, and in courses with Baur and others he fell gradually and unwittingly under the "scientific spell," of Schleiermacher's "dialectics": Schleiermacher posited, namely, that all phenomena must correspond to the existing world and fit within a coherent view of God and nature, or the infinite and finite. Admittedly, Schleiermacher was a romantic thinker and defender of religious faith: he emphasized the paramount significance of religious feeling; he drew on Schelling and offered a monistic conception of the cosmos as a living and evolving totality; he worked

---

45. Strauss, *Zwei Friedliche Blätter*, 11 (quoting Goethe, *Faust*).
46. Ibid., 13.
47. Ibid., 17.
48. Ibid., 18.
49. Ibid., 19.

against the negative tendencies of the Enlightenment to bring scientific rationality and religious faith into a complementary unity. But he also opened a decidedly critical approach to the Bible and theology. Schleiermacher felt that the most relentlessly scientific study would not contradict religious truth. Furthermore, he claimed that devout feeling and scientific analysis offered grounds for perceiving distinct religious truths, a claim which granted authority—as much as Kant's philosophy—to the experience of the subject, over and against any religious object, event, or person. Strauss would soon come into conflict with Schleiermacher about numerous points of historical analysis and Christology in the Gospels; however, the *Glaubenslehre* first convinced him to set his own self-consciousness above mystical experience and biblical authority.

With this critical turn back to the grounds of self-consciousness, Strauss and his friends felt their old world *inverted*: "we stood on new spiritual terrain, from which, looking back on the old enchanted land [*Zauberland*] of clairvoyance, magic, and sympathy, everything appeared turned on its head [*auf den Kopf gestellt*]."[50] He would begin to express this changed, inverted perspective in 1830 with the piece on the distinct views of Hauffe's clairvoyance. He attributes his compulsion to write this work to the sudden popularity of Kerner's *Seeress of Prevorst* as well as a need to reconcile his discordant experiences over the previous years. "I was driven by a need to make sense of a phenomenon which had preoccupied me for so long."[51] He did not entirely dismiss the truth of Hauffe's revelations in this work; however, he sought to analyze her experiences strictly on this-worldly terrain. As such, the article already "plainly betrayed an author whom Schleiermacher had just taught to think and to speak."[52] It led to a short-lived falling out with Kerner.

When Strauss began to study Hegel, his demystifying inclinations fixed even more firmly in place. Here as in his study of Schleiermacher, Strauss not only gravitated to a thinker who offered critical resources for theological study, but also interpreted these resources in a one-sidedly critical light. Hegel and Schleiermacher's attempts to reconcile *Wissenschaft* and *Glaube* left some room for interpretation. When Hegel argued that philosophy and theology led to the same truths, for example, some conservative theologians took this to mean that Christian dogmas were philosophically

---

50. Ibid., 22.
51. Ibid.
52. Ibid., 22–23.

true; Strauss, on the other hand, ultimately took it to mean that theology had to be translated—and dissolved—into the higher, scientific truths of philosophy. When Schleiermacher posited that historical criticism did not impinge on the truth of Christ, Schleiermachians such as August Neander, for example, and Olshausen claimed the historical "facticity" of supernaturalistic ideas;[53] for Strauss, the "spell of Schleiermacher's dialectics" already worked like an inoculation against these views.

In the piece on Kerner and in later writings, Strauss presents his critical turn in the late 1820s as a decisive break with his early attraction to everything occult and mystical. But his early mysticism and later skepticism stood in a more difficult and intimate connection than this picture suggests. Nast's characterization offers indications to that effect: "To the question whether Strauss indicated, while in the preparatory seminary, his extreme skeptical bent," he writes, "it is difficult to give a categorical reply," but he adds, "In a peculiar, *yet disguised or equivocal way*, I may say that he did."[54] Strauss admittedly shared the "chilly" and rationalistic bent of the other seminarians. Nast locates the real sign of his skepticism, however, in the very intensity of his interest in everything strange and supernatural. Strauss pursued occult phenomena with an earnest curiosity that outpaced that of his friends. And yet, even at the height of this pursuit, his words and actions always appeared tempered throughout with "a vein of fine irony": "We were never sure he fully meant what he said. We could not take his words to mean what they appeared to mean."[55] One could not be sure even if this ironic detachment fell to the credit of Strauss's religiosity or skepticism. After Strauss wrote the *Life of Jesus* in 1835, Nast half expected him to follow with a work that gathered together and systematized the rebuttals from his opponents.[56]

Nast's account is anecdotal but incisive. This ironizing blend of serious, frank engagement with esoteric religious matters, and, as Nast would have it, "chilly" rationality forms an integral part of Strauss's critical orientation. His 1839 account of the trip to Weinsberg ten years earlier is tinged

---

53. August Neander, *Das Leben Jesu Christi in seinem geschichtlichen Zummenhange und seiner geschichtlichen Entwickelung*, 4th ed. (Hamburg: Perthes, 1837); Hermann Olshausen, *Biblical Commentary on the New Testament*, trans. A. C. Kendrick (New York: Sheldon, 1857); trans. of *Biblischer Commentar über sämmtliche Schriften des Neuen Testaments zunächst für Prediger und Studirende* (Königsberg: Unzer, 1830).
54. Nast, "Recollections of David Friedrich Strauss," 345.
55. Ibid., 344–45.
56. Ibid.

1. THE NOCTURNAL SIDE OF NATURE 43

with irony. The repeated, romantic references to his search for a "direct vision," for example, should be read in light of his statement, a few pages later, that he eventually lost interest in this search altogether. Jean-Marie Paul suggests that letters that he wrote to his friend Binder at the time manifest a similar "ironic distanciation," including tongue-in-cheek references to Weinsberg as "Mecca nostra."[57] In the broader scope of his work in the 1830s, including the *Life of Jesus*, Strauss's method and tone are equally ironic. His methodological irony takes two related forms. First, there is the simple sense in which Strauss embraces orthodox and Pietist beliefs and practices only to reconceive their significance or to demonstrate where they break down. His 1839 account of his youthful romanticism in his trip to Weinsberg ten years earlier is ironic in this sense. If Strauss presents his *Bildung* as a mystical initiation, it is an ironic initiation. After he completes his passage toward the "living presence" or "direct vision" of the divinity, he finishes this "mysterious and terrifying consecration" by abandoning his mystical impulses. This first mode of irony opens onto a second mode, one that Marilyn Massey first analyzed in detail in Strauss's work.[58] For Strauss, irony consists in the movement by which whatever appears to be immediately given and objective is revealed to be mediated by subjective, individual or collective consciousness. The ironist follows the principle of subjective freedom. He or she demonstrates that seemingly fixed, external "givens"—esteemed institutions, for example, authoritative political orders, or established interpretations of the Bible—are open to revision and transformation.[59] Schleiermacher and Kant established the grounds of this ironic orientation when they set the authority of individual self-consciousness above that of religious objects. Thus Strauss's ironic exposition of his mystical initiation culminates when he reads Schleiermacher,

---

57. Paul, *Strauss et son époque*, 143.

58. In "The Literature of Young Germany and D. F. Strauss's *Life of Jesus*" (*JR* 59 [1979]: 298–323) and *Christ Unmasked*, Massey shows that Strauss shared this understanding of irony with the literary authors of Young Germany. Among his contemporaries, the *Life of Jesus* provoked comparisons in particular with Karl Gutzkow's notorious ironic novel that appeared in the same year, *Wally the Skeptic*. In the second part of his *Streitschriften* or "Polemical Writings" in defense of the *Life of Jesus* in 1837, Strauss defended irony in contemporary literature as well as in his own approach to the New Testament ("Literature of Young Germany," 312–16).

59. Vischer theorized this understanding of irony, as the dissolution of objective givens in subjective freedom, in his Hegelian writings on aesthetics (Massey, "Literature of Young Germany," 309–12).

after which the whole "magical realm" of somnambulism et cetera appears inverted, "turned on its head." For Strauss, Schleiermacher's dialectics had inverted the priority of religious objects over the subjective consciousness that mediates them. He could no longer seek the unmediated "living presence" of the divine. He could only conceive religious phenomena as mediated. They had to fit within a subjective, rational, and internally coherent conception of the cosmos.

Thus Strauss's autobiographical coming-of-age story presents a distinct, modern and scientific vision of *Bildung*, understood as both "culture" and "education." In romantic thought and in the philosophy of history, individual development mirrors that of human culture in history writ large. For Strauss, *Bildung* encompasses the general process by which a scientific worldview supplants an archaic or youthful affinity for mysticism, miracle, and immediate revelation. In the introduction to the *Life of Jesus*, he traces this process of *Bildung* on the historical stage. In the modern age, people stop taking the world in a naive and immediate way; they learn to see the mediated chains of this-worldly causes and effects that make up the natural order.[60] Education and the progress of research enable them to uncover these mediations in the heart of any idea, no matter how extraordinary: "Because *Bildung* is in general mediation, the progressive *Bildung* of the people will always know more clearly the mediations which an idea requires for its efficacity."[61] The idea of God as a personal and transcendent miracle-worker, in particular, gives way over time to the scientific view that nothing can break or transcend the laws of nature.

At the same time, Strauss's *Bildung* narrative models a scientific disposition and critical affect. When confronting an obscure, "horrifying" or arcane religious subject, one may be tempted to turn away in fear or scoff in disbelief. But a scientific theologian should engage it with earnest respect—even as doing so may turn a dearly-held world of belief on its head. Strauss writes in 1836 that the scientific study of possessed people, for example, requires a "sharp, but not already unbelieving testing of the facts."[62]

---

60. *LJ* 1835 1:1–2; *LJ* 1892, 39–40.
61. *LJ* 1835 1:2; *LJ* 1892, 40.
62. Strauss, *Charakteristiken und Kritiken*, 307.

From an Equivocal Affinity to an "Inverted Image" of the Nocturnal Side of Nature

Strauss's writings on the nocturnal side of nature between 1830 and 1839 epitomize his equivocal approach. He takes the accounts by Kerner and others of esoteric phenomena seriously, even as he demystifies many of their claims. In the 1836 response to Kerner and Eschenmayer's *Accounts*, he defines this alternative as an "inverted image" (*verkehrte Abbild*) of their theory, analogous to Copernicus's inversion of Ptolemaic astronomy.[63] The trope of inversion brings together the scientific disposition that he represented in his *Bildung*-narrative with his critical adaptation of romantic theories of mind and nature. It echoes his youthful turn away from the topsy-turvy "magical realm" of clairvoyants and sympathetic cures under the spell of Schleiermacher's dialectics; however, it also defines his altered, monistic, and materialist turn to an embodied, human subject.

Strauss advocates for the nocturnal side of natural science, often in terms that echo Schubert, Kerner, Meyer, and other romantic physicians. He insists on the quality of Kerner's work in particular. He could confirm the trustworthiness of Kerner and Hauffe firsthand. In the opening lines of the 1830 article on Hauffe, he writes,

> We cannot accept the opinion of those who attack the facts of Kerner's writing by supposing in that a sick woman means to deceive us and that the doctor falsifies his observations. The writer of the present essay, and in fact all impartial readers of Kerner's work, can attest that this supposition is groundless.[64]

The young Strauss regarded Hauffe with a degree of esteem that bordered on reverence. He could not believe she was insane. When not in her magnetic state, she was an entirely "sensible" (*verstandige*) and "pleasant" person.[65] Furthermore, she was beyond the point of fabricating her afflictions. Later he would write, "She was certainly not a swindler, but an unfortunate woman, deeply to be pitied."[66] Kerner, on the other hand, he recognized

---

63. Ibid., 304.
64. Ibid., 391.
65. Strauss, *Zwei Friedliche Blätter*, 19.
66. Strauss, *Kleine Schriften*, 320–21.

and admired as a painstaking empiricist, one who spoke frankly about the sometimes crude facts of human physiology and psychology.

In his response to the *Accounts*, Strauss also follows Kerner's lead and emphasizes the sheer weight of evidence for nocturnal phenomena. Whatever modern people make of demons, ghosts, or clairvoyants, the writings of Kerner, Eschenmayer, and others record "a series of extraordinary facts [*Thatsachen*]" that demand to be reckoned with.[67] Strauss points out that Kerner, like Gassner a century earlier, was only one among the many credible, cultured experts to bear witness to these phenomena. When ghosts appeared to a group of prisoners in Weinsberg, for example, Kerner observed the events in the company of other doctors, court officers, and professors.[68]

Occult phenomena deserve priority, for Strauss as much as for Schubert, in the study of natural science. The fact that they stand at the limits of existing knowledge about nature only proves that we should apply the tools of science to their investigation. He acknowledges that most cultured, modern readers turn away in "aversion and contempt" when they come upon ideas about demons and ghosts. But their neglect of these matters is "a shame, since Kerner's writings are for the doctor, the philosopher, in general for those who seek knowledge of the hidden depths of human nature, of the highest significance." They shed light on blind spots in existing knowledge about human health and sickness.[69] Antipathy to the occult can therefore mask an underlying, unscientific bias: many skeptics fear ridicule, if not the phenomena in question. In an ironic inversion of Enlightenment rhetoric, the fact that Kerner and others take "superstitions" seriously demonstrates their scientific discipline and disinterest. Kerner makes similar claims in the *Seeress of Prevorst*—he quotes Meyer, for example, and writes, "our knowledge of the higher natural phenomena would have progressed much further, if we did not fear the rod of quotidian reason, like children."[70]

Similar rhetoric pervades Strauss's work in the 1830s. In his writings on early Christianity as in his work on the nocturnal side of nature, he fixates on subjects that provoke learned people's feelings of "aversion" or "timidity." In the introductory lines of the 1835 *Life of Jesus*, he stakes his

---

67. Strauss, *Charakteristiken und Kritiken*, 301.
68. Ibid., 329, 331.
69. Ibid., 301–2.
70. Kerner, *Seherin von Prevorst*, 292.

credibility as a scientific critic on the fact that he keeps his eyes open to those alienating, ancient elements of the Gospels that provoke a "sense of repulsion"[71]—primitive stories about demons, resurrections, angels, and the imminent end of the world, for example. Contemporary apologists, including many rationalist theologians, covered over these elements or explained them away. Strauss focuses on them and claims they are the most essential parts of Christianity. Strauss's dogged fixation on repulsive religious facts in the mid-1830s recapitulates his youthful, unflinching pursuit of a direct vision and "horrifying ... consecration" in the encounter with Hauffe.

Nevertheless, Strauss also manifests the same skepticism, in his psychological writings, that Nast detected in his early affinity for the occult. The crux of his equivocation appears, ironically, at the point of the romantic physicians' commitment to empirical data. For Strauss, Kerner and others came to the wrong conclusions because of their strict scientific empiricism, their reflexive submission to the facts at hand. In the 1830 piece on Hauffe, he maintains that Kerner's experiences had proven stronger than his theoretical faculties. Kerner's views on ghost seeing "must emerge naturally in those overwhelmed by their direct viewing of such matters"[72]—an experience to which Strauss could personally attest.

This criticism reappears in his response to Kerner's *Accounts* six years later. The *Accounts* included some of Kerner and Eschenmayer's most audacious claims, beginning with the thesis "that it is a fact, that there are spirits, which appear to men, and demons, which take hold of them."[73] They maintained that age-old popular religious beliefs about ghosts and demons provided the only explanation that was adequate to the empirical results of their studies. "The theory which they put forward, they say, is not added by them," Strauss explains, "but lies already in the facts, and imposes itself so irresistibly with these, that only arbitrary violence can sunder it from them."[74] Kerner excuses himself from theorizing entirely. He claims that experience leads inexorably to his conclusions in two ways. On the one hand, the hypothesis of actual demons corresponds with uniform consistency to the testimonies of possessed people—as in his writings on Hauffe, Kerner grants significant authority to his subjects' claims.

---

71. *LJ* 1835 1:2; *LJ* 1892, 40.
72. Strauss, *Charakteristiken und Kritiken*, 391.
73. Ibid., 305.
74. Ibid., 303–4.

On the other hand, this hypothesis explains the strange, difficult facts of the matter in one sweep, with remarkable ease and clarity.

Strauss concedes that Kerner's appeal to actual demons keeps him from becoming entangled in a whole "web of difficulties."[75] From the perspective of common sense, Kerner's is the *most* compelling and plausible explanation. But his conclusions are still wrong. Kerner errs when he attempts to suspend any theoretical presuppositions or reasoning about the existing world. Ironically, he falls back onto the strict, sensualist materialism that he despised in contemporary medicine and theology: Kerner begins from "the claim, which outstrips even the crassest empiricism, that the scientific explanation can be only the tautological repetition of experience."[76] A scientist cannot fail to think about the theoretical coherence of his or her account—just as he or she must consider its correspondence to the existing world of established facts. Strauss offers the Copernican analogy by way of explanation. Kerner and Eschenmayer stand in the same position as proponents of the pre-Copernican astronomical system. The older astronomy "speaks with invincible persuasiveness for the turning of heaven and the resting of the earth," and "all appearances can be explained sufficiently from this presupposition." Copernicus's novel hypothesis, on the other hand, had led modern people to accept ideas that were contrary to their experience—the "invisibility and imperceptibility of the turning of the earth," for example, and "the fact that a portion of its inhabitants periodically hang upside down."[77] Matters are not always as they appear at first glance. Modern science had learned accordingly to pass "beyond the appearance to the essence." After Copernicus, we must accept that "the correct theory of the fact is not always the exact one, but rather from time to time is its inverted image."[78]

But what is this "inverted image"? The analogy echoes a famous passage from the preface to Kant's *Critique of Pure Reason*, one with which Strauss was familiar. Here Kant elaborates on his postulate that objects are formed through the a priori forms supplied by subjective cognition. He explains that it resembles Copernicus's heliocentric theory. Previous philosophers had tried to resolve the separation between subject and object by making cognition correspond to objects in the world; Kant suggests instead that

---

75. Ibid., 304.
76. Ibid.
77. Ibid., 303.
78. Ibid., 304.

objects have their grounds in consciousness: we receive impressions of the world that our cognition forms into what we perceive and understand. We do not need to search for a universal ground for knowledge, then, since we can rest secure on the universality of the forms by which we cognize them. He adds,

> This would be just like the first thoughts of Copernicus, who, when he did not make good progress in the explanation of the celestial motions if he assumed that the entire celestial host revolves around the observer, tried to see if he might not have greater success if he made the observer revolve and left the stars at rest.[79]

Kant claims that he and Copernicus both devised their scientific views of the world by considering how observers constitute phenomena.

Like Kant, Strauss emphasizes the mediating role that a subject plays in shaping objective experience. The correct, inverted view comes when we step back from the object onto the grounds of subjective self-consciousness. This correction would apply first to the perspective of the scientific observer. Kerner needs to slacken his fixation on the objective facts at hand in order to see how his theories mediate them. The experiences of possessed people can be explained on the same grounds. Claims about demons and ghosts may seem satisfying, just like the old Ptolemaic system of astronomy. However, even clearer explanations will ensue if we consider that ghost appearances are "merely subjective"—just as Copernicus provided the most satisfying view of celestial bodies when he considered that their observed movements "have their (likewise subjective) ground in the yearly motion of the earth."[80] As in Copernicus's heliocentric theory and Kant's critical philosophy, this is not to suggest that subjective perceptions are illusions. In the article on Hauffe, Strauss rejects the "contagion theory," for example, the notion that Hauffe's visions were hallucinations that she communicated to the imaginations of present observers. Rather, the consciousness of observers and patients gives form to the real world that they see and describe.

The "subject" to whom Strauss wishes to turn, however, differs from that of Kant. Strauss's subject, including its consciousness, is embed-

---

79. Immanuel Kant, *Critique of Pure Reason*, ed. and trans. Paul Guyer and Allen W. Wood (Cambridge: Cambridge University Press, 1998), 110.

80. Strauss, *Charakteristiken und Kritiken*, 305.

ded wholly within the organic order of nature. He embraced the organic monism of Schelling and Schleiermacher. He could not accept a separation between ideal consciousness and the actual world of things-in-themselves. In addition, he was influenced by romantic medical studies of human physiology and psychology. He adopted many of Kerner's theories about bodies and souls—including ideas about magnetism, for example. Above all, he embraced Kerner's attempt to localize spiritual phenomena in the organic, individual body. Consequently, Strauss's "subject" is not only the subject of "consciousness," but a living body that exists in nature. It is an embodied, historical individual.

Hauffe and the Embodied Limits of Spirit

The 1830 piece on Hauffe offers a first image of this inverted view. Strauss's new perspective shows through especially in his response to Hauffe, Kerner, and Eschenmayer's notion of the "nerve-spirit" (*Nervengeist*): an obscure, spiritual-material organ that Kerner credited Hauffe with having discovered. In the *Seeress of Prevorst*, Hauffe appears at times in the role of a theorist alongside Kerner and Eschenmayer. Kerner records numerous statements in which Hauffe bases her capacity to see ghosts, demons, and spiritual realms on the work of her nerve-spirit. She presents the nerve-spirit as an embodied spiritual force, embedded in our physical nerves, that enables us to perceive the world. The eye receives impressions of objects, for example, through its mediating work.[81] Hauffe claims that because the nerve-spirit stands at the height of organic nature, it establishes contact between bodies and souls as much as bodies and the world.[82] It lingers on therefore after death, at which time it takes the shape of a "hull of ether" around the dead person's soul. Ghostly beings in the intermediate realm between life and death can use this ethereal hull to manipulate ethereal matter in the atmosphere by which they produce sounds audible to humans. Kerner adduces people's sensations of phantom limbs as evidence for the existence of the nerve-spirit.[83] Hauffe's nerve-spirit gives a semitangible, natural ground for links between subjects and objects, like animal magnetism. But the nerve-spirit also resem-

---

81. Kerner, *Seherin von Prevorst*, 265.
82. Ibid., 187.
83. Ibid., 92–93.

bles magnetic forces in that it is mysterious and opens a broader, nocturnal spectrum of perceptive powers.

This psychophysical account of the nerve-spirit draws on many of the key topoi of romantic medical theories of magnetism and somnambulism. Hauffe claims that in a normal, waking state, a person cannot hear the sounds made by the dead or see their corresponding souls. Our perceptive powers remain imprisoned in our material body and rational brain. A healthy brain protects the body from the perceptions of the epigastric region, the seat of magnetic forces. Moreover, we cannot make spiritual matter an object of perception because it is what enables us to perceive in the first place: simply put, "the subject cannot at the same time be the object."[84] Hauffe and Kerner posit that her illness had diminished the brain's protective-dominating power and loosened her nerve-spirit to an abnormal degree from its bodily support. Hauffe's perceptions of the inner spiritual realm are part and parcel with her relative proximity to physical death.[85] Thanks to this loosening, she can turn her spiritual gaze inward, back on her soul, in the somnambulic state of trance. This inward turn creates an echo-chamber of soul and spirit, in which her spiritual energies and sensitivity are heightened. As she passes into the inner realm, she begins to see and hear things that are normally hidden from waking perception, including the souls and voices of the dead.[86]

Strauss rejects the hypothesis of the nerve-spirit. He claims, first, that no organic phenomenon can exist without living, material support; second, that any autonomous, living being is a closed unity of its various organs and members. Even the nerves, for example, which find their center in the brain and are therefore among the highest expressions of organic life, stop working without a living body to sustain and reproduce them. Why, then, would the "nerve-spirit" be any different? It must stand in the same relation to the nerves as that in which they stand to the body; without living nerves, there is no nerve-spirit.[87]

Strauss admits that Kerner and Eschenmayer could object to this account of bodies and souls on the basis of analogies from nature. Kerner regularly explains spirit beings through the analogy of a butterfly, for example, which casts off its pupa and lives on independently; human

---

84. Ibid., 253.
85. Ibid, 252.
86. Ibid., 253.
87. Strauss, *Charakteristiken und Kritiken*, 395.

children also live on without the parents who produced them. But these "products," Strauss counters, are precisely examples of closed, independent organisms "whose various parts are organized and grounded into a living unity, by which they are capable of an autonomous life"; the nerve-spirit, on the other hand, "is essentially a simple thing, without hands or feet … a disconnected Spiritus."[88] The same reasoning would apply if we conceded the existence of a nerve-spirit but took it only as a "principle" and "grounding force" or if we placed it even more firmly within the natural-material order. A bodily principle only can be said to exist where there is a body on which it operates. And if the nerve-spirit is a part of nature, then what do dead souls eat, for example?[89] The critique rests as such on a monistic and materialist view of the subject: an individual is an autonomous totality of the processes and organs that constitute it; the operation of these various members is limited to the material life of the body.

At this point, we can see how Strauss's altered conception of the subject and its limits also alters Kant's critical epistemology. When Kant located the universal foundations of knowledge in cognition, he placed boundaries on what we could know. Our understanding cannot pass beyond the organizing work of our minds to grasp things as such, as they exist out there in the world. When dealing with objects of science, we deal only with appearances. In Strauss's view, on the contrary, things-in-themselves are accessible to scientific understanding. He appears to undermine the limits that Kant had set on scientific knowledge. For Strauss as for Schelling or Hegel, our consciousness is bound up with the universe itself, and if humans are part of nature, then human "self-consciousness" is also the self-consciousness of the organic cosmos. It is objective spirit coming to know itself. There is consequently no reason to limit what we can know to the realm of appearances. Thus, while Strauss's appeal to Copernicus

---

88. Ibid.

89. Ibid. Hauffe and Kerner claimed that spirits consumed people's religious words, which are also formed from the ethereal matter of their nerve-spirit. As spirits heard Hauffe's pious expressions, these spirits—trapped in the intermediate realm—were drawn more and more toward reconciliation with God. For Strauss, this view only confuses natural and supernatural phenomena. It grants a too-material form to words as also to the spirits that would consume them. He also objects to the notion on theological grounds: how could a just God force these spirits to be content for the possibility of their salvation with the "crumbs which fall from the richly laid out tables of living humanity"? (Strauss, *Charakteristiken und Kritiken*, 396).

resembles Kant's in many respects, it also includes the very un-Kantian claim that the inverted view "*passes beyond the appearance* to the essence."[90]

In fact, Strauss sets his own critical limits on epistemology. But he does not place these limits at the gap between consciousness and the world. Rather, they are part of the world itself. The bounds of epistemology are the same, in effect, as those of ontology. *Naturphilosophie* prepared the way for this view. Schelling claimed that distinctions between subjects and objects or finite beings are real, but are part of a dynamic, evolving totality that exceeds and constitutes them. The distinct, finite subjects that make up the world are hypostatized eddies in the productive flow of the world-soul. As the world-soul presses onward and evolves, the hypostatized eddies dissolve back into it. Kerner similarly claims that the living, rational subject is a calcified extension of the totality and that in death the subject is immersed once again in the grand totality of nature. Hence broken, dying bodies and minds have special access to the hidden order of the cosmos. Strauss recognizes with Kerner and Schelling the hierarchy of polarities between distinct beings or products within the organic totality. But he also adds a Kantian, critical twist: he insists on and radicalizes the limits of these distinctions. The action of any magnetic forces, human spirits, or world-soul cannot exceed the limits inscribed in the natural order of life. When Strauss inverts Kerner's theory and turns to the subject, he turns back to a unitary being that is closed, mortal, and embodied. For Kant, legitimate scientific knowledge stops at the limits of subjective consciousness; for Strauss, it stops at the dead human body.

Kerner could still appeal approvingly to Kant's work. In a discussion of the spirit-world in the *Seeress of Prevorst*, Kerner recalls that Kant, "that deep thinker," states in his "Dreams of a Ghost-Seer" that he could not bring himself to reject the credibility of all ghost stories. Individual stories might be improbable, but taken together they offer some weight of evidence. Even more, Kant refuses to make any certain claims about bodies and souls in life and death:

> Kant ... expresses that he knows as little of how the human spirit passes beyond a person, [that is], its condition after death, as he knows of how it enters into the world, [that is], how to explain its generation and propa-

---

90. Ibid., 303.

gation; or even how it exists in the present world, [that is], how it could be an immaterial nature in a body through which it is effective.[91]

This reticence stands in stark contrast with Strauss's approach to the nerve-spirit. Strauss too claims that ghost stories may have some basis in fact, and he cites the weight of the evidence; but he presents a priori limits on the organic nature of the facts in question. Strauss's architectonics of living and dead bodies and souls establishes an insuperable boundary against the possibility of certain spiritual phenomena.

Strauss's vision of the scientific method differs accordingly. From the 1830s onward, he repeatedly affirms his commitment to experimental method: a scientist must abstain from conclusions until he or she has all of the facts in hand and works with as few presuppositions as possible. When, in the *Accounts*, for example, he commends "a sharp, but not at the outset already unbelieving examination of the facts," he then adds that one should begin with an epoche "in regard to the theory ... which does not let the conclusion be rushed, but rather allows its further development be deferred to further, unknown observations and investigation."[92] "Ghosts" and "demons" belong to a class of obscurely known phenomena at best; it is better for us to rest content with only one known and accessible presupposition: the condition of the "suffering subject," the possessed individual.[93] But Strauss's caution does not lead him to suspend his monist and materialist worldview: the turn to a knowable, "suffering subject" keeps us firmly in its bounds. Experimental method, like subjective consciousness, forms part of the natural order of embodied life. While Strauss remains tenaciously open to new facts, any theoretical explanation of them must keep to the confines of that order.

Grombach, Anna U, and the Psychophysical Condition of Demonomania

Strauss's 1836 response to the *Accounts* presents a series of examples in which his openness to spiritual phenomena enables him to define in turn radical limits on their possible authenticity. He focuses in his response on the two cases that Kerner had observed personally: that of Magdalena Grombach, "the girl from Orlach," and "Anna Maria U," also from Württem-

---

91. Kerner, *Seherin von Prevorst*, 293–94.
92. Strauss, *Charateristiken und Kritiken*, 307.
93. Ibid., 306.

berg. Kerner diagnoses their conditions as a form of demonomania, specifically the "*kakodämonisch-magnetisch*" (evil-demonic magnetic) variety. He adduces precedents for this designation from the New Testament and modern history. At the same time, he distinguishes their "demonic paroxysms" from Hauffe's somnambulic-magnetic trance. Strauss agrees that no better term exists for the diagnosis of these women than to call them "possessed," but he adds that the name should not imply that we are dealing with cases of literal demon possession.[94]

Grombach and Anna U's conditions began in distinct ways. Anna U's seemed to spring from within. Her experiences resembled those of the demoniacs in the New Testament. She suffered from seizures for four months before she began to speak in a demonic voice. In Grombach's case, on the other hand, the demonic activity began outside of her. Before her possession, she witnessed a series of paranormal occurrences. She first saw visions of sinister animals and the form of a white ghost. At the same time, strange things began to happen on the farm where she lived—cows were released from their pens, for example, or found with their tails tied mysteriously together. The "black form of a monk" soon began to appear to Grombach. Her full-fledged demonic state began when this figure wrapped his fingers around her neck and entered into her body.

In spite of their differences, key, shared features of the women's experiences enabled Kerner to categorize them together. In particular, in their "paroxysms," both Anna U's and Grombach's consciousnesses seemed totally displaced.[95] They sought to resist the demons as hated attackers, but the spirits usurped their organs and voices and forced them to move and speak. Grombach's demon spoke in a rough, bass voice that did not resemble her own. She identified this demon as the soul of a monk who had died centuries earlier after he raped and murdered a nun. The women were also visited by good, tutelary spirits—in Grombach's case, the ghost of the nun—who protected them from the attacks. These similarities set the women equally apart from Hauffe. Kerner found, for example, that magnetic passes were less effective with them. In fact, the demon sometimes responded to these attempts at healing by compelling its host to perform counterstrokes. When he passed his hand upward to move magnetic forces toward Grombach's brain region, the demon compelled the

---

94. Ibid., 309.
95. Ibid.

patient to move her hand down along her body in the opposite direction.[96] Kerner therefore supplanted this treatment with exorcisms. In addition, although Hauffe and other somnambulists spoke at times of good, tutelary spirits and encounters with souls of the dead, these other women never experienced a wholesale displacement of their native consciousness—an "exchange of self"—like Anna U and Grombach did.

This displacement forms the crux of Kerner and Eschenmayer's views on demon possession. Kerner appends to the study of Grombach a reflection by a friend, a Pastor Gerber, who voices their shared sense of wonderment at this aspect of demonic states:

> Most marvelous is the exchange of personality. It is difficult to find a name for this state. The girl loses consciousness, her "I" disappears or rather another "I" takes its place. Another spirit now takes possession of this organism, of its sense organs, of its nerves and muscles, speaks with its throat, thinks with its brain nerves.[97]

In an allusion to the New Testament gospel accounts of demons, Gerber then adds, "it is just as if someone stronger comes and chases the owner out of the house and then looks comfortably out of the window as if it were his own."[98] Kerner records numerous incidents that give evidence of this displacement. He emphasizes that the demonic personalities differ from the customary dispositions of the two women and that they can recall buried memories and obscure events in the town's history. Gerber adds that we should distinguish their experiences from those of insane or dreaming people—the man so convinced he is caesar, for example, that he forgets he is a cobbler. The demoniacs suffer from a divided consciousness: the demonic ego and possessed individual remain aware of one another even as one prevails over the other at different times.[99] With these details in hand, Gerber, Kerner, and Eschenmayer class demon possession apart from insanity. Like Hauffe, the demoniacs' magnetic propensities grant them access to souls in the Hades region and vice versa. In their case, however, the souls in question are often manifestly evil. In his concluding

---

96. Kerner and Echenmayer, *Geschichten Besessener neuerer Zeit*, 31.
97. Ibid., 50.
98. Ibid.
99. Ibid.

reflections, Eschenmayer argues that possessions form part of the cosmic, religious struggle between good and evil spiritual forces.

Strauss embraces the nuance with which Gerber and Kerner distinguish between types and degrees of psychological disorder. But he brings the Manichean drama that they use to support it within the immanent frame of the women's individual bodies and minds. To begin, he localizes the demoniacs' spiritual battle in their subjective bodies. He takes his cue from the very romantic theories of physiology that Kerner, Eschenmayer, and others developed. The fact that demonomania would bewilder these physicians, Strauss says, surprises him:

> The only person who could marvel at the fact that the diseased inner life disintegrates into duality, one so to speak subjective and one objective, one dominating and one suppressed "I," is who does not know, or does not think clearly, that the "I" is already in itself and in a healthy condition this duplicity of a subject-object.[100]

The "I," the Ego, namely, is divided between the cerebral and ganglion systems, the brain and the epigastric region. These two distinct parts form a closed unity—the individual self or subject. It is surprising to see people familiar with magnetic conditions present the dualistic, "crass postulate" that an Ego and its body could be split, "as if a log or a wedge were driven in between."[101] Magnetism offers a clear alternative explanation. In somnambulic trance, for example, the ganglionic system prevails over the brain and nerves; the rational mind appears suppressed or driven out entirely. Why then could we not assume that a similar derangement occurs in possession, "an imprisonment of the brain's activity in that of the ganglia … in which the former remains in consciousness as what is suppressed and human, the latter as the prevailing demonic aspect?"[102] He offers as evidence of this view the mediating, tutelary spirits that appear to both of the women alongside their demons: these figures, who draw the women back toward a healthy state, are objectified representations of the underlying unity of their mind—just as the divided "demon" and "self" represent the internal divisions of their own consciousness. The presence of these medi-

---

100. Strauss, *Charateristiken und Kritiken*, 310.
101. Ibid., 311.
102. Ibid.

ating figures demonstrates that these women have not succumbed entirely to the dominance of the epigastric forces.

Contrasted with this subjective psychophysical explanation, the hypothesis that a demon usurps the demoniac's subjective consciousness must appear, he says, as an unnecessary "*deus ex machina*."[103] Strauss uses the same phrase to describe the theory of the nerve-spirit.[104] In both cases, it connotes the unfitting, superfluous character of these hypotheses: demons and the nerve-spirit come on the scene without precedent to tidily solve and explain the conditions in question. But the *machina* also conveys the closed nature of the self, its composite and autonomous totality in a unity of interlocking and mutually sustaining parts. As a principle of subjective life, any soul or spirit is only as real as the living parts that comprise it. Strauss's passage through romantic medicine and philosophy defines a remarkably negative[105] approach to spiritual matters. Ironically, Kerner, Schelling, and Schubert had opened for him a radical antisupernaturalism that extended to souls, nerve-spirits, and world-souls.

It bears insisting, however, that the rigor of this materialism rests precisely on the fact that it is not strictly mechanistic. In a reply to Strauss's *Life of Jesus* in 1836, Christian Hermann Weisse remarks that "speculative observers of nature" had made possible a more definitive counter to miracles than previous Enlightenment materialism had done. For the latter, natural law stands over and against any ostensible rupture in its opera-

---

103. Ibid., 306.

104. Ibid., 327.

105. Strauss's approach is negative in an ambivalent way. On the one hand, it serves to establish limits on spirit. On the other hand, this negative criticism does not follow the course of previous rationalism or deism. The negative movement is recuperated. It does not turn away from or reject what it identifies as irrational, sick, dead, or disordered (e.g., the Bible, superstitious people, demonomania). Rather the progress of science and culture depends, for Strauss, on our ability to grasp and make sense of what defies reason. As we confront the unsettling or seemingly irrational facts of nature and human experience, we define the limits of spirit and transform our own consciousness; we drive on the development of culture. The negative movement of criticism comprises irrationality, sickness, error, and fanaticism within a humanistic economy of spiritual development. In the third and fourth chapters, I will consider where this approach leads Strauss into proximity with Hegel's view of negativity and the progress of modern spirit, especially as these appear in the *Phenomenology of Spirit*. Here negativity signifies the creative capacity to think in opposition to or beyond what already exists. Strauss was one of the first major figures in his day to interpret this work, and Hegel's philosophy, in a resolutely humanistic and critical fashion

tion only as a superficial, external limit. The speculative philosopher of nature, on the other hand, places spirit wholly within nature as a closed but infinite and universal totality. Consequently, any break with the natural law would demand a radical contradiction—it would "fully negate and suspend the actual self, the substance and concept of nature."[106] Strauss develops this view into a systematic form.

Strauss defines the limits of *Geist*, mind or spirit, in effect, by making room for it within the confines of an immanent order. Psychological and spiritual phenomena are real and efficacious for Strauss. Even magnetic healings and clairvoyance are possible within embodied limits. His first premise, that demon possession can be traced to a unitary subjective Ego, sets the boundaries of his subsequent analysis, but he goes on to interpret an array of Kerner's individual observations on these immanent grounds. In some cases he appeals directly to theories about somnambulic states. He grants Grombach certain powers of precognition, for example, which might have allowed her to know that a neighbor would help her with building her barn or that a stranger would give her some gold. Tellingly, he presents this as a counter to alternative, supernaturalistic religious explanations: magnetic precognition gave an objective form to what Grombach took as a "revelation of spirit."[107] When Anna U's demon instructs her that the pot from which she will eat is cracked and lets her know where she can find another, Strauss explains this as well as an example of the "far-seeing" powers of magnetic individuals.[108]

But this startling elasticity within the immanent order only illuminates more starkly its boundaries. If clairvoyance is possible, nerve-spirits are an unnecessary *deus ex machina*. Although magnetism is possible, "demons" and "tutelary spirits" are better understood as projections of people's inner magnetic lives. Strauss's appeals to paranormal phenomena blend invariably into psychological explanations that feel more modern and critical. For example, when Kerner emphasizes how strange it is that the poorly-educated Grombach's tutelary spirit can remember obscure Bible verses, Strauss counters, "Among somnambulists scenes from earliest childhood,

---

106. Christian Hermann Weisse, quoted in August Tholuck, *Die Glaubwürdigkeit der evangelischen Geschichte: Zugleich eine Kritik des Lebens Jesu von Strauss: Für theologische und nicht theologische Leser* (Hamburg: Perthes, 1837), 95–96.
107. Strauss, *Charakteristiken und Kritiken*, 318.
108. Ibid., 319.

long hidden from the healthy mind, often appear in the most clear light."[109] His view of somnambulism does not lead back to romanticism and mysticism. Rather, it anticipates a modern theory of repression: when the defensive forces of the rational mind fade away, buried memories come to the fore. The contents of these memories are often matters of scandalous import, moreover—crimes and taboo behavior. The ghost's descriptions of "deceit, drunkenness, fornication, denial of paternity, brawls, and murder" are typical of the lower class of people to whom the ghost was supposed to belong, Strauss claims, but also "can be fabricated unconsciously in diseases belonging to people in the same class, when their imagination is excited to the point of a pathological production."[110] The limits of spirit are defined by the embodied life of the subject in a second sense, then: spiritual phenomena are possible, but only as long as they are consistent with a person's cultural, physical, and psychological experience.

Esslinger and the Cultural Conditions of Paranormal Experience

At the same time, these psychological and cultural aspects of Anna U and Grombach's experiences become objects of analysis in their own right. Strauss's turn to the subjective grounds of paranormal experience not only underwrites his critique of spiritual phenomena; it opens onto the psychological and social conditions through which these phenomena took shape. If we cannot accept demons or nerve-spirits, we must nevertheless account for people's experience of them. Where a phenomenon presses up against the limits of nature, Strauss asks that we refocus our attention from the event in question to the subjective mind that conceived it. Because Strauss embraced a monistic worldview, this turn to the subject would also lead back to the objective body. It led in addition to the objective world of culture and history that shaped consciousness. He turns first to the disordered psychophysical state and life experiences of the patients in question, as in the cases of Anna U and Magdalena Grombach. He then considers the role that culture, education, and gender play in shaping their perceptions. Demonomania is a psychophysical disease, but its expression is mediated by culture. Thus Grombach's evil monk makes his confession in the idiom of the class and community that she shared with him.

---

109. Ibid.
110. Ibid., 321.

Strauss develops this psychological and cultural analysis explicitly in another piece from 1836 on a series of ghost sightings at a rural prison. The phenomena in this case began with a woman named Elisabeth Esslinger, a ghost seer and treasure seeker whom Kerner visited in the prison at Weinsberg in 1835. She claimed that she was visited regularly by the ghost of a fifteenth-century priest who had stolen money from his parish. This dead priest begged her to visit the spot to which his soul remained bound to the material world and, when she had done so, to pray for his salvation.[111] After her release from prison, she granted the request in a well-attended ceremony with many miraculous occurrences.[112] A variety of witnesses attested to evidence of the ghost's presence and communications with Esslinger. During the same period, fellow prisoners, court officials, Kerner, and people in the nearby town all perceived unusual, seemingly related phenomena in or around the prison. Other prisoners heard strange tones and loud noises, smelled a musty odor, or saw flickering lights and vaguely human forms appear. Those at a further remove described eerie flashes of electric light, diffuse phosphorescence, and a gray mist. Others heard similar tones and smelled the same musty odor.[113]

Confronted with these various and well-attested strange occurrences, Strauss follows the same course he had taken with Hauffe and Grombach. He does not dispute, with one exception, that the witnesses really perceived what they claimed to have perceived. Uncharacteristically, he admits that Esslinger alone might have engaged in some intentional deception—she had been arrested for duping people, he explains, as part of her divination and treasure-seeking business.[114] Aside from the possible exception of Esslinger, however, it is not a question of deception but of self-deception; we are pitched back from the phenomena to the underlying subjective mentality that shaped them.

This is a different order of self-deception, moreover, from that which we saw in the case of Grombach and Anna U. Their false perceptions were shaped by life experiences, but were still partly pathological. They resulted from the disordered state of their bodies and minds. There is no question

---

111. Justinus Kerner, *Eine Erscheinung aus dem Nachtgebiete der Natur: Durch eine Reihe von Zeugen bestätigt und dem Naturforschern zum Bedenken mitgetheilt* (Stuttgart: Cotta, 1836), 12–13.
112. Ibid., 205–11.
113. Strauss, *Charakteristiken und Kritiken*, 329–31.
114. Ibid., 333.

of mental illness or irrationality per se among the witnesses at Weinsberg. He describes even Esslinger, for example, "as a widow, uncultured, but still of sound natural reason."[115] Rather, he explains the events in terms of distinctions between the witnesses' genders, on the one hand, and levels of culture and education, on the other.

Strauss distinguishes between a series of groups of observers whom Kerner names in his report: Esslinger and other female prisoners, the male prisoners in the next room, those who perceived phenomena in nearby locales, and the group of "learned and scientific men," for example, the district court judge, other civil officials, doctors, and professors of mathematics and physics who witnessed the events.[116] Distinctions in physical distance stand as such alongside distinctions in gender, class, and education. These distinctions correspond to discrepancies in how the witnesses perceived the events—discrepancies, in particular, in how solid and present the ghosts and their voices appeared to individuals in each group. During one of the ghost's appearances, the men in the adjoining room saw only an "indeterminate luminosity," for example, where the women in the room itself saw a human figure. The educated observers heard only "inarticulate tones," when the prisoners thought they heard words being spoken. But Strauss does not linger on the question of relative distance. He asks, rather, whether "it is not clear, that fear and superstition allowed some to see and hear more than was really to be perceived?"[117] In effect, gender and education have as much of a mitigating influence on how people perceive paranormal phenomena as their physical distance from them.

Strauss asserts as such that subjective experience is shaped from its roots by distinctions in class, culture, and gender. He does not distinguish between the witnesses' capacity for reason per se. Rather, polarities between genders and levels of culture define a relative capacity to mediate and make sense of what the witnesses perceive. They determine the shape of subjective, rational minds, as much as the interactions of the ganglionic and brain systems. Kant had argued that all our perceptions of the world are mediated and made possible by subjective consciousness; for Strauss, this consciousness is also historical, cultural, and contextual. Ideas about ghosts are not pure fantasies, because they coalesce within the frame of a particular mode of cultural thought. It is therefore

---

115. Ibid., 329.
116. Ibid., 329.
117. Ibid., 336.

irresponsible for science to dismiss the claims of ghost seeing clairvoyants and demoniacs, because they give us new information about human minds and the way that culture shapes them. They lead from the critical study of facts to the scientific study of human consciousness.

This scientific perspective also serves, however, to define and reinforce the cultural hierarchy that Strauss uses as an analytic. Each individual sees, smells, and hears from the vantage of his or her relatively advanced or delayed position in the course of spiritual *Bildung*. Strauss demands that science take seriously the ghost visions of uneducated, lower-class women, but only in the light of hierarchical distinctions between classes, genders, and levels of education. As such, Strauss adopts and alters Schubert and Schelling's accounts of culture. He traces analogies between the microcosm of individual subjective minds and the macrocosm of culture. Polarities between the rational mind and material body mirror those between educated and unenlightened people, or between men and women. Furthermore, these polarities are hierarchical. The progress of spirit in history leads from the worldviews of those dominated by the *Herzgrub* to educated people in whom it stands entirely under the direction of reason. Unlike Schelling or Schubert, however, Strauss does away with any romantic concessions to the more intuitive or divine inner life of those on the lower end of the hierarchy. One cannot support their claims or perceptions, any more than we should avoid them. Disordered ideas must be taken seriously, but they can only be fully comprehended within a correct, modern and rational worldview.

The work of science parallels as such the process of development that takes place in education and culture. Critical science ensures the ongoing movement of *Bildung*. It stands at the avant-garde of modern progress. Only an educated, critical person can stare religious phenomena in the face without being overwhelmed by them. If, on the one hand, physical distance keeps us from perceiving the nocturnal side of nature and, on the other hand, education keeps us from being overwhelmed by it, then it is up to educated people to draw as near as possible to these phenomena without putting off the critical resources of modern culture. An unflinching science alone can mediate their truth; education can stave off the lingering traces of premodern mentalities. Strauss's youthful *Bildung*-narrative models a kind of heroic, critical disposition. His ironic rapprochement with romanticism serves as a badge of modern honor, a testament to his scientific nerve. Strauss knows he is modern and critical, because he can confront directly the temptations of faith and emerge utterly skeptical.

It bears recalling in addition that Strauss was writing at a time when new institutions of spiritual authority and inquiry had begun to dominate the cultural landscape—the university, in particular, and the asylum. Strauss struck out against the dogmatic and apologetic views of orthodox theologians, but he also challenged the views of rural folk healers and clairvoyants. In the context of rural nineteenth-century Germany, a "demoniac" could exercise a surprising degree of authority within his or her milieu. Studies of possession across cultures have highlighted the influential social positions that possessed women often occupy in their societies.[118] Rural nineteenth-century Germany was no exception. Kerner describes the various women who were the subjects of his reports—Hauffe, Grombach, Anna U, and Esslinger—accessing secret knowledge about the cosmos, prophesying the future, and interacting with dead souls. At times, they act as mouthpieces and even confessors for these souls.[119] Grombach's tutelary spirit, for example, asks for aid in her salvation the first time that they meet. On March fourth, she appears to her in her room, just after the demolition of the house has begun. She explains that no one can bring spirits into heaven except for the savior, Christ; however, "the earthiness which holds me here below can be taken from me by you: through your mouth I can tell the world the atrocities that weigh on me." She then tells the story of her relationship with the monk. After she finishes, her soul disappears from the earth. When Grombach relates this story, she presents it as a parable of salvation for the living. Before the spirit departed, she says, it twice exclaimed, "no one should wait until after the end, but should confess his guilt to the world before he dies!"[120] This and other similar revelations exercise extraordinary sway over the women's friends, their families, and religious authorities. After the tutelary spirit tells Grombach that she will be cured only if she promises to tear down her house on the fifth of March, her father, a person of stature in her community, dutifully arranges for the house to be demol-

---

118. See, for example, Janice Boddy, "Spirit Possession Revisited: Beyond Instrumentality," *Annual Review of Anthropology* 23 (1994): 407–34; Susan Starr Sered, *Priestess, Mother, Sacred Sister: Religions Dominated by Women* (Oxford: Oxford University Press, 1994); Mary Keller, *The Hammer and the Flute: Women, Power, and Spirit Possession* (Baltimore: Johns Hopkins University Press, 2002); and Erika Bourguignon, "Suffering and Healing, Subordination and Power," *Ethos* 32 (2004): 557–74.

119. Kerner and Echenmayer, *Geschichten Besessener neuerer Zeit*, 43–44, 90–94.

120. Ibid., 41.

ished on the assigned date.[121] Kerner also accepts the spirit's promise; he gives up on magnetic cures in the meantime.

Strauss grants a certain legitimacy to the subjects of ghost seeing and demon possession: they are not irrational, stupid, or insane. But he undermines their credibility as spiritual authorities. If they are not, with the exception of Esslinger, hopeless liars or outright mad people, they should be subject to corrective education: "it is now the endeavor of all rational educators to expel from the youth," he writes, in the response to Kerner, "opinions about demon possession and magic."[122] His appeal comes during an era of campaigns of *Volksaufklärung*, popular Enlightenment, in the eighteenth and nineteenth centuries. These campaigns sought to colonize and systematize the symbolic worlds of the German peasantry. The peasantry appeared to public officials and *Aufklärern* to be especially prone to superstition and fanaticism; they needed to be educated. Pastors, state administrators, and school teachers set out to disabuse people of enthusiastic beliefs. Ecumenical, rational, and tolerant religious views formed a cornerstone of the curriculum.

Although *Aufklärers* opposed religious intolerance and political tyranny, their work often served the interests of an absolutist state. German state officials and aristocrats enthusiastically embraced and supported the *Volksaufklärung*.[123] It played a crucial role in state formation: it not only defined the illegitimacy of competing models of spiritual authority, it helped to unify a diverse people. Those who were not ready to be inducted into the enlightened public sphere, on the other hand, were subject to a different, often more painful model of reformative education. Ann Goldberg's study of the Eberbach asylum in the German *Vormärz* has shown the extent to which campaigns of popular Enlightenment in the churches and schools went hand-in-hand with a growing discourse

---

121. Kerner says that he was an upright, honest farmer. He eventually became the mayor of Orlach (Kerner and Echenmayer, *Geschichten Besessener neuerer Zeit*, 20).

122. Strauss, *Charakteristiken und Kritiken*, 302.

123. Jonathan B. Knudsen notes for example that princes, administrators, and rural pastors played a far more substantial role in freely distributing Rudolf Becker's *Noth- und Hülfsbüchlein für Bauersleute*, a novel on the education of the peasantry, than its intended audience ("On Enlightenment for the Common Man," in *What is Enlightenment? Eighteenth-Century Answers and Twentieth-Century Questions*, ed. James Schmidt [Los Angeles: University of California Press, 1996], 277–78). See also Ann Golderg, *Sex, Religion, and the Making of Modern Madness*.

on religious pathology and the rise of the asylum.[124] Medical, psychological explanations of religious disorder transformed potential threats from inspired charismatics into objects of education, psychiatric treatment, and imprisonment.

Conclusion

In his writings on the nocturnal side of nature, Strauss develops a distinct approach to the scientific study of religious belief and experience. The scientist is to take the most esoteric spiritual phenomena and claims totally seriously; however, this engagement should lead from the occurrences in question to the modes of consciousness that shape religious experience. It should bring the world of spirit wholly within the frame of an immanent, material cosmos. This model of critique mirrors his account of his early *Bildung*. At the start of his career, he feels an attraction to the nocturnal side of nature. He approaches it with sincerity, openness, and even piety. This movement culminates when he brings religious objects into a systematic monist vision of the cosmos, bodies, and souls. For Strauss as for his romantic contemporaries, this subjective and scientific process is reflected in the macrocosms of culture and the progress of spirit in history. Education, critique, and history follow the same course. Strauss breaks with romanticism, however, and characterizes this movement as one-sidedly critical and progressive. He defines in the process a hierarchy of culture, with critical, modern science at its apex and serving as its guiding light. It is crucial that we stare the strange regions of religious belief in the face. Only then do we pass fully into the modern age.

In each of these respects, Strauss defines a demystifying, secularizing approach to religion. Still, we can affirm with Nast that the roots of this skeptical project lay in an early affinity for romantic thought and paranormal phenomena. If his writings reflect the context of campaigns of popular Enlightenment, it bears considering how the theories and revelations of Hauffe and Grombach shaped Strauss and Kerner's views of science, God, and nature. In the chapter that follows, I turn to Strauss's most famous work, his *Life of Jesus*, to pursue this question. I turn as such from his work on contemporary German religious belief and experience to that of

---

124. Golberg, *Sex, Religion, and the Making of Modern Madness*, 63–71.

the ancient, biblical world. Here too we can trace complex ways in which Strauss's critical, secularizing approach intersected with nocturnal regions of religious belief.

2

The Nocturnal Side of Strauss's Historical Critique of Miracle Stories

Strauss's *Life of Jesus* was published in two volumes in 1835–1836. The first volume appeared five years after the first essay on Hauffe; the second appeared in 1836, the year that he wrote his response to Kerner's case studies of Anna U and Grombach. In the previous chapter, I argued that in the psychological writings Strauss developed a scientific, critical approach to questions about medical and religious pathologies and that he did so by way of the romantic study of paranormal religious phenomena—ghost seeing, possession, clairvoyance, and magnetism. I consequently affirmed with Nast that the roots of Strauss's "extreme skeptical bent" were tangled up with his early affinity for esoteric regions of belief. In what follows, I pursue the implications of Nast's suggestion in regard to Strauss's better known work on the gospels and the historical Jesus. I continue as such to trace the unfamiliar religious field in which his materialist, scientific worldview and critical methods took root.

The *Life of Jesus* became a touchstone in the demystification and rationalization of religion soon after its publication. Strauss's attempt to carry out a historical critique without "presuppositions" defined an ethos and rhetoric of *Wissenschaft* in the fields of history and theology. He laid out the consequences of modern philological and historical criticism for the historicity of the gospels in an especially thoroughgoing fashion. Many of his conclusions presaged those that dominated in historical criticism of the Bible from the turn of the twentieth century onward. Contemporaries as otherwise distinct as Marx, Baur, and the orthodox theologian August Tholuck recognized the irreversible impact the *Life of Jesus* had in what Marx would famously go on to define as "the criticism of religion."[1] Nevertheless, here as in Strauss's writings on the nocturnal side of nature, demystifying critique involved a complex negotiation of sometimes arcane religious arguments. His shift from "religious" to "scientific" psychological or historical conceptions was by no means straightforward. Strauss had to draw and contest lines between these regions at every turn.

Since the start of the twentieth century, commentators have debated whether Strauss's conclusions in the *Life of Jesus* reflected a legitimate, scientific conception of history or were side-effects of his speculative perspective, that is, his youthful interest in the philosophy of Hegel.[2] This framing obscures Strauss's place in the broad field of romantic thought. His views on the limits and possibilities of the natural world and human body were reflected as much in the work of Schelling, Schubert, and Kerner as in that of Hegel. I argue that Strauss did in fact define a lasting and modern scientific approach to historical criticism. But in his work on history as in that on psychology, his critical ethic and method only became possible by way of romantic cosmology and medicine. Specifically, his studies in these regions enabled him to define the limits of "history" and "nature" against which he measured the authenticity of the gospel reports. This was among the most controversial aspects of the work, especially as it touched on the miracle narratives—the resurrection and Jesus and his disciples' healing ministry, for example.

In the *Life of Jesus*, as in the writings on demon possession and clairvoyance, romantic medicine initially widened the spectrum of credible strange and wondrous events. Strauss had, after all, witnessed firsthand "possessions" and "miraculous" cures like those in the New Testament gospels. But here again the nocturnal side of natural science closed in

---

1. Marx, "Toward the Critique of Hegel's Philosophy of Law: Introduction," in *Writings of the Young Marx on Philosophy and Society*, 249.

2. Hans Frei claims, for example, that Hegel's philosophy led Strauss to important historical critical conclusions in the *Life of Jesus*, but that by the 1860s he had "thrown off the Hegelian incubus" in favor of "the strong conviction that the empirical and historical-critical sense of *Wissenschaft* was the most important" (Frei, "David Friedrich Strauss," 248). Ernst Troeltsch asserts that historiography should not need the "Hegelian-tinted thought" of Strauss: "historical method" provides its own principles of interpretation (Troeltsch, "On the Historical and Dogmatic Methods in Theology," in *Gesammelte Schriften*, trans. Jack Forstman, (Tubingen: Mohr Siebeck, 1913), 2:731. See also Sandberger, *David Friedrich Strauss* and Harvey, "Strauss's Life of Jesus Revisited." Sandberger and Harvey consider his status as a Hegelian thinker in light of his historical critical approach and value as a historian in light of his Hegelianism, respectively.

practice what it had opened in principle. At the heart of his account of Jesus's miracles, Strauss places the same conception of a unitary, mortal, embodied subject that we saw in his contemporary responses to Kerner. This placement enabled him to twist the monist and organic cosmology that he used to set limits on the miracle stories in a critical, materialist direction. His view of bodies and souls forms the crux of a radical historical critique. It extends outward, moreover, to form a global vision of the limits of spirit in space and time. As such, his writings on possession and ghost seeing in the ancient and modern world converge in an essential way with his better-known, lifelong obsession with immanence and the limits of Christian eschatology.

Strauss on Historical Critical *Wissenschaft* in the *Life of Jesus*

The results of Strauss's historical critical analysis of the gospels were dramatic and negative.[3] Many authors had written "lives of Jesus" before him. But their efforts were largely reconstructive. Enlightenment criticism had taken a devastating toll on the gospel histories. Critics had exposed their contradictions and rejected as unhistorical their patently miraculous elements. But they still took the gospels as credible eyewitness sources. Most theologians in Strauss's day admitted that the events might have been tangled in their retelling or that the evangelists' understanding of them was colored by their ancient view of the world; however, interpreters continued to attempt to sort through these confusions in order to craft a realistic, rational biography of the life and death of Jesus.[4] Orthodox theologians hoped to prove thereby that a modern person could still see the gospels as literally true and inspired; interpreters of a more liberal, rationalist inclination sought to uncover an image of the historical Jesus on which modern

---

3. Here as in the psychological writings, the first face of Strauss's negativity appears in the radical limits that he sets on spirit. At the same time, this unflinchingly negative confrontation with limits will comprise in turn the progressive movement of spirit. It secures the ongoing development of human science and culture in history.

4. Schweitzer surveys many of the best-known examples, including the works by Paulus and Schleiermacher cited below, in Albert Schweitzer, *The Quest of the Historical Jesus*, trans. W. Montgomery (Mineola, NY: Dover, 2012), 27–67. See also Hans Frei, "Hermeneutical Options at the Turn of the Century," in *The Eclipse of Biblical Narrative: A Study in Eighteenth and Nineteenth Century Hermeneutics* (New Haven: Yale University Press, 1977), 245–66.

faith could rest—Jesus was a protomodern ethical teacher, for example, or a man endowed with a unique consciousness of the divine.

In his *Life of Jesus*, on the other hand, Strauss moves through the narratives in a systematic fashion to set limits on their credibility. At each point, he describes other interpreters' attempts to authenticate the narratives and shows why they fail. He makes use of a more exacting philological and historical critique, in which he adduces as evidence the narratives' plain sense, their internal contradictions, and their many evident violations of the laws of nature, history, and human psychology. Finally, he turns to the "mythical interpretation" as a compelling alternative. He argues that the stories are not mainly eyewitness accounts but myths, blends of legendary material that coalesced around the person of Jesus soon after his death.

In the preface to the first edition of the *Life of Jesus*, Strauss lays out the "scientific" and "critical" foundations of his distinct approach. He states that his qualifications for this undertaking have nothing to do with either his learning or critical skill; rather, they lie in his freedom from "presuppositions." He writes,

> The majority of the most learned and acute theologians of the present day fail in the main requirement for such a work, a requirement without which no amount of learning will suffice to achieve anything in the domain of criticism—namely, the internal liberation of the feelings and intellect from certain religious and dogmatical presuppositions; and this the author early attained by means of philosophical studies. If theologians regard this absence of presupposition from his work, as unchristian: he regards the believing presuppositions of theirs as unscientific.[5]

Science had to set aside two presuppositions held by the ancient church in particular: "first, that the gospels contained a history, and secondly, that this history was a supernatural one." Rationalist theology had rejected the second presupposition, "but only to cling more tenaciously to the former, maintaining that these books present unadulterated, though only natural, history." This was not enough: "the other presupposition also must be relinquished, and the inquiry must first be made whether in fact, and to what extent, the ground on which we stand in the gospels is historical."[6] Theological *Wissenschaft* must be prepared to undertake an unflinching

---

5. *LJ* 1835, 1:vi; *LJ* 1892, xxx.
6. *LJ* 1835, 1:v; *LJ* 1892, xxix.

historical critique of the gospels; it must put the historicity of every narrative to the test.

In this passage, Strauss distills a modern ethic and rhetoric of historical science. He draws on a well-established trope of Enlightenment discourse, one that had defined the modern era as an "age of criticism," in the words of Kant[7]—criticism takes human reason as its principle and refuses to exempt even authoritative religious texts from examination. Strauss learned early from Baur and Schleiermacher to turn back from the ostensible mystical authority of religious objects to the grounds of critical self-consciousness. When considering the texts of the New Testament or events in rural Württemberg, Christian beliefs and reported "facts" about demon possessions or healing miracles could not trump the rational criteria by which one would test and limit their historicity.

At the same time, he set the tone for an array of critical work to come. He expressed this commitment to a freedom from presuppositions at a time when experimental models from the natural sciences were beginning to reshape the ethos of humanistic inquiry. Over the coming decades, thinkers in a variety of fields would conceive free, objective science in opposition to dogma and ideology, including even the ideology of speculative philosophical thinkers like Schelling or Hegel, which were too riddled with presuppositions. Positivist approaches to historiography and natural science would soon dominate in nineteenth-century Germany. In Strauss's own later writings on the New Testament, he takes up a more exclusively positive, empiricist model of science and criticism.

Not all of Strauss's contemporaries were convinced by his claims to this effect, however. After the *Life of Jesus* appeared, some demanded to know in what, precisely, this "freedom from presuppositions" consisted. In one of his *Polemical Writings in Defense of the Life of Jesus*,[8] Strauss credits Ernst Hengstenberg, the conservative and orthodox editor of the *Evangelische Kirchenzeitung*, with articulating this criticism with particular clarity. In the introduction to an 1836 piece in defense of the authenticity of the Pentateuch, Hengstenberg asserts that Strauss's *Life of Jesus* was as "full

---

7. Kant, *Critique of Pure Reason*, ed. Guyer and Wood, 100 n.*.

8. David Friedrich Strauss, *Die Evangelische Kirchenzeitung, die Jahrbücher für wissenschaftliche Kritik und die theologischen Studien und Kritiken in ihrer Stellung zu meiner kritischen Bearbeitbung des Lebens Jesu.* Vol. 3 of *Streitschriften zur Vertheidigung meiner Schrift*, 7–54. Hereafter cited as *Streitschriften*.

of irreligious presuppositions as it was void of religious presuppositions."[9] Strauss's initial claim to an unbiased scientific perspective was only a pretense. His approach led inexorably to his negative results, because his philosophical perspective predetermined it. The *Life of Jesus* only proves, therefore, that we should free ourselves "from the prejudgment that there is some abstract science of entirely unbiased critique; there is only believing or unbelieving critique."[10] Abstract science is as prejudiced as faith. Unlike faith, however, it presumes to avoid prejudice.

Strauss concedes that there is some truth to Hengstenberg's argument. Historical critique has to bring along the scale by which it weighs historicity; it can therefore be said to rest on one fundamental presupposition: "One can express with a word what makes up the presupposition of historical critique: it is the essential homogeneity of all occurrence [*die wesentliche Gleichartigkeit alles Geschehens*]."[11] Historical critique begins by asserting that miracles are impossible. Events, objects, and persons inhere in a network of causes and conditions. Consequently, no radically unique events can occur. Real differences exist and new events take place in history, but only within the same homogeneous field of possibilities. Strauss makes the same point in the footnote that he adds to the second and later editions of the *Life of Jesus*:

> To an absence of presupposition we lay claim in the following work; in the same sense as a state might be called free from presupposition where the privileges of station, etc., were of no account. Such a state indeed has one presupposition, that of the natural equality of its citizens; and similarly do we take for granted the equal amenability to law of all events.[12]

This singular presupposition emerges from and mirrors the best aspirations of Enlightenment critique and science. Critical historiography rejects miracles in the same way that critical politics rejects privilege. The democratic aspirations of the age of criticism are reflected in the flat and even canvas on which it draws historical events.

---

9. Hengstenberg, *Evangelische Kirchen-Zeitung*, June 1836, 48:36, quoted in Strauss, *Streitschriften* 3:35.

10. Hengstenberg, *Evangelische Kirchen-Zeitung*, June 1836, 48:36, quoted in Strauss, *Streitschriften*, 3:35–36.

11. Strauss, *Streitschriften* 3:37.

12. *LJ* 1840 1:84 n. 5; *LJ* 1892, 80 n. 5.

He goes on to submit, however, that Hengstenberg's objection goes too far. If this conception of a homogeneous cosmos is a presupposition, it is not of the same order as the theological, dogmatic presuppositions that he rejects. "Because it is not drawn subjectively," he explains, "from the mind of the critic, but objectively, from its subject matter, history, it cannot actually be called a presupposition."[13] History provides its own principles of interpretation. This claim presages later historiographers' commitment to attend to history itself, on its own terms. It seems to push back against the speculative and theoretical turn of idealism.

Romantic Cosmology and the Modern Critique of Miracle

But what does "history itself" mean for Strauss? And how does he arrive at the principle of the homogeneity of all occurrences? Strauss's position on miracles and history did not stand ready to hand. He had to work it out in and through the speculative regions of theology and philosophy. In the *Life of Jesus* and in his later *Polemical Writings*, Strauss traces the critique of miracle to an immanent, monistic conception of sacred history and revelation—of the operation of God and spirit in the organic world of mundane life. In both writings, his references to his freedom from presuppositions crop up accordingly in the context of overtly religious and speculative discussions. The passage from the *Polemical Writings* includes a reflection on magnetism, presentiment, and miraculous healings.[14] The footnote from the *Life of Jesus* closes an account of how God works in and through nature. Here again, romantic and mystical thought play a key role in Strauss's articulation of humanistic science. The fundamental presupposition of historical criticism does not reflect any objection to idealism per se; rather, it emerges out of a radical, systematic pursuit of the consequences of romantic cosmology.[15]

---

13. Strauss, *Streitschriften* 3:39.
14. Strauss, *Streitschriften*, 3:37–39.
15. Vischer characterizes Strauss's immanent worldview as both the driving force behind his vision of scientific critique and a prime example of the influence that Württemberg Pietist theosophy had on him. On the one hand, the two begin from the same cosmological and theological principle: "How is mysticism related to the speculative worldview which lies at the root of Straussian critique? Common to both is the principle of God's immanence in relation to the world. The world should not have an essential independent substance separate from God, nor should it be directed externally by God. This is an entirely nonsensical representation. Rather, it is permeated throughout by God" ("Dr.

In the introduction to the *Life of Jesus*, he traces the evolution of the modern critique of miracles through a series of interconnected shifts in modern theology and historical criticism. The credibility of miracles had, of course, been put to the test many times over the preceding centuries. Scholars had come to accept that the world was subject to inviolable natural laws. In Hume's famous formulation in his *Enquiry Concerning Human Understanding* in 1748, a miracle would be a violation of the laws of nature—it is a supernatural, transcendent, and therefore inconceivable event.[16] The rational grounds for rejecting miracles from this perspective are both theological and empirical. On the one hand, it is inconsistent to suggest that a just and omnipotent creator would break the very laws it had instantiated. It is equally difficult to explain why God would limit miracles to peculiar, local cases. Often, the biblical miracle accounts reduce God to an undignified position. He chooses flawed humans as his agents, carries out morally questionable acts, and saves some people while leaving others to suffer and perish. On the other hand, miracles contradict our rational understanding of experience. Hume uses death and resurrection as an example. We know the laws of nature from the overwhelming, consistent testimony of our own senses: objects fall, fire burns, and people die. We see people die suddenly and unexpectedly all the time. Hence our experience teaches us that this is not a miracle. A resurrection, on the other hand, which has never been observed, would constitute a genuine breach in the natural order as we know it. Consequently, a rational person will not accept testimony about a resurrection, unless not doing so would demand a still greater violation of experience. It is more consistent to believe that a witness is lying or deluded than to accept such a unique fact.[17]

The Enlightenment polemic against belief in miracles developed substantially in the field of biblical interpretation. Strauss locates the origins of the modern historical critique of miracles among deists in the late seventeenth and early eighteenth centuries. Deism comprised for Strauss the broad range of Enlightenment theologies that removed divinity from the

---

Strauss," 99). On the other hand, they diverge radically from that point. We should by no means conflate Straussian critique with mysticism. Strauss arrives at this immanent vision through mediated thought, where mystics and Pietists experience it in the immediacy of religious ecstasy. Consequently, the latter continue to embrace the flawed, older belief in immediate divine intervention (ibid.).

16. Hume, *Enquiry Concerning Human Understanding*, 86.
17. Ibid., 133–34 (§90).

historical world in order to do justice to both God and natural law. A remote, supreme God acted immediately on the world of finite things at its creation; he then left it to work toward its ends on its own devices. In a sense, God still interacted with nature and human beings, but only through the mediation of the laws he put in place. Hence, deists did not believe that religious truth appeared in specific historical incidents. The divine reveals itself only indirectly, in the workings of nature, which we comprehend through natural human reason. This Enlightenment theology gravitated toward a universal "natural religion" in place of those "positive religions" that rested on unique, special revelations in the course of history.

In England, deists such as John Toland, Thomas Chubb, and Thomas Morgan criticized the miracle stories in the Bible. Strauss credits them with showing just how widely the texts diverged from modern views of nature, history, and psychology. They interpreted the Hebrew Bible in particular as a collection of fantasies and lies. The work reflected the superstitions of antiquity; it had been crafted by power-hungry religious leaders, beginning with Moses, who wished to bring a credulous laity under their control. Other critics leveled similar polemics against the New Testament, where the apostles and Jesus took the place of Moses.[18]

Deist interpretation made its way gradually from England into Germany in the middle of the eighteenth century, following a 1741 translation of Matthew Tindal's 1730 *Christianity as Old as Creation*.[19] A number of translations of English works followed suit. In 1774–1778, Lessing presented full-fledged deist criticism to the German reading public. He published a controversial series of short pieces by an anonymous author, later discovered to be Reimarus, who had died in 1768. The pieces formed part of a larger unpublished work. Reimarus argued that Moses manipulated his followers. He performed false wonders and claimed to have received revelations from God. Reimarus's Jesus was a Jewish messianist with political ambitions: he hoped to bring about a new kingdom on earth. His efforts failed, however, and his final words in Mark and Matthew—"My God, my God, why have you forsaken me?"—show the disappointment that he and his disciples must have felt at the crucifixion (Matt 27:46; Mark

---

18. *LJ* 1835, 1:12; *LJ* 1892, 45.
19. Matthew Tindal and Jacob Foster, *Beweis, dass das Christenthum so alt als die Welt sey: Nebst Herrn Jacob Fosters Widerlegung desselben*, trans. Johann Lorenz Schmidt (Frankfurt: n. p. 1741).

15:34). The supernatural elements in the stories, beginning with the resurrection, served as a compensation for this loss.[20]

For many German scholars, Reimarus's fragments appeared to mark a decisive rupture between modern historical science and faith. Lessing maintained that they showed that Christians should look for the truth of Christianity outside of historical investigation.[21] Truth appears in the sphere of universal reason, not mired in the contingencies of history—contingencies of which miracles, as random breaches in the order of nature, would offer the clearest examples. The deist critique of miracles not only showed that special divine interventions were impossible, but that universal truth and religious faith should not rest on them. Similar conclusions led Kant to set apart historical and philosophical criticism of the Bible. Historical analysis could only uncover limited, particular truths. A rational, philosophical approach, however, could unlock its universal symbolic meaning.[22]

Nevertheless, Reimarus, Kant, and Lessing were exceptions among German scholars. Most rejected deist interpretation. In general, they were reluctant to sever the truth of Christianity from the Bible's ostensibly historical referents, especially those in the New Testament gospels. On the one hand, they did not wish to insult the apostles, evangelists, or Jesus. They could not accept that the narratives resulted from delusion or deception. On the other, German Protestants were committed to a historical, positive faith grounded in the Scriptures.[23] If the New Testament did not describe literal miracles in the way that previous generations had believed, it still bore witness to a unique and transformative series of events in the history of humanity. Many even of the most critical German scholars believed the Bible was centrally important for the culture and religion of modernity.

Strauss traces this reaffirmation of the Bible to a revised conception of God's role in history and nature. German theologians and higher critics in the late eighteenth and early nineteenth century joined the romantic

---

20. Reimarus, *Von dem Zwecke Jesu und seiner Jünger: Noch ein Fragment des Wolfenbüttelschen Ungenannten*, ed. Gotthold Ephraim Lessing (Braunschweig: n.p., 1778). This was the final fragment that Lessing published.

21. Lessing, *Theological Writings*, 53.

22. Immanuel Kant, "Religion within the Boundaries of Mere Reason" in *Religion and Rational Theology*, 57–215.

23. Frei, *Eclipse of Biblical Narrative*, 54–65 discusses the particular German Protestant commitment to "positivity," namely, that historical facticity constitutes an essential part of the truth of Christian revelation.

2. STRAUSS'S HISTORICAL CRITIQUE OF MIRACLE STORIES

philosophers and physicians who took aim at the dualistic tendency of Enlightenment thought. They rejected cosmologies that divided God and the world, the infinite and finite, or subjects and objects. In particular, they objected to the deist representation of God as a being who stands wholly apart from the realm of nature and its laws. Strauss explains in the introduction to the *Life of Jesus* that while Deism does justice to the natural world, it in effect makes God a mere "finite artist," that is, one species of limited being among others.[24] Deism leaves the universe in as much of a fragmented state as Cartesian objectivity and Kantian rationalism.

Biblical interpreters, like romantic philosophers, looked first to Spinoza's metaphysics for an alternative view. Spinoza's philosophy underwent a renaissance and became a source of controversy in late eighteenth-century Germany. His *Tractatus Theologico-Politicus* had already played a seminal part in the historical critique of the miracle stories in the gospels. Schleiermacher, in particular, helped to bring it fully back into the field. For Spinoza as for Strauss, Schleiermacher, and the "rationalist" Paulus, criticism of biblical miracles begins with a strictly immanent view of previous dualisms. God and nature constitute one and the same substance. The infinite foundation of finite things is nothing other than the totality of what exists. Consequently, God does not either create or act against the laws of nature; they are one and the same. In Spinoza's formulation, if God and nature are united, then any occurrence that violates natural laws also violates the will of God; in fact, this idea would require God to violate his own proper nature, which would be an absurdity.[25]

Modern critics took this position a step further, however. Strauss and other interpreters began, as he also had in his writings on the nocturnal side of nature, from the romantic, organic, and monist cosmology that developed in the generation of Hegel and Schelling. In their dynamic conception of the absolute, God and nature do not form a fixed or static substantial unity. If God is truly in the world, then the finite is bound up in the ebb and flow of the infinite. Strauss explains that the divine cannot be separated from the finite chain of its operations in history; God never breaks at once into the finite world, because the infinite is nothing other than the ongoing interaction and mutation of all finite things: "the absolute cause never disturbs the chain of secondary causes by single arbitrary acts of interposition, but rather manifests itself in the produc-

---

24. *LJ* 1840, 1:81; *LJ* 1892, 79.
25. Spinoza, *Tractatus Theologico-Politicus* (London: Trübner, 1862), 123.

tion of the aggregate of finite causalities, and of their reciprocal action."[26] The divine need not enter the chain of mutually conditioning causes and effects, because the name "God" designates this chain. The principles of spirit and freedom are inscribed in nature. In Hegel's formulation, the "substance" of Spinoza is also "subject." Strauss would later say that Schelling and Hegel had discovered "objective spirit," a notion with which modern science had only begun to grapple.[27] Many theologians in his day accepted the broad contours of this worldview. Strauss cites works by de Wette, Julius Wegscheider, Philipp Marheineke, and Schleiermacher as precedents for his own view.[28] Paulus embraced it as well.[29]

The organic and monist conception of nature and its laws transformed the critique of miracles from the ground up—just as it had transformed the critique of demons and ghosts. It affirmed the limits of nature in a new way. What was for Hume an external, subjective consideration becomes a constitutive feature of reality for Strauss. We do not only reject miracles because they are inconsistent with our experience; we recognize a priori that the natural order is a homogeneous field in which no breach is possible. It is only by this route that we arrive at Strauss's claim that historical criticism rests on one crucial presupposition, "the essential homogeneity of all occurrences." One has to presume that in every moment in time the same laws and forces are at work. A historian can never rest easy with a miracle. If the critic does not reject stories about strange, new events, he or she must at least question their historicity until a fitting analogy can be found.[30]

In principle, at least, this view radicalized the limits that deists had set against miracles. Hence Weisse contended that Strauss went beyond the deists.[31] A mechanistic conception of the universe only restricts God's immediate intervention from the outside. The monist alternative reduces miracle and transcendence wholly to the natural order. For Strauss there was no infinite beyond the world; there was only the infinite evolution and interconnection of finite things. And if the infinite is the system in which

---

26. *LJ* 1840, 1:100; *LJ* 1892, 88.

27. Strauss, *In Defense of My Life of Jesus*, 8–9.

28. *LJ* 1840, 1:83, n. 4; *LJ* 1892, 79, n. 4.

29. Heinrich Paulus, *Das Leben Jesu als Grundlage einer reinen Geschichte des Urchristentums*, 2 vols. (Heidelberg: Winter, 1828), 2.2:xxxix.

30. Strauss, *Streitschriften* 3:37–39.

31. See above, ch. 1 n. 105.

all distinct beings inhere, no single event can stand out above or against the rest. A miracle demands not only a breach but an internal contradiction. Conversely, revelation and miracle are in a sense "real," but only within this immanent framework. Schleiermacher claims in his early *Speeches on Religion* that "miracle" is the religious word for any event whatsoever—all of nature speaks to the infinite and divine with which it is bound up.[32]

Nevertheless, organic monism did not automatically lead theologians to reject the authenticity of the gospel miracle narratives. On the contrary, it had salutary consequences for those who wished to affirm them. To begin, it led them to reaffirm the credibility of the gospel authors. If the divine and "spirit" are inscribed in the whole objective, substantial order of nature and human history, one can no longer treat human religious ideas as mere outdated or fabulous chaff to be discarded. From a Hegelian or Schellingian perspective, reason does not oppose history, texts, and nature as if they were dead objects that need to be reconciled to the rationality of living human subjects. Strauss explains, "Just as we no longer accept Descartes's theory of animals as machines or Kant's view that purpose in organisms is a rationality merely imported by the subject into nature, we no longer consider popular religion as the outgrowth of madness and trickery." In place of those views that divided rational human subjects from an irrational nature, people had grown more accustomed to the view that "rationality and truth exist in all reality."[33] Thus abstract speculative claims about God and nature confirmed what eighteenth-century German classical scholars were beginning to claim in the study of antiquity. They refuted the deist view that ancient, primitive texts and ideas were simply stupid or insane; rather, these texts were earnest productions of human art, poetry, and religion. Even stories about impossible miracles deserve, consequently, to be taken seriously as sources of religious truth.

Strauss gathers the major alternatives to the deist critique of miracles in early nineteenth-century Germany under two broad headings: "rationalism" and "supernaturalism." Both meant to redeem the two founda-

---

32. Schleiermacher, *On Religion: Speeches to Its Cultured Despisers*, ed. Richard Crouter (Cambridge: Cambridge University Press, 1996), 49. See also idem., *Christian Faith*, §46–47. Strauss argues in a similar vein that whoever wishes to speak of "miracles," should first consider the great wonders of human history. He asks at the end of the *Life of Jesus* how we should compare "the cure of a few sick people in Galilee" to "the miracles of intellectual and moral life belonging to the history of the world ... the almost incredible dominion of man over nature ... [and] the irresistible force of ideas" (*LJ* 1836, 2:737; *LJ* 1892, 781).

33. Strauss, *In Defense of My Life of Jesus*, 9.

tions of historical faith, that is, the gospels and the person of Jesus. Strauss uses "rationalism" to denote the work of theologians like Wegscheider and Paulus, who believed the essential truths of religion and the Bible corresponded with reason and could be affirmed on rational grounds.[34] In the field of biblical interpretation, these figures continued on the path set out by "neologian" critics like Semler in the eighteenth century. Like the deists, rationalists took seriously the limits of nature and gave a this-worldly, human account of the biblical narratives. But they also opposed the deists and meant to redeem the integrity of the gospel authors.[35] They were informed directly by the study of classical antiquity: the evangelists did not write to deceive; rather, they composed their narratives, and even experienced the corresponding events, in the light of their primitive, unscientific age. Rationalists recognized that ancient people did not yet understand natural law and therefore did not view or experience the world in the same way that English deists or German theologians might. Furthermore, they believed that the universal truths of reason were made manifest in the facts of Jesus's life. Although a natural human being, Jesus was still a unique and semidivine figure, "a hero, in whose fate Providence is in the highest degree glorified."[36] The gospel writers were not only honest and credible, then, but had provided vital information about the extraordinary person and actions of the historical Jesus.

Paulus offers the classic and most thoroughgoing example of this mode of interpretation in his 1828 *Life of Jesus* and 1830–1833 *Exegetical Handbook*. He retells each one of the gospel stories in a this-worldly idiom and in such a way as to preserve their basic historical truth. His account turns on the distinction between ancient and modern mentali-

---

34. E.g., Heinrich Paulus, *Exegetisches Handbuch über die drei ersten Evangelien*, 3 vols. (Heidelberg: Winter, 1830–1833); Julius August Ludwig Wegscheider, *Institutiones theologiae Christianae dogmaticae* (Halle: Gebauer, 1815). Terms like "supernaturalism" and "rationalism" capture imperfectly the real state of affairs. There was often overlap between approaches, with only rare consistent examples of either one. My analysis does not concern representatives of these categories, however. It focuses rather on how Strauss developed his own position in and through them. Consequently, in what follows I will maintain Strauss's distinction for the sake of clarity.

35. Hence Strauss credits Johann Gottfried Eichhorn's rebuttal to Reimarus, "Uebrige Ungedruckte Werke des Wolfenbüttlischen Fragmentisten," in *Allgemeine Bibliothek der biblischen Litteratur*, 10 vols. (Leipzig: Weidmanns, 1787), 1:3–90, with initiating the modes of rationalist interpretation that dominated German biblical theology at the turn of the nineteenth century (*LJ* 1835, 1:16; *LJ* 1892, 47).

36. *LJ* 1836, 2:708; *LJ* 1892, 767.

2. STRAUSS'S HISTORICAL CRITIQUE OF MIRACLE STORIES 83

ties. The gospel writers are blameless for Paulus; they represented events in the light in which they naturally perceived them as ancient, uneducated people. He therefore sets out to separate the "facts" of their narratives from their mere "opinions," the embellishments with which these ancient eyewitnesses spontaneously colored what they saw. He argues, for example, that a tame bird had alighted on Jesus when, at his baptism, the disciples saw "the spirit descending upon him like a dove";[37] or that Jesus's disciples mistook his near death and revival on and after the cross as a "resurrection." Jesus had only entered a death-like trance; he was healed and revived by the combined effects of the surface wound from the spear thrust, the ointments in which he was buried, and the earthquake, which also helpfully rolled the stone away from his tomb.[38]

Furthermore, if the divine is inscribed in nature, this opens the range of miracles that can be deemed historically plausible. Some rationalists looked to the study of romantic medicine, psychology in particular, to explain strange phenomena like exorcisms. The nocturnal side of natural science played a still more pervasive role in the writings of "supernaturalists." These figures were more prevalent in Strauss's day; the rationalists had dominated German universities in the first decades of the nineteenth century. In their most consistent form, supernaturalists looked to revelation as a source of eternal truth, reaffirmed the divine authority of the Bible, and maintained the literal authenticity of the miracle narratives. These orthodox figures stood alongside many "mediating" theologians who combined rationalism with concessions to supernatural belief. In fact, most supernaturalists took a mediating stance. By the late eighteenth century, it no longer sufficed to appeal directly to the inspired character of the Bible. Even the most dedicated supernaturalists had to provide rational or natural explanations of the miracles in order to shore up their claims about inspiration and revelation. The designation "supernaturalism" is consequently something of a misnomer. Rather, early nineteenth-century supernaturalism often took the form of what Schweitzer designated "spurious rationalism."[39]

Some adopted a romantic cosmology in the vein of Kerner, for example: They accepted that an immanent, natural chain of causes and effects ties together the whole order of being; however, it is comprised of mul-

---

37. Paulus, *Exegetisches Handbuch*, 1:370.
38. Paulus, *Leben Jesu als Grundlage einer reinen Geschichte*, 1:266–70.
39. Schweitzer, *Quest of the Historical Jesus*, 101.

tiple levels and includes interstices in which God and other spiritual forces intervene immediately in human affairs. Neander makes this claim in his *Life of Jesus*, which he published as a rebuttal to Strauss in 1837. Although in general miracles "transcend" the laws of cause and effect, he explains, they do not "contradict" them: "Nature has been so ordered by divine wisdom as to admit higher and creative energies into her sphere; and it is perfectly *natural* that such powers ... should produce effects beyond the scope of ordinary causes."[40] God can disrupt the normal course of nature without disregarding nature per se. In Tholuck's rebuttal to Strauss's *Life of Jesus*, he makes a similar case and appeals directly to the nocturnal side of nature. He grants that "no fact exceeding nature could have come out of the life of Christ"; however, his miracles might represent those "mysterious powers of nature, as in namely the magnetic powers which project from mystical depths into our time, like a ghost of the night in the light of day."[41]

The Nocturnal Side of Nature and Strauss's Concessions to Rationalism and Supernaturalism

In the *Life of Jesus* as in his writings on Hauffe and Kerner, Strauss follows the lead of supernaturalism and romanticism to a remarkable extent. Nor, for all of his disdain of rationalism, does he reject every element in the gospels as unhistorical. His critical analysis produced certain positive results. He provides a distant, blurred image of Jesus's life and activity. Strauss finds little objectionable about judging the basic facts of Jesus's life—his baptism, for example, his crucifixion, and his healing ministry—to be historical. In the case of the miracle narratives, Strauss distinguishes from the outset between *Wundern*, extraordinary events and actions that could be explained in natural terms, and *Mirakeln*, real disruptions in natural chains of cause and effect. Only the latter would be strictly speaking impossible. Within this framework, he places the miracles along a continuum, a "progression in the marvelous," as he says, which is "at the same time a gradation in inconceivability."[42] Starting from the exorcisms, Strauss adds the other healing cures and ends with miracles as such, direct actions against nature such as walking on water or stilling a storm. Exorcisms and the resurrection serve as limit cases among the *Wundern*. The exorcisms are

---

40. Neander, *Life of Jesus Christ in Its Historical Connexion*, 137–38.
41. Tholuck, *Glaubwürdigkeit der evangelischen Geschichte*, 101.
42. *LJ* 1836, 2:153; *LJ* 1892, 486.

2. STRAUSS'S HISTORICAL CRITIQUE OF MIRACLE STORIES 85

the most historically plausible "miracles," while the resurrection would be the first miracle proper. At the lower end of this ladder, Strauss's account overlaps with rationalist interpretation, to a point. He refuses to reconstruct the precise events behind the stories. But he grants that a tenuous thread connects "supernatural" phenomena in the healing narratives to actual occurrences.

Strauss's monist cosmology and studies of the nocturnal side of nature contributed to this concession to rationalism. Romantic medicine widened the range of credible natural and historical events. His experiences with Kerner and Hauffe had proven that one should not dismiss reports of bizarre or incredible facts outright. Furthermore, Strauss had witnessed firsthand possessed people; he had seen the therapeutic power of charismatic healers and exorcists. Unlike the stories about resurrections or the stilling of the storm, clear contemporary analogies existed for Jesus's healing miracles. Strauss had only to think of Kerner's "magnetic passes" or the psychosomatic exorcisms he had read about in Kerner's *Accounts*. In fact, the earliest Christians could have had the same confused religious view that Strauss saw among peasants in the German countryside and romantic physicians: they misunderstood internal human spiritual disorders as external demons and psychosomatic cures as exorcisms.

Stories about possessed people play a prominent role in the Synoptic Gospels, which Strauss treats as more credible sources than John, and in Acts. These texts place exorcisms at the heart of Jesus and his disciples' healing ministry. In both Mark and Luke's Gospel, Jesus's first miracle is an exorcism. Immediately after Jesus's baptism, temptation, and first preaching he heals a demoniac at the synagogue in Capernaum (Mark 1:21-28; Luke 4:31-37). As he is teaching in the synagogue, a possessed man cries out in the voice of his demon, "What have you to do with us, Jesus of Nazareth? Have you come to destroy us? I know who you are, the Holy One of God" (Mark 1:24 // Luke 4:24). Jesus orders the demon to be silent and commands him to come out of the man. After sending the man into convulsions, the demon obeys and exits his body. The narrative exemplifies many of the features of the gospel possessions. Strauss analyzes it in detail along with two other relatively long accounts of exorcisms, the story of the Gadarene or Gerasene demoniac ((Mark 5:1-20 // Matt 8:28-34 // Luke 8:26-39) and of the epileptic boy (Mark 9:14-29 // Matt 17:14-21 // Luke 9:37-43).

Modern analogies for ancient possessions were not difficult to find in eighteenth- and nineteenth-century German culture. Anna U's possession resembled those in the New Testament, for example. Kerner took the similarities as evidence that we should not reject New Testament stories about demons. Olshausen, one of Strauss's main supernaturalist foils in the *Life of Jesus*, cites Kerner and Esquirol's studies of demonomania to argue that gospel stories about "demons" reflected the workings of actual diffuse forces of evil in his *Biblical Commentary on the Complete Writings of the New Testament*. But even Olshausen considered the idea that demons were discrete, personal entities to be the vestige of a bygone era. Most critics claimed simply that the gospels' descriptions of "possessions" represented real events, but these were based on natural mental and physical illnesses. With advances in medicine and philosophy, Strauss explains, "epilepsy, insanity, and even a disturbance of the self-consciousness resembling the condition of the possessed described in the New Testament could all be reduced to disorders of the human mind and body."[43]

The basic tenets of this analysis had venerable precedents. The nocturnal side of natural science allowed Strauss to fill out the image in greater detail. Ancient physicians already debated whether demonic conditions were manifestations of better-known physical illnesses. Semler's 1769 *Commentary on the Demoniacs Mentioned in the New Testament* had given the argument from analogy with natural diseases a decisive modern form.[44] Semler's contributions to the controversy over the case of the possession of Anna Elisabeth Lohmann directly shaped this work.[45] Strauss's work on the nocturnal side of nature also equipped him with a robust medical vocabulary with which to draw these analogies. He describes possession not only as a "disturbance in self-consciousness," for example, but also as "a species of madness accompanied by a convulsive tendency of the nervous system."[46]

---

43. *LJ* 1836, 2:14; *LJ* 1892, 419.

44. Johann Salomo Semler, *Commentatio De daemoniacis quorum in N.T. fit mentio* [*Commentary on the Demoniacs that Appear in the New Testament*] (Magdeburg: Hendel, 1769).

45. Johann Salomo Semler, *Abfertigung der neuen Geister und alten Irrtümer in der Lohmannischen Begeisterung zu Kemberg* (Halle: Gebauer, 1760). For discussions of Lohmann, the controversy, and Semler's response see Jeannine Blackwell, "Controlling the Demonic: The Possession of Anna Elisabeth Lohmann," in *Impure Reason: Dialectic of Enlightenment in Germany*, ed. Daniel Wilson and Robert Holub (Detroit: Wayne State University Press, 1993), 425–42; Midelfort, *Exorcism and Enlightenment*, 87–89.

46. *LJ* 1836, 2:47; *LJ* 1892, 435.

2. STRAUSS'S HISTORICAL CRITIQUE OF MIRACLE STORIES   87

The exorcisms, in turn, could be explained by way of analogy with modern psychosomatic cures. Jesus did not in fact possess miraculous curative powers. But sick people who believed he was the Messiah may well have been healed "solely through the strong confidence ... that he possessed this power."[47] Healings of mental and physical ailments are theoretically possible if they are not too deeply rooted in the body. Those who suffered from relatively superficial nervous disorders, for example, could have felt the effects of "the surpassing dignity of Jesus as a prophet, and eventually even as the Messiah himself."[48] Strauss names the healing of a demoniac at Capernaum in Mark and Luke as a concrete example. Although the story is entangled with legendary elements, Strauss claims, it lends itself to psychological interpretation. Aside from his physical convulsions, the demoniac manifests only a "fixed idea that he is possessed." His condition may therefore have been "of the lighter kind, which is susceptible to psychological influence."[49] Here as in the case of the demons, Strauss could appeal to significant precursors for this analysis. He specifically cites de Wette's *Biblical Dogmatics* and Paulus's *Exegetical Handbook to the New Testament* as models for his approach.[50] "We cannot but agree," he writes, when "Paulus remarks that cures of this kind ... were the easiest in themselves," and "even De Wette sanctions a psychological explanation of the cures of the demoniacs."[51] These interpreters were also passingly familiar with romantic medicine and psychology. Paulus anticipates Strauss's psychosomatic reading of the Capernaum demoniac. The possessed man was overcome by the idea that Jesus could cure his possession, Paulus explains, when he watched him speak in the synagogue. This conviction caused him to fall into a "paroxysm." Jesus noticed and decided to use the man's "fixed idea" to heal him: "what was more natural than that [Jesus] should make use of the man's persuasion of his power?" When Jesus ordered the demon to depart, in other words, he "laid hold of the

---

47. *LJ* 1836, 2:101–2; *LJ* 1892, 461.
48. *LJ* 1836, 2:47; *LJ* 1892, 435.
49. *LJ* 1836, 2:48–49; *LJ* 1892, 435, trans. modified.
50. W. M. L. de Wette, *Biblische Dogmatik: Alten und Neuen Testaments: Oder kritische Darstellung der Religionslehre des Hebraismus, des Judenthums und Urchristenthums* (Berlin: Reimer, 1831).
51. *LJ* 1836, 2:47; *LJ* 1892, 435.

maniac by his fixed idea; which according to the laws of mental hygiene might very well have a favourable effect."[52]

In the third edition of the *Life of Jesus* in 1838, Strauss makes still more remarkable concessions to historicizing interpretations. In this case, however, he moves in the direction of Tholuck and Neander's supernaturalism: the gospels include records of paranormal, unusual powers of nature. In a new introduction to the second volume, he explains that we must allow for extraordinary forces that elude observation in the light of everyday life (*Alltäglichkeit*)[53]—that is, manifestations of the nocturnal side of nature. Some of Jesus's miracles fall within the sphere of magnetic healing, for example. This new category of miracles stands between the strictly supernatural *Mirakeln* and ordinary *Wundern.* In a contemporary essay, he explains that magnetic endowments are no different than other natural talents, for example, great strength or eloquence.[54] But neither are they part of the ordinary, everyday order. Rather they take us from the realm of *miraculum* to *mirabile*—from the supernatural as such to "unusual and striking" but nevertheless natural phenomena.[55] This view enables Strauss to upgrade certain cures that he had deemed unhistorical in the first edition—involuntary cures, for example, and healings of paralytics.

At this point, we might be tempted to conclude that Strauss's experience with the nocturnal side of natural science had a regressive influence on his historical critical approach. In the third edition, this is evidently the case. He gravitates toward the same conception of miracles that Tholuck and Neander presented in their 1837 rebuttals to his first edition. His old affinity for romantic medicine was no doubt enlivened by their appeals to this familiar territory, as well as by the three years of bitter condemnation that followed his initial publication. Even in the first and fourth editions, we can see affinities between Strauss's work on the nocturnal side of nature and rationalist approaches to the gospels. Strauss, Paulus, and de Wette's psychological explanations of exorcisms all resemble aspects of his contemporary writings on possession and ghost seeing. Paulus's explana-

---

52. *LJ* 1836, 2:22; *LJ* 1892, 423, trans. modified; Paulus, *Exegetisches Handbuch* 1:474–75.

53. *LJ* 1838, 2:7.

54. Strauss, "Vergangliches und Bleibendes im Christentum," in *Zwei Friedliche Blätter*, 91.

55. Ibid., 94.

tion of the Capernaum demoniac not only anticipates Strauss's treatment of this ancient exorcism in the *Life of Jesus*, but also his 1836 response to Kerner's *Accounts*. Both reject the eyewitnesses' flawed explanation of the events but grant the basic facts of the narrative. They interpret exorcisms as natural therapies, in which the "exorcist" enters into and exploits a patient's "fixed ideas."

But the majority of Strauss's concessions to rationalism and supernaturalism comprise only hypothetical possibilities. When he analyzes specific events in the narratives, his conclusions are overwhelmingly negative. What he admits in general—that, for example, Jesus could have healed people psychosomatically—he refuses to affirm or rejects outright in individual cases. With the exception of the Capernaum demoniac, Strauss refrains from authenticating the exorcism narratives. Nor does he grant more credibility to those miracles that occupy the succeeding rungs of his ladder. Even in the third edition of 1838, he hesitates to verify most accounts.

The Nocturnal Side of Natural Science and the Limits of the Gospel Stories in the *Life of Jesus*

In the first and third editions, as in the responses to Kerner, Strauss's embrace of the nocturnal side of natural science only opens a path toward romantic and apologetic interpretations of religious phenomena. It does not compel him to follow it. On the contrary, the same dynamics appear here that we have already seen in the ironic or equivocal inclination that Nast detected in Strauss's youth. At first, Strauss willingly embraces the possibility of nocturnal phenomena. He sets out in the direction of romantic and orthodox views of religious phenomena. But he arrives at the opposite conclusions. In the *Life of Jesus* as in his studies of possession and ghost seeing, Strauss opens up the nocturnal region of nature and it leads him to draw radical boundaries.

Strauss had developed a more extensive, systematic understanding of psychology and physiology than other contemporary biblical critics. In the *Life of Jesus*, he tests the historicity of healings and other miracles more exactingly and with less hesitation. Even in the third edition, he tempers his concessions to supernaturalism in this way. He still distinguishes carefully between more and less credible kinds of healings. Animal magnetism might have allowed Jesus to exercise an influence over the damaged nerves of paralytics, for example, but Strauss refuses to weigh in on whether he could affect deeper ailments, especially "corrupted humours."[56] Furthermore, he sounds significant notes of ambivalence throughout his revised analysis. After all, magnetic powers are often found in individuals who suffer from mental illness. We must be wary not to identify the gospel protagonist with Kerner's patients. At the very least, we should not use his magnetic powers as evidence of a unique moral or semidivine character. To grant Jesus magnetic powers is only to bring him more firmly into the world of natural and fallible human beings.

In the first and fourth editions, analogies from the nocturnal side of natural science define still clearer limits on supernaturalizing interpretations. Strauss rejects all miraculous healings of a manifestly physiological variety. No analogies exist for magnetic healings of blind people, for example.[57] But even stories that lend themselves more readily to paranormal explanations are inauthentic. For example, Strauss rejects the authenticity of the story of a woman who suffered from hemorrhages for twelve years. In this pericope, which appears in the Synoptic Gospels, the woman is healed miraculously when she touches the hem of Jesus's garment (Mark 5:24–34 // Matt 9:20–22 // Luke 8:42–48). In Mark's and Luke's accounts, Jesus feels his power leave him at the woman's touch. Strauss, Olshausen, and Paulus all concede that the story lends itself to an interpretation based on animal magnetism. Jesus resembles a magnetic healer, "who in operating on a nervous patient is conscious of a diminution of strength, or like a charged electrical battery, which a mere touch will discharge."[58] Paulus and Olshausen reject this interpretation, however, in order not to diminish Jesus's authority. They wish to avoid reducing the savior's power to a merely physical capacity, as if he had no willful control over it. Strauss condemns this apologetic reasoning as a failure of critical nerve. He appears poised, for a moment, to accept the magnetic explanation, but he rejects it as well. Analogies from the realm of medical science offer no clear confirmation, he explains, of this particular miracle: magnetism would not usually endow people's clothes or the region around them with power.[59]

Strauss raises and rejects paranormal explanations again in a number of cases, usually in opposition to Olshausen. For example, Olshausen claimed in his *Biblical Interpretation* that the story of Jesus healing a cen-

---

56. *LJ* 1838, 2:74.
57. *LJ* 1836, 2:67; *LJ* 1838, 2:87; *LJ* 1892, 445.
58. *LJ* 1836, 2:97; *LJ* 1892, 459.
59. *LJ* 1836, 2:102; *LJ* 1892, 461.

2. STRAUSS'S HISTORICAL CRITIQUE OF MIRACLE STORIES 91

turion's bed-ridden servant without being present in the room can be explained by way of analogy with animal magnetism. In this instance, "Christ, without personal contact, merely by the magic power of his will (if I may use the expression), exercises an active power at a distance—a fact which again has its analogies in magnetism."[60] Strauss counters and presents himself as the better-informed critical expert. In general, "I will not directly contest this," he writes in response, "but only point out the limits within which, so far as my knowledge extends, this phenomenon confines itself in the domain of animal magnetism." Analogies from his experience with magnetic healers allow him to define these limits:

> According to our experience hitherto, the cases in which one person can exert an influence over another at a distance are only two: first, the magnetizer or an individual in magnetic relation to him can act thus on the somnambule, but this distant action must always be preceded by immediate contact,—a preliminary which is not supposed in the relation of Jesus to the patient in our narrative.[61]

He follows the same approach to counter Olshausen's claim that the Capernaum demoniac recognized Jesus as the Messiah through clairvoyant perception. Olshausen adduces as evidence, namely, "the preternaturally heightened nervous system, which, in demoniacs as in somnambules, sharpens the presentient power, and produces a kind of clear-sightedness." By this means, he claims, "such a man might very well discern the importance of Jesus as regards the whole realm of spirits."[62] Strauss responds that this explanation presses us toward supernatural, otherworldly terrain. For the demoniac to recognize Jesus as the Messiah before anyone else, including Jesus himself, would demand a strictly transcendent aptitude. It would far exceed the more modest forms of clairvoyance we typically see in those who suffer from nervous disorders—no matter how excited their nervous systems might be.[63]

These more precise analogies rest in turn on a more rigorous a priori conception of human psychophysiology. As in Strauss's contemporary response to Kerner's *Accounts*, physical, mortal bodies define the limits of what is historically possible. Divisions between the successive rungs of his

---

60. Olshausen, *Biblical Commentary on the New Testament*, 343.
61. *LJ* 1836, 2:121; *LJ* 1892, 470.
62. *LJ* 1836, 2:29; *LJ* 1892, 424; Olshausen, *Biblical Commentary on the New Testament*, 364.
63. *LJ* 1836, 2:30–31; *LJ* 1892, 424.

ladder of miracles reflect the extent to which the diseases being cured affect "the entire corporeal system." The ladder begins with "cures of mental disorders," then moves on to "all kinds of bodily maladies, in which, however, the organization of the sufferer was not so injured as to cause the cessation of life and consciousness," and finally arrives at "the revivification of bodies, from which the life has actually departed." The exorcisms are the most historically credible miracles, because they only concern the nervous system, that is, that part of the human body "which is immediately connected with mental action" and is therefore the most susceptible to change. In cases of insanity or epilepsy, and even, he says, in some cases of physical illness, "leprosy, blindness, lameness, etc ... there was always something present, to which the miraculous power of Jesus could apply itself; there was still a consciousness in the objects, on which to make an impression—a nervous life to be stimulated."[64] When facing an actual dead body, in which no spiritual activity remains, there can no longer be any question of a cure.

The progression centers on the same view of embodied, mortal subjects that appears in the writings on modern demon possession. He cites it from the outset of his treatment of miracles, when he turns to the question of demon possession. Strauss claims that a properly modern antipathy to belief in demons rests only in part on empirical research and modern analogies. It has a second and more essential, conceptual foundation: our revised, modern image of the human subject's body and mind.

> Whatever theory may be held as to the relation between the self-consciousness and the bodily organs, it remains absolutely inconceivable how the union between the two could be so far dissolved, that a foreign self-consciousness could gain an entrance, thrust out that which belonged to the organism, and usurp its place.[65]

Self-consciousness and the physical organs of the body form one closed, unified, and singular totality. The idea is familiar from his response to Kerner's *Seeress* and *Accounts*—when he rejects the possibility of the "nerve-spirit," for example, or reprimands Eschenmayer for the "crass postulate" that an alien consciousness could cram itself between the "I and its organism ... as if it were something like a log split in the middle—a split into which then a wedge taken from some other lumber might be

---

64. *LJ* 1836, 2:153; *LJ* 1892, 486.
65. *LJ* 1836, 2:14–15; *LJ* 1892, 419–20.

allowed to be driven in."⁶⁶ Ironically, Kerner, Eschenmayer, and other romantic physicians had provided the surest grounds on which to reject these hypotheses. Individual self-consciousness unifies the brain and "epigastric" region within a singular body. The limits of this individual body are the limits of spirit.

The same principle determines the limit of possible historical events at the opposite end of his ladder of miracles, when he turns to the question of resurrection. For Strauss, this is the most elementary example of a miracle proper. In the third edition, he states that it represents the "supernatural as such."⁶⁷ In the gospel stories about Jesus's death and resurrection, he says, modern culture (*die neuere Bildung*) consequently faces a stark dilemma: "either Jesus was not really dead, or he did not really rise again."⁶⁸ As in the exorcisms, Strauss plays the role of the modern medical expert. For Strauss, unlike Hume, the impossibility of resurrection is not a question of experience, but of an a priori conception of the immanent human subject, the "correct opinion of the relation between soul and body."⁶⁹ This view inverts the ancient, but still popular, dualistic image of the soul inhering in the body like a bird in its cage or the contents of a box. Strauss reiterates the coextensive portrait of bodies and souls that he was simultaneously bringing to bear in his writings on possession:

> What we call the soul is the governing centre which holds in combination the powers and operations of the body; its function [*Thatigkeit*], or rather the soul itself, consists in keeping all other processes of which the body is susceptible in uninterrupted subjection to the superior unity of the process of organic life, which in man is the basis of his spiritual nature.⁷⁰

Strauss's psychophysically reductive, immaentizing tendency is in full evidence here. The soul is nothing but the ordering function or "regulating power" that keeps the body's "inferior principles" from their inevitable drift toward entropy, corruption, and dissemination. In general, the spiritual nature of humanity is only the unity assumed by particular constellations of organic processes. As such, the body and soul must die together:

---

66. Strauss, *Charakteristiken und Kritiken*, 311.
67. *LJ* 1836, 2:7.
68. *LJ* 1836, 2:647–48; *LJ* 1892, 736.
69. *LJ* 1836, 2:645; *LJ* 1892, 736.
70. *LJ* 1836, 2:646; *LJ* 1892, 736.

"the soul [*die Seele*] as such ceases in the same moment with its dominion and activity, which constitute its existence." Even, Strauss writes in a backhanded concession to the popular views of his day, "if it should occur to the departed soul, or be imposed on it by another, to re-enter its former dwelling place: it would find this dwelling, even after the first moments, uninhabitable in its noblest parts, and unfit for use."[71]

In itself, this view of bodies and souls was widely accepted. Indeed, in order for Strauss to be able to claim that it was the "correct," modern view, it could not have been without precedent. Most theologians were familiar with the underlying medical concepts. In his 1819 lectures on the life of Jesus, Schleiermacher also claimed that where diseases are more deeply rooted in people's physiology miracles are correspondingly less likely, for example.[72] Even Olshausen's analyses of demons were not antiscientific in this respect. He took to heart the modern concept of self-consciousness, namely, that the self is a subjective unity, one that cannot be dislodged by or cohabit with an alien spirit. Even for him, Strauss writes, "Personal demons are too repugnant ... the comprehension of two subjects in one individual is too inconceivable to find a ready acceptation."[73] Likewise, although Paulus and de Wette accepted psychosomatic explanations of the exorcisms, they were reluctant to extend it to those miracles that were too manifestly physiological in nature.

But Strauss carries out the limiting consequences of their shared view in an especially ruthless way. Baur claimed that in the *Life of Jesus* Strauss had not surpassed the insights of the modern, historical critical age; he had only followed their lead without flinching.[74] The miracle narratives offer a case in point. Other interpreters used analogies from medicine to explore where Jesus's miracles might be possible; Strauss, instead, metes out the consequences of the concepts of bodies and spirits on which these possibilities rest. Every event in every story had to be measured against the limits of a human subject's embodied life. This approach already shaped

---

71. *LJ* 1836, 2:647; *LJ* 1892, 736.

72. Friedrich Schleiermacher, *Das Leben Jesu: Vorlesungen an der Universität zu Berlin im Jahr 1832*, ed. Karl August Rütenik (Berlin: Reimer, 1864), 214–23.

73. *LJ* 1836, 2:17; *LJ* 1892, 421.

74. Ferdinand C. Baur, *Paulus, der Apostel Jesu Christi: Sein Leben und Wirken, seine Briefe und seine Lehre: Ein Beitrag zu einer kritischen Geschichte des Urchristenthums* (Stuttgart: Becher & Müller, 1845), 2.

2. STRAUSS'S HISTORICAL CRITIQUE OF MIRACLE STORIES

his responses to Kerner and Eschenmayer. Rather than reject their psycho-physical, romantic concept of the subject, he turned it against them.

He follows the same course when he turns in the *Life of Jesus* to Olshausen's and Paulus's interpretations of the story of the Gadarene demoniac, for example. This narrative, versions of which appear in the three Synoptic Gospels, presents an array of difficulties for modern interpreters. Matthew, Mark, and Luke disagree on its most rudimentary elements—on how many demoniacs were in question, in particular. Even were we to decide which of these should take precedence, the narrative outstrips the other possessions in incredible elements. It describes a man who is isolated from his community, lives among the tombs, hurts himself with stones, and has extraordinary strength. As in the story of the Capernaum demoniac, the Gadarene's demon recognizes Jesus and asks, "What have you to do with me, Jesus, Son of the Most High God?" (Mark 5:7 // Matt 8:29 // Luke 8:28), after which Jesus performs an exorcism. But this individual is not only possessed by one demon; a whole host inhabits him. When Jesus expels them, they rush out into the bodies of a nearby heard of swine whom they compel to drown in the nearby sea.

The medical view of bodies and souls demonstrates from the outset that the story's most basic element is unhistorical. The notion of one possessing demon is difficult to conceive in a rational, modern light; two or more is outright ludicrous:

> For as possession means nothing else, than that the demon constitutes himself the subject of the consciousness, and as consciousness can in reality have but one focus, one central point: it is under every condition absolutely inconceivable that several demons should at the same time take possession of one man.[75]

If the unity and singularity of the embodied subject militates against one possessor, it certainly could not bear an entire legion of them.

Of course, Paulus would agree in principle with this view, and even Olshausen admits it. But both attempt to find the story's historical foundation. Paulus attempts to set it on strictly natural grounds. He claims that it is a historical record of a psychosomatic healing that ancient witnesses misunderstood, in the vein of the Capernaum demoniac.[76] Olshausen, on

---

75. *LJ* 1836, 2:31; *LJ* 1892, 427–28.
76. Paulus, *Exegetisches Handbuch* 1:438, 475.

the other hand, turns to the immanent world of spirit. His perspective is not unscientific. He presupposes that "possessions" reflect psychophysical illnesses and that self-consciousness cannot be dislodged by or cohabit with an alien spirit. But he argues that the references in the gospels to demons signify the workings of a diffuse, impersonal "kingdom of darkness," which exerts a "controlling foreign influence on the [suffering person's] nervous life."[77] Satan remains real, in Olshausen's view, as both a personal and supernatural entity. But demons are only the impersonal, dark forces at work in people's struggles against immorality and sensuality.[78] By giving in to their worst appetites, these individuals, who are not evil per se, allow the kingdom of darkness into their souls.[79] For Olshausen as for Kerner, this contact with the spirit world has physical consequences—even in the more benign New Testament examples of speaking in tongues or "being in the spirit," the body and mind are subjected to an "overpowering holy force."[80] In the case of the demoniacs, the combination of a foreign, evil influence and the individuals' own debilitating pangs of remorse leads to an intensification of physical and mental suffering. "Hence," he writes, "the common opinion, which pronounces the demoniacs to be sick people, is partially true; but only partially, as it confines itself to the outward effects, while the representation of Scripture regards the phenomena in their moral origin."[81] For Strauss, both interpretations fail to do justice to the modern medical conceptions they presuppose. Paulus's psychosomatic explanation is out of the question in this instance. The demoniac in the tale suffers from an especially "intense and deep-rooted mania."[82] "Spirit," no matter its natural, psychological form, could not exercise such force on a material body. The demoniac's illness would not have dissipated from a mere word from Jesus, no matter his charisma. The same objection applies to the third major exorcism narrative that Strauss considers, the story of

---

77. Olshausen, *Biblical Commentary on the New Testament*, 353.

78. Ibid., 362.

79. Olshausen accordingly distinguishes between the forms of evil and suffering to which demoniacs fell victim and the more calculated, "intellectual" evil of those—he uses Judas as an example—who suffered no corresponding disruption in the unity of their consciousness. Where Judas was eventually led to despair, the struggle of the demoniacs against evil contributed to their physiological degeneration, even as this opened them up in turn to contact with the spirit realm (ibid., 363).

80. Ibid., 364.

81. Ibid., 363.

82. *LJ* 1836, 2:49; *LJ* 1892, 435, trans. modified.

the epileptic boy, "since an epilepsy which had existed from infancy and the attacks of which were so violent and regular, must be too deeply rooted in the system for the possibility of so rapid and purely psychological a cure to be credible."[83] It also applies to Paulus's psychosomatic explanation of the healing of the woman with a hemorrhage. Paulus claims that when the woman touched Jesus's garment her illness abated as a result of her faith in Jesus. "She was seized with a violent shuddering in her whole nervous system," which led her to be healed.[84] Strauss concedes that such an explanation could be possible in theory—the historical Jesus may have healed people through "the power of imagination and faith." But he rejects this specific explanation for two reasons. First, it is unlikely that the confidence of a timid person, hidden away from the sight of Jesus, would have sufficed to free her from her disorder. Second, once again, this was an especially deeply-rooted and stubborn illness, one that had lasted for twelve years.[85] It is not the sort of superficial nervous disorder that is normally susceptible to psychosomatic influence. Strauss considers it possible and even likely that stories about Jesus healing people charismatically reflected his real historical ministry. But no single element in them could be traced to a historical fact.

Strauss's objection to Olshausen's analysis is still more firm: "this shifting of the question from the ground of physiology and psychology to that of morality and religion," he writes, "renders the discussion concerning the demoniacs one of the most useless which Olshausen's work contains."[86] In making vague claims about a "controlling foreign influence on the nervous life" or an "overpowering holy force," Olshausen, like Kerner and Eschenmayer, supplies needless religious causes for phenomena that can be explained on natural terms. Olshausen grants the modern philosophy of subjectivity and self-consciousness; he fails, however, to carry out its negative consequences for the historicity of the gospels, those that followed from his own psychophysical view of spirit.

The problem is not simply that Olshausen leaves room for strange, immanent forces at work in the natural order. After all, any magnetic interpretation would do the same. Rather, Strauss objects to the fact that he treats his spiritual, moral, or religious view as the primary lens for

---

83. *LJ* 1836, 2:49; *LJ* 1892, 436.
84. *LJ* 1836, 2:99–100; *LJ* 1892, 460.
85. *LJ* 1836, 2:102; *LJ* 1892, 461.
86. *LJ* 1836, 2:20; *LJ* 1892, 422.

making sense of the narratives. Here we can trace the roots of Strauss's more exacting approach to another distinct feature of his cosmology and method; namely, he applies his limiting view of bodies and souls more precisely, because he situates it at the heart of his whole account of revelation and miracle. It constitutes the crux of his taxonomy of miracles—the primary, deciding factor by which he tests their credibility at each level. The embodied human subject marks the final, decisive restriction on the operation of spirit in history. No other interpretive lens or criteria can trump the first, limiting factor that extends from "the ground of physiology and psychology."

Olshausen is not the only interpreter from whom Strauss diverges on this point. Schleiermacher, for example, in his lectures on the life of Jesus, divides between credible and impossible miracles primarily by their relative "humanness." Miracle narratives are likely authentic, he claims, when they exhibit a moral dignity and love of humanity that befits Jesus's extraordinary character.[87] He acknowledges a distinction between psychosomatic and miraculous physical cures, but only grants it a secondary role in his analysis. Furthermore, he uses it in support of his claim that some narratives *could* be possible, although, unlike Paulus, he does not affirm that they are necessarily authentic. Thus Schleiermacher's position on this point is precisely the inverse of Strauss's. He places physical and psychological analysis in a supplemental role and argues that certain miracles might have taken place as described, though he does not authenticate them outright. Strauss uses the medical analysis as the leading, essential criterion by which to demonstrate that the narratives could not have happened as they are described in the gospels, though he acknowledges that some real event might lie in the inaccessible past behind them.

The distinction between Strauss and Schleiermacher's approaches is especially evident in the case of the resurrection. In spite of its patently supernatural character, critics in Strauss's day could draw on substantial scientific and philosophical resources here as well to explain Jesus's resurrection. Romantic science played a key role in this effort. Strauss could testify to its persuasive power as well as anyone: seven years before publishing the *Life of Jesus* during his early years at Tübingen, he wrote a prize essay in which, as he put it in a letter to his friend Vischer in 1838, "I proved exegetically and through natural philosophy, with full conviction,

---

87. Schleiermacher, *Leben Jesu*, 214–23.

the resurrection of the dead."[88] Some of the most influential rebuttals to Strauss's 1835 Life of Jesus began from a similar view. Neander, for example, made use of an immanent but tiered romantic cosmology in the vein of Schelling or Kerner to explain how Christ might have died and risen again. He claimed that when Jesus died, he entered into a "higher region" in which the laws of corporeal existence no longer held sway. Here, in this higher state of existence, the body and soul that had tenuously separated in death reunited once and for all.[89]

Alongside these supernatural interpretations, a host of commentators offered natural explanations. Enlightened readers widely agreed that the gospels misreported the incident: Jesus had not really died on the cross, but the historical core of the story was true. This view was already prevalent in deist criticism. Reimarus famously revisited the ancient argument, attested in the Gospel of Matthew (27:64) and Origen's *Against Celsus* that Jesus's disciples stole his body from the tomb in order to deceive the people.[90] Rationalists turned the naturalist explanation to apologetic ends. In the early 1780s Karl Bahrdt wrote an imaginative life of Jesus, for example, in which he argued that the gospel protagonist had collaborated with an order of Essenes to stage the resurrection. The Essenes rightly sought, in doing so, to lead the people beyond the narrow messianic representations of their age.[91] We have already considered Paulus's equally sympathetic and less imaginative account, in which Jesus fell unconscious during the crucifixion but revived afterward while alone in his tomb.

Schleiermacher adopts a similar view, but only to show that the story might be plausible. The most we can say is that Christ appeared to have died. The gospels mention nothing about his body decomposing, for example. Whether or not he was actually dead is impossible to know: "We need not go further into the fact, because nothing is to be ascertained about it."[92] As such, Schleiermacher's mediating view leaves open a space for the supernaturalism of Tholuck as much as for the rationalism of Paulus. In a response to the published edition of Schleiermacher's lectures in 1864,

---

88. David Friedrich Strauss, *Ausgewählte Briefe*, ed. Eduard Zeller (Bonn: Strauss, 1895), 52.
89. Neander, *Life of Jesus in Its Historical Connexion*, 436–37.
90. Reimarus, *Von dem Zwecke Jesu und seiner Jünger*.
91. Karl Friedrich Bahrdt, *Briefe über die Bibel im Volkston: Eine Wochenschrift von einem Prediger auf dem Lande* (Halle: Dost, 1782).
92. Schleiermacher, *Leben Jesu*, 486.

Strauss objects directly to his hedging claim: "That sounds like an excuse, but it is a warning, like a skull erected at a dangerous swimming hole."[93] Schleiermacher had refused in effect to render a verdict on the dilemma that Strauss already identified in 1836: "either Jesus was not really dead, or he did not really rise again." By 1836, Strauss had of course reversed his view of 1828, namely, that resurrections could be proven on the grounds of natural philosophy. His subsequent view of bodies and souls rebuts directly Neander's claims. Even in the third edition, where he makes so many other concessions to Neander and Tholuck, he remains firm on this point. A dead body still represents the unbreachable limits of spirit. Souls and bodies do not break apart and reunite. They are one organism, and they die together. If Schleiermacher does not wish to stare too long at the scene of the cross, Strauss demands that we go looking for a corpse.

Bodies, Souls, and the Global Limits of Spirit in Strauss's Cosmology

Strauss's treatment of the resurrection leads us in turn beyond the individual miracle reports. The limits that he sets here form part of a global vision of the operation of spirit in space and time, nature and history. If souls and bodies are inseparable, then modern ideas about the immortality of the soul, in particular, are untenable. This is not a marginal concern. "The belief in immortality," Strauss would go on to say in the second volume of his *Glaubenslehre* in 1841, "is the soul of the current religiosity of feeling and understanding," that is, of modernizing theologies based on the work of Schleiermacher and Kant, respectively—"More than God and Christ, the educated pious person takes on the hope for continuance after death. What use for me is a God, what ground do I have to take Christ's yoke upon myself, when in death all is finished?"[94] Strauss saw this idea of subjective immortality—no matter how philosophically well-conceived—as the last remainder of the old eschatological hopes for Christ's second coming and the transformation of heaven and earth: "Out of the concrete fabric of biblical and churchly representations of a return of Christ, resurrection, judgment, heaven and hell, modern reflection has drawn the abstract central

---

93. Strauss, *The Christ of Faith and the Jesus of History: A Critique of Schleiermacher's "The Life of Jesus,"* trans. Leander E. Keck (Philadelphia: Fortress, 1977), 124.

94. David Friedrich Strauss, *Die christliche Glaubenslehre in ihrer geschichtlichen Entwicklung und im Kampfe mit der modernen Wissenschaft*, 2 vols. (Tübingen: Osiander, 1840–1841), 2:697.

thread of immortality, and affixed its I to the same, over the dreaded abyss of annihilation." Beyond the odd millenarians and Pietists who held fast to ancient and medieval apocalypticism, these modern eschatological beliefs were mainstays of theological and philosophical anthropology. He notes that Kant, in particular, set personal immortality as the highest postulate of practical reason. For Strauss, this modern residue of ancient eschatological views was "the last enemy, which speculative critique has to battle and where possible to overcome."[95]

Thus the architectonics of souls and bodies that underlies Strauss's writings on the nocturnal side of nature is tied up with the questions of immanence and eschatology that obsessed him throughout his career. In 1830, the same year that he published his first article on the "Seeress of Prevorst," he wrote his short dissertation on the Christian doctrine of the ἀποκατάστασις πάντων, the "restoration of all things" (Acts 3:21), in which he traces the evolution of eschatological thought from ancient Judaism into modern theology and Hegelian philosophy—where, he argues, it would finally be liquidated.[96] Five years later, eschatology became the guiding theme of the *Life of Jesus* where he sets the gospel narratives squarely within the apocalyptic worldview of first-century Judaism. It remained central in the *Glaubenslehre* of 1840–1841 and in his *The Old Faith and the New* of 1872.

Conclusion

It is fitting that Strauss later represented his 1828 prize essay on the resurrection, *De resurrectione carnis*, as the crux of his turn to a more rationalistic view: "as I dotted the last period," he wrote in an 1838 letter to Vischer, "it was clear to me that there was nothing in the entire story."[97] Strauss's experience in composing this essay, ending with his realization that "there was nothing to" the resurrection, proved to be prototypical for his subsequent negative, limiting, and critical approach to Christianity. In the *Life of Jesus* as in the *Glaubenslehre* of 1840, Strauss meticulously traces the course of narratives and dogmas, but now in order to show that there is nothing to them. As in the writings on modern cases of demon possession, he takes

---

95. Ibid., 2:739.
96. Strauss, "Die Lehre von der Wiederbringung Aller Dinge in Ihrer Religionsgeschichtlichen Entwicklung," in Müller, *Identität und Immanenz*, 50–75.
97. Strauss, *Ausgewählte Briefe*, 52.

the narratives seriously and brings them within a radically circumscribed frame. In writing the "resurrection of the flesh" of 1828, Strauss had inadvertently put the point on a death certificate for Jesus Christ—he would spend much of his following career, including the *Life of Jesus* in particular, taking up this accidental act of coronership as his proper vocation.

This critical approach coalesced around the concept of bodies and souls that Strauss developed in conversation with romantic medicine and natural philosophy. A monist view of bodies, souls, and the world enabled him to radicalize the critique of gospel miracles, even as he left open the possibility of certain paranormal phenomena. Nor do the parallels between his writings on ancient and modern religion stop there. In the next chapter, we will see that, as in his writings on the nocturnal side of nature, the first, limiting critique of supernatural occurrences opens onto a critical theory of mind and the progress of culture. Strauss's analysis of "demons" and "ghosts" led him to analyze the psychological and cultural condition of the subjects of ghost seeing and possession. In the *Life of Jesus*, Strauss's critique of stories about miraculous healings, resurrections, and imminent apocalyptic transformation also leads to an account of the subjective cultural mentalities that shaped these tales. It leads, specifically, to his famous interpretation of the gospels as "myths." In the following chapter, I will consider his seminal treatment of the gospel authors and myth in light of his work on religious belief and paranormal experience among demoniacs and ghost seers in the German countryside.

3
Strauss on Myth and the Nocturnal Side of Nature

Over the last two chapters, we have seen how Strauss defined and secured limits on spirit in history and nature throughout his writings in the 1830s. His conceptions of embodied subjects and an immanent cosmos led him to critique reports of supernatural events and beings—demons, for example, ghosts, and resurrections—in the ancient and modern world. In the first chapter, we saw that, in his writings on the nocturnal side of nature, this critical view led from the phenomena in question to the psychological and cultural condition of their subjects: from ghosts and demons to the minds and experiences of clairvoyants and the possessed. In the *Life of Jesus*, Strauss's critique of miracle stories follows a similar course. It leads to the cultural worldviews that shaped these narratives. And it sets them within an overarching account of the progress of spirit and culture. In the pieces on demoniacs and ghost seers, Strauss relates the progress of *Bildung* to distinctions in gender, spiritual disorder, and levels of education. In the *Life*, he considers the difference in historical cultures. He traces lines between ancient and modern mentalities.

In this chapter I move accordingly from the first major critical and scientific aspect of Strauss's *Life of Jesus*, his critique of miracles, to a second, his adaptation of mythical interpretation. Myth theory had flourished in German romantic thought and biblical criticism before Strauss. It turned biblical scholars' attention to the consciousness that shaped ancient writings and the narrative form and functions of these accounts. With romantic thinkers, it came to redefine in a positive light the religious worldview of ancient people. The scientific study of antiquity, as much as that of nature or medicine, would have to recognize how spirit infuses and unifies the totality of the cosmos. All phenomena, texts, and mentalities have meaning and value; they deserve to be explored seriously on their own terms. For romantically-inclined thinkers like Schelling or Herder, myths were the spontaneous, poetic expressions of people who stood in a closer unity with God.

Strauss drew explicitly on these romantic insights and brought them to bear on the gospels. His work here converged in specific, essential ways with his studies of the nocturnal side of nature. Kerner, Schubert, and others had already drawn parallels between modern somnambulists and ancient seers and poets. Strauss's firsthand experience with these individuals deepened his engagement with the mentalities at work behind the gospel narratives. In both the *Life of Jesus* and the writings on the nocturnal side of nature, he confronts the nonmodern, alien aspects of religious thought from which enlightened interpreters turned away in revulsion.

In the process, he develops a critical application of myth theory in two key areas. He does so first in the realm of historical criticism. Myth interpretation forms a second stage in his critique of miracle stories. Strauss first shows that elements in the gospels are impossible; he then demonstrates that they can be better explained as products of an ancient mythical worldview. This movement guarantees the ruthless, negative results of his tests of authenticity of the gospels. But for Strauss this is only a first axis of the negative movement of critique in his *Life of Jesus*. As he rules against the historicity of gospel narratives, he also turns a glaring light on each point at which a breach had opened between modern, critical reason and the ancient mentality shared by Jesus, the disciples, and the gospel writers. He follows the lead of romantic theorists and moves from a history of events to a history of consciousness. Here again, Strauss's ironic affinity for the margins of Christian belief plays a consequential role. He insists on those portions of the gospels that other theologians sought to downplay. In the realm of first-century Jewish thought, this meant emphasizing apocalyptic representations in particular. He holds fast to the plain sense and meaning of the texts, but does so in order to mark out the divergent territories of the ancient and modern world. Criticism of the gospel narratives serves as such to educate modern people about what they are not. The *Life of Jesus* operates as a critique of culture and consciousness. Critique demands an internal reckoning in the religious worldview of an age and enacts the process of *Bildung* by which modernity would emerge fully on the stage of history. He would later theorize this aspect of the work explicitly through his interpretation of the philosophy of Hegel. In this chapter, I consider these dimensions of Strauss's *Life of Jesus* and call attention to those points where they interlace with his work and experience in the nocturnal side of nature.

3. MYTH AND THE NOCTURNAL SIDE OF NATURE

German Romanticism and the Scientific Study of Biblical Myths

Scholarship on myth in Germany developed significantly in the middle of the eighteenth century. Mythical interpretation began in the study of classical antiquity. Studies of the Hebrew Bible by the Oxford Professor of Poetry Robert Lowth and the Göttingen classicist C. G. Heyne brought it into the field of biblical theology.[1] For Heyne "all the history and philosophy of the ancients proceeded from myths," including the Old Testament.[2] Johann David Michaelis, a seminal biblical scholar, helped to bring Lowth's lectures into the German context with his annotated editions of them.[3] Herder expanded on Heyne's research and presented Israelite mythology as the expression of a shared national spirit.[4] In contrast to previous Enlightenment thinkers, Herder and Heyne did not use "myth" in a pejorative sense. It designated the poetic and philosophical form of ancient stories in distinction from their ostensibly historical content. In antiquity, religious, aesthetic, and national interests came before any ethic of accurate historiography. The stories were primitive but had their own truth and value. Mythical composition formed the basis, for example, for ancient and modern art and religion. It therefore deserved to be taken seriously and analyzed without modern prejudice as an ancient form of expression.

Theories of myth flourished in German romantic thought. They constituted a historical, cultural counterpart to speculative reflections on God, spirit, and the cosmos. Recall that for Schubert, Kerner, and Schelling, ancient humanity's unity with God and the universe formed a first stage in the dynamic movement of the world-soul. They believed that modern thought constituted an ambivalent advance on ancient worldviews; they also claimed with Herder that ancient people stood in a more

---

1. In his 1740 lectures, later published as *De sacra poesi Haebrorum* (1753), Lowth read the Hebrew Bible as a collection of ancient poetry. Its truth lay as much in its art as in its sacred history. Heyne drew on Lowth to argue that the Hebrew Bible contained "philosophical myths," reflections on origins, alongside "historical myths" that focused on events (C. G. Heyne, *Apollodori Atheniensis Bibliothecae Libri Tres et Fragmenta*, 2nd ed. [Göttingen: Dietrich, 1803]).

2. "*A mythis omnis priscorum hominum tum historia tum philosophia procedit*" (Heyne, *Apollodori Atheniensis Bibliothecae*, 1:xvi, quoted in Strauss 1835, 1:28; 1892, 52).

3. Robert Lowth, *De Sacra poesi Hebraeorum*, ed. Johann David Michaelis (Göttingen: Dietrich, 1770). Sheehan, *Enlightenment Bible*, 184.

4. Herder, *Vom Geist der Ebräischen Poesie*.

immediate relation to God and nature. This connection to the universe shaped the stories the ancients composed. A similar dynamic appears in romantic writings on myth to that which we saw in the polarities of romantic medicine and cosmology. Modes of consciousness dominated by the *Herzgrub* and brain stand in a hierarchical relation. A rational, modern worldview is healthier; it leads to a more accurate account of the living, material world. Nevertheless, ancient people, the mentally ill, women, the uneducated, and children have special intuitive access to the nocturnal life of spirit. Kerner could write, for example, that old age and childhood stood within the circles of the spirit world along with "the childhood of the human race" and "saints, poets, and, still closer to the center, seers."[5] The experiences of somnambulists put them in touch with this ancient world—in her trances Hauffe even reverted to a strange "inner" language resembling those of antiquity.

Romantic myth theory formed part of the reaction to the Enlightenment. Like speculative cosmologies and romantic medicine, it offered new means by which German scholars could redeem faith, and the Bible in particular, for modern thought and culture after the devastation of Enlightenment criticism. It enabled theologians to admit in good conscience that these were not modern texts—the Bible does not offer the same kind of rigorous, scientific truths we expect from a contemporary historian or philosopher. But that does nothing to diminish its value for faith and reason. The truth of ancient texts did not lay in their historical content but in their poetic expressiveness or in their capacity for conveying deep human feeling and religious intuition. When Semler argued, for example, that the book of Revelation was too irrational and Jewish to be part of a canon of modern Christianity,[6] Herder countered that we must consider how John and his ancient audience would have experienced its apocalyptic prophecies. The truth of John's Apocalypse was not to be found in any particular prediction; rather, it lay in the underlying feeling it generated—that God was near and would see the universe through its most harrowing tribulations.[7]

---

5. Kerner, *Seherin von Prevorst*, 197.

6. Semler, *Christliche freye Untersuchung über die so genannte Offenbarung Johannis* (Halle: Hendel, 1769).

7. Herder, *Maran Atha oder das Buch von der Zukunft des Herrn* (Riga: Hartknock, 1779).

3. MYTH AND THE NOCTURNAL SIDE OF NATURE

This model of interpretation redefined the task of the study of antiquity and religion. It opened an historical science of culture and historical mentalities. According to myth theory, science worthy of the name must grasp ancient thought and belief on their own terms. Scientific historiography could no more dismiss myths as fables and delusions than a natural scientist could dismiss the psychophysical phenomena associated with somnambulism and possession. At the same time, this concept of myths shifted the focus of scientific historiography from the history of events to that of narratives, on the one hand, and of the collective modes of consciousness that shaped them, on the other. It pushed back against those deists, rationalists, and orthodox defenders of inspired Scripture who sought only bare facts behind the biblical narratives. It expanded the already growing study of the Bible as a cultural, historical text and underwrote the rise of the scientific university, in the place of the church, as a privileged site of inquiry into the truth of Christianity.

Theories of myth exerted a formative influence on the science of higher criticism. By the time Strauss composed the *Life of Jesus*, a number of interpreters had used mythical interpretation to distinguish historically authentic and inauthentic material in the Bible. In the introduction to the *Life of Jesus*, he names as precedents in this vein the work of the "mythical school," figures like Johann Gottfried Eichhorn, G. L. Bauer, J. P. Gabler, and others,[8] who argued that the composition of the Old and New Testaments had been colored by ancient modes of thought. Eichhorn had determined, for example, that the New Testament gospels were not exclusively eyewitness accounts. The stories were transmitted for a short time after Jesus's death before being written down. They consequently underwent some supernaturalizing alterations. He argued that in a few instances writers had crafted biblical stories from the ground up.[9] Although Eichhorn originally maintained that the Eden narrative in Gen 2 and 3 was an account of an ancient poisoning,[10] for example, he eventually changed his mind and developed a full-fledged mythical reading: the story embodied

---

8. Following Hartlich and Sachs's *Ursprung des Mythosbegriffes*, modern scholars usually group these three together as the "mythical school" in higher criticism.

9. Eichhorn, "Uebrige Ungedruckte Werke des Wolfenbüttlischen Fragmentisten."

10. Eichhorn, *Urgeschichte*, ed. Johann Philip Gabler (Altdorf bei Nürnberg: Monath & Kussler, 1793), 3:98–310.

a philosophical thought "that the desire for a better condition than that in which man actually is, is the source of all the evil in the world."[11]

For the most part, however, Eichhorn's later account of the fall narrative was an exception. His earlier, euhemeristic version was more typical of the mythical school. He, Gabler, and others argued that the biblical narratives, the gospels in particular, were "historical myths." They recorded real events; only these records were inflected by the ancient worldview of their writers. Though Eichhorn acknowledged that biblical narratives were written down after the fact, he insisted that, with a few exceptions in the Hebrew Bible, this compositional work was not too far removed in time from its subjects. If the gospels were not immediate eyewitness accounts, they were based nevertheless on the experiences of eyewitnesses. They preserved in a relatively faithful manner the history of Jesus's life and death. He and other members of this mythical school in historical criticism set out accordingly to separate the historical kernel of the stories from its supernaturalistic chaff. They set the stage for Paulus's thoroughgoing rationalism. Eichhorn "agreed with Paulus," Strauss explains, "in considering the miraculous in the sacred history to be a drapery which needs only to be drawn aside, in order to disclose the pure historic form."[12]

Strauss believed that this mode of historical criticism betrayed the romantic and scientific impulses from which it began. Admittedly, Paulus and Eichhorn recognized the distinction between ancient and modern mentalities. But they put this insight to a selective use: they pressed it into the service of a positive history of events. In their haste to unearth historical facts, they failed to take biblical texts seriously on their own terms. They lost sight of their poetic forms, religious meanings, concepts of truth, and underlying cultural interests. They forced the accounts into the mold of a modern historical worldview that their composers would not have recognized.

The gospel narratives about demons differed in one crucial respect, in that vein, from Kerner's accounts of demoniacs in the German countryside: ancient people did not set out to write exacting empirical records. Modern interpreters mangled the meaning of the stories when they reduced them to archives of facts. Compared with Eichhorn's later account of the Genesis fall narrative as the vehicle of an idea, for example, Strauss claims that "nothing could be worse" than his original, historiciz-

---

11. *LJ* 1835, 1:25; *LJ* 1892, 50.
12. *LJ* 1835, 1:25; *LJ* 1892, 50.

ing interpretation: "In considering the tree of knowledge as a poisonous plant, he at once destroyed the intrinsic value and inherent meaning of the history."[13] Rationalist interpretation led to absurd distortions of the plain sense of the narratives.

In contrast, he cites approvingly two major recent scholars of myth in the Hebrew Bible: Johann Severin Vater and de Wette.[14] These authors broke with Eichhorn and the others in two respects. First, they claimed that biblical stories were not based at all on eyewitness accounts; they were products of a lengthy tradition of transmission. Second, they emphasized the genre of the texts and intentions of their authors. Vater argued that we "do violence to the original sense of the compilers of these narratives"[15] when we take them as eyewitness accounts. De Wette affirmed still more strenuously that the Hebrew Bible should not be mined for bare historical facts. Its composers never set out to write that kind of history. Even when their work took a historiographical form, their interests lay elsewhere.

Strauss credited de Wette with bringing the romantic conception of myth fully to bear on the Bible. De Wette followed Schelling's early work on myth[16] and argued that they were spontaneous and poetic religious expressions. He affirmed with Herder that ancient authors were guided by national, *völkische* commitments—the biblical stories articulated their patriotic, religious feelings. In effect, he attended to the shape of the narratives, as well as to the ancient mentalities and cultural contexts behind them. He undermined the historical credibility of the narratives almost entirely in the process. But the analysis carved out a space for faith. It furnished new forms of religious and historical truth. If the Pentateuch did not record particular historical events, it reflected the culture in which it was composed—along with that culture's religious and poetic conceptions of God and humanity. Consequently, Strauss says, the rationalists not only found "the web of facts they had so ingeniously woven together torn asunder," but also "all the art and labor expended on the natural interpre-

---

13. *LJ* 1835, 1:54; *LJ* 1892, 66.

14. Johann Severin Vater, *Commentar über den Pentateuch*, 3 vols. (Halle: Waisenhaus, 1802–1805); W. M. L. de Wette, *Beiträge zur Einleitung in das Alte Testament*, 2 vols. (Halle: Schimmelpfenig, 1806–1807).

15. *LJ* 1835, 1:32; *LJ* 1892, 54.

16. Schelling, "Ueber Mythen, historische Sagen, und Philosopheme," 1:43–83. Ironically, the essay was originally published by Paulus in his *Memorabilien* (Leipzig: Crusius, 1793), 5:1–68.

tation at once declared useless."[17] Paulus complained that, where he sought to laboriously separate fact from opinion in biblical narratives, this mode of criticism resolved the historical question at once by dissolving them entirely back within "the *camera obscura* of ancient sacred legends."[18]

Strauss took the insights of de Wette, Schelling, and Herder to heart. In the introduction to the *Life of Jesus*, he asserts that scientific critics must heed the purpose that the gospels had for their ancient composers. Christian and Jewish Scriptures formed in eras of religious and social agitation, not unlike the modern age, in which novel modes of life intersected with rapidly shifting worldviews. But ancient people were not modern philosophers or scientists. The first Christians, like their contemporaries were "a community of Orientals, of mostly unlearned men, who as such were in no condition to admit and indicate that idea in the abstract form of the understanding and concept, but rather in the concrete manner of the imagination, as image and history."[19] Ancient religious thinkers could not conceive ideas in abstract philosophical terms; they could only articulate them as stories, that is, as sacred narratives. Like other mythical stories, the gospels were meant to capture new ideas in an imaginative, history-like form.

To make sense of the narratives, a modern scholar would therefore have to lay bare the ideas behind them. Mythical interpretation inverts the historicizing approach of rationalists and deists: the latter, Strauss explains, "sacrifice all divine meaning in the sacred record," but "uphold its historical character," where mythical interpretation rather "sacrifices the historical reality of the narratives in order to preserve their absolute truth."[20] Reimarus and other deists uncovered real events behind the narratives to show that they lacked religious value for a modern person; the rationalists did so in order to hold onto a core of positive historical revelation. Both elided in the process their underlying, ideal meaning. Eich-

---

17. *LJ* 1835, 1:54; *LJ* 1892, 66. Strauss only clarifies that he had de Wette's mythical interpretation in mind specifically here in later editions (*LJ* 1840, 1:56–58).

18. *LJ* 1835, 1:55; *LJ* 1892, 67.

19. *LJ* 1835, 1:71–72. This passage only appears in the first edition. In later editions, he revised and expanded on his explanation of myth in section 12 of the *Life of Jesus*. He adds four subsequent sections (13–16) in which he responds more thoroughly to his critics. Section 12 of the first edition still provides a succinct synopsis of this view, however. It affirms the same basic premises as the longer passages in later editions.

20. *LJ* 1835, 1:52; *LJ* 1892, 65.

horn's reading of the fall narrative as a story about an ancient poisoning typified this approach.

Full-fledged mythical interpretation, like Eichhorn's later reading of the narrative as the shell of a noble idea, attends to the concepts that ancient people struggled to represent by using concrete, historical imagery. To that extent, it returns to ancient and medieval forms of allegorical interpretation in the vein of Origen. Both consider that "something historical lay at the foundation of the histories; however, whether the composer was conscious of the fact or not, a higher spirit made use of this historical element as the mere shell of a transcendent truth or meaning."[21] Both sought the true idea behind the external, historical narrative.

Nevertheless, mythical interpretation does not break altogether with history. It differs from allegorical interpretation in this one crucial respect: "according to the allegorical view, this higher spirit," namely, the spirit that drove the composer to press an idea into a historical shell, "is the immediate influence of the divinity; for the mythical it is the spirit of a people or a community."[22] The mythical view, like Strauss's psychological interpretations of demon possession, attends openly to the world of *Geist*, mind or spirit, as well as to religious truth; however, it remains within the immanent historical and cultural order. The modern speculative conception of the universe determines this approach. God does not intervene directly in particular cases, but moves everywhere and at once through the dynamic evolution of nature and humanity. As for miracles, so also for revelation in general: truth and spirit emerge within human thought in history. A mythical interpreter who seeks ideas in the stories "is controlled," therefore, "by regard for the conformity with the spirit and modes of thought of the people and of the age."[23] The "ideas" behind the narratives are neither strictly ideal nor strictly historical religious truths; they are ancient people's way of making sense of the universe, as seen and expressed from the vantage of their particular stage in the intertwined evolution of God, humanity, and nature. Science must attend to local historical and cultural contexts. Like Herder and de Wette, Strauss drew romantic speculation into the service of a more rigorous historicism.

As collective compositions, myths take shape spontaneously and unconsciously. The "intention" and "meaning" that Strauss and de Wette

---

21. *LJ* 1835, 1:52; modified in later editions.
22. *LJ* 1835, 1:52–53; *LJ* 1892, 65.
23. *LJ* 1835, 1:52–53; *LJ* 1892, 65.

set out to expose does not lie on the surface of the biblical authors' consciousness. The ancients composed without the reflexive intentionality of modern, individual writers. If the substance of a myth narrative is not revealed by a transcendent God, neither "is it the work of an individual, but rather of the universal individual of that community, by whom it is also produced without consciousness or intention."[24] Strauss follows Schelling and affirms that they were "unartificial and spontaneous productions" in opposition to any "artistic product of intentional design."[25] In later editions, he cites as a precedent for this view the work of Karl Otfried Müller, a scholar of Greek antiquity who also drew on myth theory to develop a historicist view of ancient narratives. Müller had asserted that the lack of analogies in contemporary writing should not blind us to the unconscious way in which ancient people composed. These stories are not the products of individual consciousness, but of "a higher communal consciousness."[26] Popular traditions could emerge and transform dramatically in the course of oral transmission.[27] In passing from one mouth to another and a third, Strauss explains, a story may change only a little; however, these small changes can coalesce into major, dramatic alterations without any of their narrators being the wiser.[28]

Müller, Schelling, and de Wette's notions of spontaneous, collective composition gave Strauss resources to consider that the gospels were composed without intention from a shared stock of cultural ideas. His firsthand experiences with people whose consciousness had not reached the level of modern *Bildung* lent still more certainty to this approach. Strauss knew from Grombach and Anna U that strange history-like narratives could form, seemingly out of thin air, in the minds of people who were neither lying nor, strictly speaking, insane. While Strauss believed Grombach and Anna U suffered from disordered psyches, they were a far cry from the cobbler who believed he was caesar, for example. Their somnambulic-demonic states, in which the *Herzgrub* dominated over their brain, was not so different than the condition of the ancient poet or seer as he or she drew verses seemingly out of the ether. And Grombach and Anna U, these otherwise relatively rational and sincere individuals, managed to

---

24. *LJ* 1835, 74, removed from later editions.
25. *LJ* 1835, 1:31; *LJ* 1892, 54.
26. *LJ* 1840, 1:89; *LJ* 1892, 82, translation modified.
27. *LJ* 1840, 1:88–89; *LJ* 1892, 82.
28. *LJ* 1835, 1:74, removed from later editions.

dream up accounts of the lives of their possessors, in particular, including specific details about their personal histories. As in ancient myths, it was a question of unconscious composition. As we recall from the first chapter, when Anna U spoke in her possessor's voice and confessed a series of his sins, these were "fabricated unconsciously" in her agitated condition from a stock of ready cultural material. The deeds she described, "deceit, drunkenness, fornication, denial of paternity, brawls and murder—were in fact typical of the class of people" to whom the dead soul was supposed to belong, as well as to her own class.[29]

First Critical Aspect of Strauss's Adaptation of Romantic Myth Theory: The Critique of Miracles

In the *Life of Jesus* Strauss follows Müller and de Wette, and he develops these insights from myth theory and his own experience into a concrete historicist application. He claims that the stories emerged after Jesus's death and enabled his followers to engage unconsciously ideas about the relation between God and humanity. They elaborated this narrative in the idiom of first-century Jewish apocalyptic thought. This is not to suggest that Jesus's actual existence was irrelevant to the traditions behind the gospels. Rather, it provided a "framework" for them, in scanty concrete events of his life: he was raised in Nazareth, for example, was baptized by John, assembled disciples, preached about the messianic kingdom, entered into debates with contemporary Jewish thinkers, and was crucified. From the first, "this framework was wreathed around with a manifold of deeply meaningful threads of earlier reflection and imagination;" soon after his death, "these threads interwove with ideas about [Jesus] ... and transformed into facts about his life."[30] The Hebrew Bible furnished the most substantial of these threads. Its stories and prophetic types of the Messiah converged with Jewish apocalyptic thought. Together they formed the fabric of the social and religious cosmos in which the early Christian community lived and moved.

Over the course of this analysis, Strauss puts a critical twist on previous views of myth. Here as in his writings on the nocturnal side of nature, the foray into romantic territory supplies the material of a demystifying science. To begin, he carries mythical analysis into a region of the Bible

---

29. Strauss, *Charakteristiken und Kritiken*, 321.
30. *LJ* 1835, 1:72, removed from later editions.

where other interpreters hesitated to tread. Orthodox and rationalist theologians objected to de Wette's claims that the Hebrew Bible included myths; they would respond still more vehemently to Strauss's mythical reading of the gospels. There were a number of reasons to take their objections seriously. The stories had a more this-worldly form, for example, than Greek legends about the exploits of the gods. Furthermore, they emerged at a period when historiography was fairly well developed. There was finally the lengthy Christian tradition that attributed the texts to disciples and fellow travelers. Strauss grants that some of these considerations are significant. But to take them as sufficient reasons not to conduct mythical analysis smacks of exceptionalism. Unscientific prejudice alone can keep scholars from analyzing the gospels in the same terms as stories from other traditions.[31]

He consequently presses mythical interpretation past the points at which other interpreters stopped short. He brings the critique of miracles together with mythical analysis to show where stories were fabricated unconsciously in ancient communities. In the introduction to the second and later editions, he uses them to define two major criteria, negative and positive, respectively, by which he tests the historical status of gospel stories. He names two negative criteria, of which the critique of miracles is the second and more weighty. The critic should ask, first, whether a narrative is inconsistent either internally or with its parallels in other gospels. Contradictions among them highlight the difficulty of uncovering a secure, shared eyewitness account. With this criterion one cannot prove that a narrative is impossible; however, it presses back against efforts at reconstruction. The second criterion is more decisive: he asks whether the narratives break the "known and universal laws which govern the course of events,"[32] including the established patterns of nature and causality, as well as of human psychology—how people customarily behave and think. From there, the single positive criterion, which constitutes the heart of the mythical interpretation, follows suit: "If the contents of a narrative strikingly accord with certain ideas existing and prevailing within the circle

---

31. *LJ* 1840, 1:62–63; *LJ* 1892, 69. He explains in this portion of the later editions that every positive faith pretends to have privileged access to God in history, through its prophets, texts, or traditions. It is not possible that these multiple and mutually exclusive beliefs are all true. Christianity's alleged roots in authentic historical revelation are just as credible as those of Judaism, Islam, or ancient Pagan religion.

32. *LJ* 1840, 1:100; *LJ* 1892, 88.

from which the narrative proceeded ... it is more or less probable ... that such a narrative is of mythical origin."[33] Strauss draws on precedents from the Hebrew Bible and other ancient texts and shows that stories about Jesus reflected their context. The miracle reports, for example, developed as Jesus's followers passed on stories about a person whom they considered to be the Messiah: "That the Jewish people in the time of Jesus expected miracles from the Messiah is ... in itself natural, since the Messiah was for them a second Moses and the greatest prophet."[34] They molded their narratives to fit these types. If Moses provided his followers with supernatural food and Elijah raised people from the dead, so must have the Messiah; if Isaiah predicted that in the messianic age people would be miraculously healed, then Jesus must have healed them.[35] All of the miracle reports are made up of mythical elements.

The positive and negative criteria work hand-in-hand throughout the *Life of Jesus*. If an element of a story meets both sets of criteria—if it transgresses the laws of nature and corresponds to the interests of Jewish thought in the first century—then the story is likely to be mythical. Strauss's treatment of the demons and the herd of pigs, in the story of the Gadarene demoniac, exemplifies this approach. Recall that in Matthew, Mark, and Luke the demons begged Jesus to expel them into a herd of pigs, a request which he granted, at which point the pigs rushed into the nearby sea and drowned. For Strauss, this element provides sure proof of the impossibility of the narrative, as much as the legion of possessing demons. It is a question of the familiar limits of bodies and spirits, now framed in terms of the relative spiritual development of humans and animals. An alien self-consciousness dividing a subject from his or her body is impossible; the idea of multiple demonic possessors is still more bizarre; equally outrageous is the claim that these intelligent spirits would enter into animal forms, that is, pigs—"Every religion and philosophy," he explains, "which rejects the transmigration of souls, must, for the same reason, also deny the possibility of this passage of the demons into swine."[36] Hence even Olshausen recognizes the story as a "scandal and stumbling block" for an interpreter who wishes to set it on natural terrain.

---

33. *LJ* 1840, 1:103; *LJ* 1892, 89.
34. *LJ* 1836, 2:1; *LJ* 1892, 413, translation modified.
35. *LJ* 1836, 2:1; *LJ* 1892, 413.
36. *LJ* 1836, 2:32; *LJ* 1892, 48.

As he often does, Strauss frames his mythical interpretation against Paulus's rationalist account. Paulus claimed that the stories conflated the possessed man and the demons. The Gadarene demoniac, frenzied under the influence of his fixed idea, rushed toward the pigs and chased them into the water. But here again, Paulus blithely disregards the plain meaning and intention of the narratives. Luke and Mark expressly describe how the demons "enter in" (εἰσῆλθον) to the pigs (Mark 5:13; Luke 8:33), while all three describe them "coming out" (ἐξελθόντα/ἐξελθόντες) (Mark 5:13; Luke 8:33; Matt 8:32). Paulus fails to explain the narrative, because he breaks with the authors: "Our Evangelists do not in this instance merely relate what actually happened in the colours which it took from the false lights of their age; they have here a particular, which cannot possibly have happened in the manner they allege."[37] And if the evangelists explicitly present a story that is not possible, we are pitched from the realm of eyewitness events to that of consciousness. We have to explain why they would craft this kind of narrative from the ground up.

Strauss passes accordingly to the realm of ancient thought and mythical narratives. Where Paulus invents natural explanations, Strauss explains, "we must rather ask, whether in the probable period of the formation of the evangelical narratives, there are not ideas to be found from which the story ... in the history before us might be explained."[38] In fact these ideas stand ready to hand in other ancient texts. We find multiple ancient accounts in which the expulsion of a demon is proven by the movement of a nearby object. Josephus, for example, describes in the *Antiquities* (8.2, §5) how a man named Eleazar, who used ancient exorcistic techniques from Solomon, would "set a vessel of water in the neighborhood of the possessed person, so that the departing demon must throw it down and thus give ocular proof to the spectators that he was out of the man."[39] Apollonius of Tyana describes an incident where a statue fell over at the moment a demon was expelled. These narratives take us from the events to their function: to prove the efficacy and reality of an exorcism. Furthermore, if other narratives had exorcists whose healing rites could affect nearby objects, those performed by the Messiah would have to include still more dramatic effects. The demons ran into the bodies of pigs because of the association in Jewish culture between unclean spirits and unclean animals.

---

37. *LJ* 1836, 2:34; *LJ* 1892, 429.
38. *LJ* 1836, 2:37–38; *LJ* 1892, 430.
39. *LJ* 1836, 2:38; *LJ* 1892, 431.

"Only by this derivation of our narrative from the confluence of various ideas and interests of the age," Strauss concludes, can it be explained and its various contradictory elements resolved.[40]

We can see here the extent to which mythical interpretation secures the devastating, negative effect of the historical-critical analysis of miracle stories. Not only are the stories impossible, they are better explained in terms of ancient thought. Consequently, they are more surely unhistorical. Like Magdalena Grombach's demons, those of Matthew, Mark, and Luke are less likely to have been real to the degree that Strauss finds more plausible immanent, historical grounds to explain them. His explanations in both sets of texts reinforce the material limits that he set on the work of spirit. If it could be better explained on immanent grounds, then a demon must appear as a superfluous *deus ex machina*. Strauss recognizes, as de Wette recognized in his work on the Hebrew Bible, that this is a sure result of his analysis. If the stories are myths, they are not historical. His work might appear therefore to share more in common with the rationalists than he admitted. For both, the goal would be to see what could be reconstructed of the gospel narratives. Only for Strauss the answer would be "very little."

The Second Critical Aspect of Strauss's Adaptation of Romantic Myth Theory: Ancient and Modern *Bildung*

But in fact this is only the first face of his analysis of myths and miracles. As in his account of Grombach and Anna U, Strauss's turn back to subjective consciousness not only fixes limits on the supernatural elements of the stories: it sheds a clear light on that consciousness and makes it an object of analysis in its own right. In his critical analyses of Grombach's demons or Hauffe's nerve-spirit, the breaches that these conceptions demanded in the immanent, psychophysical realm led him back to the minds and experiences that shaped them. He first posited, for example, that no external consciousness could force itself, like a wedge, between a person's body and her mind; he then went on to seek "subjective" grounds for Grombach and Anna U's divided consciousness and strange demoniacal symptoms. On the one hand, he sought these grounds in the women's distorted psychophysical conditions; on the other, he located them in the unlearned

---

40. *LJ* 1836, 2:40; *LJ* 1892, 431.

religious culture of the German countryside.⁴¹ Only nonmodern, undeveloped mentalities can blatantly transgress the limits of nature and human bodies without calling their own trustworthiness or sanity into question.

In the *Life of Jesus*, Strauss sets the critique of miracles to work in a similar fashion, in the service of an exploration of ancient, mythical mentalities. Even before he turns to cultural contexts in the *Life of Jesus*, supernatural elements serve as evidence, in themselves, of an alien mind at work. The presence of miracles in a narrative measures the influence of nonmodern thought. From the opening pages of the *Life of Jesus*, he connects the two. He defines sacred history "in which the divine enters without intermediation into human affairs; the ideal thus assuming an immediate embodiment,"⁴² that is, in which there are miracles, as an expression of ancient worldviews. It is the main stumbling block to a modern person's understanding of the Scriptures.

In the introduction to the second and later editions, he cites the presence of miraculous elements in the narratives as the most certain justification for applying myth theory to the gospels. After the barrage of criticism that followed the first edition's publication, Strauss felt it necessary to develop this justification in more exacting detail. He asserts, first, that the external grounds for thinking the gospels were written from eyewitness narratives are flimsy at best. There are no more substantial reasons to think the gospels were written by Matthew, Mark, Luke, and John, than that the Pentateuch was composed by Moses. The attributions are relatively late and inconsistent. We know, moreover, that pseudonymous composition was widespread in the ancient world.⁴³ This external argument shows that the gospels might, at least, not be eyewitness accounts. Still more decisive are arguments on internal grounds, namely, those that take their cue from the content of the texts. And among these grounds, one point in particular offers the most incontrovertible evidence that the gospels are mythical: they include elements that directly contradict modern conceptions of God and nature.

Strauss's discussion of changing conceptions of natural law underwrites this claim. He asks, first, whether the biblical history clashes with our idea of the world "and whether such discordancy may furnish a test of its unhistorical nature." He describes how in antiquity "the knowledge of

---

41. Strauss, *Charakteristiken und Kritiken*, 301–27.
42. *LJ* 1835, 1:2; *LJ* 1892, 39.
43. *LJ* 1840, 1:62–74; *LJ* 1892, 69–75.

nature [was] so limited, that the law of connection between earthly finite beings was very loosely regarded." The ancients did not understand the interdependence and consecutiveness of the natural order. They consequently imputed major shifts in the world to God's immediate action on them: "He it is who gives rain and sunshine; he sends the east wind and the storm; he dispenses war, famine, pestilence; he hardens hearts and softens them, suggests thoughts and resolutions." "Our modern world," on the other hand, "after many centuries of tedious research has attained the conviction, that all things are linked together by a chain of causes and effects, which suffers no interruption."[44] He then continues with the various shifting concepts of nature and God that we have seen, from the deists to Spinozan monism, supernaturalism, and dynamic monism in the vein of Hegel, Scheleiermacher, or Schelling. At the end, he asserts, simply, that this overview secures the "surprising conclusion ... that the Hebrew and Christian religions, like all others, have their myths."[45] Thus the singular "presupposition" of historical critique—Strauss's monistic views of human subjects and the cosmos—forms the measure of modern thought. The limits of bodies and souls mark inversely the presence of mentalities that transgress them.

In each of the miracle accounts that we have already considered, the patently impossible, miraculous elements in the narratives serve accordingly to illuminate the ancient mentalities at work behind them. In this piece of his analyses, Strauss diverges more radically still from contemporary rationalists and supernaturalists. For Strauss, the problem with Paulus, Schleiermacher, Tholuck, or Olshausen's interpretations is not only that they fail to set psychophysical limits firmly in place; in doing so, they fail to engage seriously the ancient worldview behind the narratives. In his haste to explain the passage of the legion of demons into a herd of pigs, for instance, Paulus fails to consider why an author would craft this narrative. But still more damning, for Strauss, is that when these interpreters obscure the ancient, alien qualities of the narrative, they blur the lines between ancient and modern thought. They overlook the sheer impossibility of miracle reports, for example, because they cling to the belief that the evangelists and Jesus shared a modern, fully rational perspective on the world. In their efforts to make them palatable objects of faith or sources of reli-

---

44. *LJ* 1840, 1:80; *LJ* 1892, 78.
45. *LJ* 1840, 1:84; *LJ* 1892, 80, translation modified.

gious truth for a modern person, they credit Jesus and the disciples with concepts that these figures could not have held.

Olshausen's interpretation of the Gadarene demoniac presents an especially glaring example. Recall that Olshausen's interpretation rested on two central claims.[46] First, he claimed that the New Testament "demons" were not personal, individual beings but part of an immanent, diffuse spiritual evil. Second, he claimed that the demoniac's disorders were at once physiological, moral, and religious; Jesus and the disciples could therefore heal them through faith. Between these two claims, Olshausen hoped in part to preserve the literal veracity of the reports. But he also hoped to affirm that the gospel stories were inspired sources of truth, in spite of their patently unscientific and unmodern representations. The disciples and Jesus may have held ancient views on demons and possession, but these beliefs were ultimately secondary matters. Their real goal in addressing these issues was to engage the underlying moral, spiritual afflictions that generated them.

Because the origin of the diseases were moral, moreover, and because the possessed individuals' wills were inadequate to shake them off, the gospel accounts of healings and exorcisms could function as parables about redemption through faith. Olshausen meant as such to grant a more universal, modern application to an ancient New Testament idea. Ancient people believed pneumatic evil could be defeated through an appeal to a higher spiritual authority—for example, the name of Jesus could serve to cast out demons. A nineteenth-century person, without necessarily believing in demons, could understand his or her own struggle with "sensual inclinations" in an analogous fashion. Olshausen's interpretation aims to draw us nearer to the authors of these ancient texts. Strange ideas about demons are only the antiquated husk of the disciples' and Jesus's more essential beliefs—beliefs that resemble at their core modern religious notions about faith and morality.

In his rebuttal, Strauss takes up a question that Olshausen had raised, but not pursued, in a footnote, namely, how the ancient apostles would have understood modern mental illnesses: "were the apostles to visit our madhouses," Olshausen says, "it is questionable how they would designate many of the sufferers in them."[47] Olshausen cites Kerner and Esquirol's studies of demonomania as a justification for the question. Olshausen had

---

46. Olshausen, *Biblical Commentary on the New Testament*, 362–64.
47. Ibid., 365 n. *.

to leave the answer to this question uncertain, Strauss claims, in order to avoid two conclusions: First, that the apostles were unenlightened by modern standards, that the idea of demon possession should be an artifact of a bygone age, no matter how we interpret it; second, consequently, that ancient stories about possessed people could not possibly have been "inspired." Strauss responds directly and writes, "they would to a certainty name many of them demoniacs," continuing, "the official who acted as their conductor would very properly endeavor to set them right: whatever names therefore they might give to the inmates of the asylums, our conclusions as to the naturalness of the disorders of those inmates would not be at all affected."[48] The ancient Christian disciple shares the possessed individual's belief in the influential power of demonic entities; the asylum official and critic work to exorcise these delusions by naming them.

In fact, this image of the asylum official as he initiates Jesus's disciples into the proper names of the modern study of psychology captures the essence of both Strauss's reproach to Olshausen and his vision of critical science. Both he and his official undertake a labor of *Bildung*. The official wants to show the disciples the truth about "demonomania." He means to prove there is no supernatural influence at work, but also to educate them about immanent, natural differences between their states of mind and body and those of the demoniacs. Strauss means to show a modern, rational person—namely, Olshausen—the truth about the disciples and evangelists, that they do not share the mentality of a modern theologian. To do so, he details features of the ancient apocalyptic worldview in which the possession and exorcism narratives took shape.

Jewish demonology in the first century emerged from apocalyptic traditions that developed over the previous three centuries, Strauss explains, around the flood narrative in Gen 6. He sums up the underlying storyline and writes, "in the Hebrew view, the demons were the fallen angels of Genesis 6, the souls of their offspring the giants, and of the great criminals before and immediately after the deluge, whom the popular imagination gradually magnified into superhuman beings." After the angels mated with humans, they gave birth to the "giants," the *nephilim* who ruled the world before the flood. This was a time of great evil, and God decided to cleanse the earth. According to later traditions, the flood destroyed the evil giants and God imprisoned or otherwise restrained their angelic progenitors; the

---

48. *LJ* 1836, 2:15; *LJ* 1892, 420.

souls of the giants and "great criminals" remained, however, to tempt and possess human beings.[49] The demons and wayward angels would only be eliminated in the last judgment at the end of time. Hence Jesus's power over the demons is part of an eschatological apocalyptic worldview. It signals the onset of the last days. When Olshausen suggests that the Capernaum demoniac might have recognized Jesus as the Messiah through presentient power, Strauss directs his attention accordingly back to the narrative's plain sense and, in turn, to this unfamiliar field of apocalyptic thought:

> The evangelical narrative … does not ascribe that knowledge to a power of the patient, but of the demon dwelling within him, and this is the only view consistent with the Jewish ideas of that period. The Messiah was to appear, in order to overthrow the demoniacal kingdom and to cast the devil and his angels into the lake of fire: it followed of course that the demons would recognize him who was to pass such a sentence on them.[50]

When he made this kind of claim, Strauss stepped well outside of the theological mainstream in his day. Theologians since the early twentieth century have grown accustomed to Jewish apocalyptic elements in Christian stories. But most of Strauss's contemporaries willfully ignored or sought to downplay these features of the texts. Schleiermacher, for example, in his treatise on Christian doctrine, stipulated that eschatological beliefs, especially in Jesus's resurrection and parousia, were incidental to Christian faith: "The facts of the resurrection and the ascension of Christ, and the prediction of his return to judgment, cannot be laid down as properly constituent parts of the doctrine of his person."[51] Christians should not look to Jesus's sayings or the gospel stories about strange miraculous phenomena and an imminent kingdom for their faith; they should focus instead on who Jesus was and on his unique consciousness of God.

For Strauss this dismissal could only do violence to the texts. He asks that interpreters "understand the statements of the New Testament as simply as they are given."[52] He insists with the old strains of orthodoxy and contemporary romanticism on the plain sense of the narratives. In the process, however, he makes clear the alien quality of their worldview. If we

---

49. *LJ* 1836, 2:13; *LJ* 1892, 419.
50. *LJ* 1836, 2:24; *LJ* 1892, 424.
51. Schleiermacher, *Christian Faith*, 417 (§99).
52. *LJ* 1836, 2:20; *LJ* 1892, 422.

3. MYTH AND THE NOCTURNAL SIDE OF NATURE 123

are to take these stories at their plain meaning, we must not embrace that meaning in turn. Olshausen fails equally on each of these counts. He tries to make the evangelists modern and devises an account of spirit that drags us back into the ancient world. Strauss deems Olshausen's effort "useless" in part because it violates the immanent limits of the natural order. But it fails just as much as an attempt "to modernize the New Testament representation of the demoniacs."[53]

When he insists on the plain sense of the narratives, Strauss means to make this kind of confusion impossible. He aims to cut off access to ancient thought—or rather to show that this access is only illusory. As in his critique of miracles, Strauss draws on the resources of Pietism and romanticism and turns them to a critical effect. His image of the exorcism stories not only shows where they are unhistorical. It takes his contemporary readers into unsettling, alien territory. It leads them, like the disciples in the asylum, to recognize and acknowledge the true, immanent, and natural form of the gospel writers' consciousness. It consequently drives a wedge between ancient and modern culture. Each of the critiques of miracle narratives doubles as a proof and examination of the differences between ancient and modern *Bildung*. Inversely, they provide Strauss an opportunity to outline the contours of modern scientific consciousness. Modern people do not believe in demons because of the conception of a unitary, embodied self-consciousness. Only in "modern times," he explains, is "the contradiction in the idea of demon possession ... beginning to be dimly perceived," namely that,

> whatever theory may be held as to the relation between the self-consciousness and the bodily organs, it remains absolutely inconceivable how the union between the two could be so far dissolved, that a foreign self-consciousness could gain an entrance, thrust out that which belonged to the organism, and usurp its place.[54]

Modern people do not believe in resurrections, in turn, because "modern culture" has taught them to conceive of bodies and souls as coextensive. If "modern culture has decisively established the dilemma: either Jesus was not really dead, or he did not really rise again,"[55] then modern culture, as

---

53. *LJ* 1836, 2:20; *LJ* 1892, 422.
54. *LJ* 1836, 2:19; *LJ* 1892, 419.
55. *LJ* 1836, 2:647–48; *LJ* 1892, 736.

well as the impossibility of the event itself, comes into clear relief when science takes on the gospel narratives.

Hence the same dynamic appears when Strauss breaks with Schleiermacher on the question of Jesus's resurrection. We have already seen that Strauss pushes past Schleiermacher's warnings and closes once and for all the doors that Schleiermacher left open to both supernatural belief and rationalist reconstruction of the historical event. Mythical interpretation adds another layer to his critique. As in Olshausen's reading of the exorcisms, the issue for Strauss was not that Schleiermacher had gotten history wrong; it was that he failed to see how truly ancient and alien the gospel narratives were. In his 1865 response to the published version of Schleiermacher's lectures, Strauss states that, like Olshausen, Schleiermacher wished to affirm the credibility of the gospel authors. Schleiermacher did not only want to give grounds for historical belief of the rationalist or supernaturalist variety. He could not believe the narratives were untrue because to do so would be to accuse the gospel writers of crafting narratives to make their point, rather than attending to the real facts of Christ's life. It would, as such, attribute to them "such a spiritual weakness that their entire testimony about Christ becomes unreliable."[56]

For Strauss, the combination of Schleiermacher's rationalist account of the resurrection and his disregard of its importance for Christian belief did the worst kind of violence, not only to the meaning of the texts, but to Christian faith itself as it actually took shape in the course of its history:

> For the belief in the resurrection of Christ is the foundation stone, without which the Christian church could not have been built; nor could the cycle of Christian festivals, which are the external representation of the Christian faith, now suffer a more fatal mutilation than by the removal of the festival of Easter: the Christ who died could not be what he is in the belief of the church, if he were not also the Christ who rose again.[57]

Strauss repeats over and again that a Christian faith worthy of the name cannot turn away in fear from the doctrines and ideas that have played such an instrumental role in its history. He believes that his work improved

---

56. Strauss, *The Christ of Faith and the Jesus of History: A Critique of Schleiermacher's The Life of Jesus*, trans. Leander E. Keck (Philadelphia: Fortress, 1977), 127, quoting Schleiermacher's *Christian Faith*, 418–19.

57. *LJ* 1836, 2:718; *LJ* 1892, 773.

on rationalism, because it took all of faith seriously, even where it made modern people uncomfortable. Yet precisely this fear and this discomfort come to serve as the grounds of a new critical exercise. As in the writings on demonomania and ghost seeing, Strauss is keen to attend to those points where modern theologians feel aversion when confronted with alien dimensions of belief. For example, Enlightenment interpreters feel "repugnance"[58] at the idea that Jesus and the gospel writers believed in demon possession, just as they felt "aversion and contempt" for the phenomena in Kerner's *Accounts of the Modern Possessed*. Strauss does not allow his readers to look away in either case.

In the introduction to the *Life of Jesus*, Strauss argues that critique begins with a breach in the historical evolution of *Bildung*. It begins where established sacred texts evoke a feeling of anachronism and decay in the face of a changing culture.

> Wherever a religion, resting upon written records, prolongs and extends the sphere of its dominion, accompanying its votaries through the varied and progressive stages of mental cultivation, a discrepancy between the representations of those ancient records, referred to as sacred, and the notions of more advanced periods of development, will inevitably sooner or later arise.[59]

As a religious culture evolves, it diverges from its fixed texts and traditions. Those who become cognizant of this breach experience a "sense of repulsion" (*unbehangliches Sichabwenden*) at the sight of the outmoded cultural artifacts.[60] At that point, an interpreter can pursue one of two courses: in an apologetic mode, he or she will "close his or her eyes to the secretly recognised fact of the disagreement between the modern culture and the ancient records;" a critical interpreter, on the other hand, "unequivocally acknowledges and openly avows that the matters narrated in these books must be viewed in a light altogether different from that in which they were regarded by the authors themselves."[61] The critic should serve as a kind of herald, then, who scrutinizes and announces the signs of the times; he or

---

58. *LJ* 1836, 2:10; *LJ* 1892, 417.
59. *LJ* 1835, 1:1; *LJ* 1892, 39. Most interpreters have neglected this affective dimension of Strauss's account of cultural memory and development in the *Life of Jesus*. An exception is Blanton, *Displacing Christian Origins*, 50–66.
60. *LJ* 1835, 1:1; *LJ* 1892, 39.
61. *LJ* 1835, 1:2; *LJ* 1892, 40.

she should also serve as a coroner: having refused to try to bring the dead cultural past to life in an immediate and artificial way, the interpreter has instead to guarantee its expiration. The critic who keeps her eyes open to the breach exacerbates the "sense of repulsion" that modern people ought to feel for the old religious representations to which they unwittingly or passively cling.

Once again, Strauss's youthful *Bildung* mirrors at once the development of culture and the work of scientific critique. Criticism calls attention to the crises of culture; it brings people into the light of the new age by exacerbating the aversion they feel for the lingering presence of calcified ideas and institutions. As the *Life of Jesus* tests the historicity of pericopes, it sheds an unflattering light, to "repulsive" effect, on the boundaries between ancient and modern worldviews. If each era's respective conceptions of history, God and nature, and bodies and souls define the distinctions between them, then Strauss's efforts to set limits on particular miracles double as attempts to draw and secure lines between ancient and modern consciousness. Only modern people understand the unbreachable unity of bodies and souls. Strauss shows that the narratives violate these natural limits at every turn. Thus historical criticism and the critique of culture converge to define a unified, radical method of scientific interpretation.

Strauss's Hegelian Exposition of His Method: An Immanent, Historical Critique of Consciousness

Soon after he published the *Life of Jesus*, Strauss would use Hegel's philosophy to theorize this movement of critical *Bildung* in one of his polemical writings in defense of the *Life of Jesus*.[62] The essay in question responds to theologically conservative Hegelian critics of his work. In this piece, Strauss claims to proceed from Hegel's postromantic adaptation of Kant's critical philosophy. The essay defines Strauss's contribution to a theologically critical reading of Hegel's philosophy—B. Bauer and Marx, for example, saw Strauss's work as a precedent to revise elements of Hegel's philosophy into an active social and religious critique. Strauss's contribution in this region is consistent with the modern critical approach that we have seen him develop elsewhere, from the time of his early *Bildung* in the German

---

62. The essay from the *Streitschriften* translated by Massey as *In Defense of My Life of Jesus*.

countryside to his application of myth theory in the *Life of Jesus*. Hegel's philosophy provided Strauss with theoretical resources by which to conceive his engagement with ancient and modern margins of religious belief and experience. In order to see how he develops this theoretical view, we have to pass by way of Kant's critical philosophy to Strauss's Schellingian and Hegelian rebuttal and finally on to his revised, historicized version of a "critique of consciousness."

Strauss's adaptation of Kantian critique forms a second axis of the "critical" dimension of the *Life of Jesus Critically Examined*, alongside historical critique. For Strauss and his contemporaries, critique (*Kritik*) had a range of meanings. Broadly speaking, it denoted practices by which one judges limits between what is legitimate and illegitimate, authentic and inauthentic. Strauss's efforts to test the authenticity of the gospels against the limits of nature, for example, fall within the realm of "historical criticism." Critique is not a strictly negative endeavor, however. As a critic sets limits, he or she determines foundations on which to secure truths, beliefs, and values. From the early modern period onward, new forms of critique developed to secure the conditions of a legitimate modern faith, one that could survive the wars of religion and sectarian divisions.[63] Critics sought to name what was original and historical in the ancient texts in order to expose the rational grounds of positive religion. Michaelis and Semler, for example, tried to show where biblical religion already converged with reason. They did not believe they were attacking the Bible, miracle, or revelation from the perspective of reason; rather they showed how and to what extent positive revelation could be intrinsically rational. This approach continued with rationalists like Paulus and Wegscheider, as well as with Schleiermacher, who used criticism to reconstruct a modern, rational, and unique historical Jesus.

Kant transplanted the philological model of critique onto the field of cognition. He set out to define the conditions of possibility of rational thought per se and to establish in the process the legitimacy of science, including historical criticism. We have considered already how his "Copernican" subjective turn led in this direction. It established how subjective consciousness, divided as it is from the world of objects around us, could guarantee the adequacy of cognitive representations to what exists. In Kant's view, science could attain firm and consistent truth from our

---

63. Legaspi, *Death of Scripture*, 3–26.

experience of nature and history, but only because all subjects rely on the same forms of consciousness to unify and make sense of their manifold impressions of the world.

This model of critique has negative functions as well. Kant deduces legitimate, canonical concepts of the human understanding, but also shows where reason cannot tread. As a condition of its universality, the horizon of subjective preunderstanding limits consciousness to the phenomenal realm, that is, to the empirical world as it appears to us. We cannot pass beyond the categories through which the world is made available to our cognition. We cannot grasp the "noumenal" realm of "things-in-themselves," that is, things as they really are out there. In particular, reason cannot fulfill our propensity to comprehend objectively supersensible realities such as God, the immortal soul, or the ends or origins of the cosmos. We can only grasp these matters tenuously, as postulates, as if they were objects, in order to orient our moral action. This approach from the realm of "practical reason" differs from "theoretical reason," which attempts to conceive God et cetera objectively, in the manner of previous metaphysics.

Kant's model of critique had implications for theology and biblical criticism. On the one hand, he granted that historical criticism, like other sciences, could produce universally verifiable truths. But these are strictly empirical truths, limited to the phenomenal realm. When an interpreter tries to pass beyond these phenomena to things-in-themselves—the will of God, for example, of the true eternal nature of the historical Jesus—he or she transgresses the limits on reason. Any attempt to grasp supersensible truth through the analysis of historical or textual particulars is bound to fail. He consequently divides philosophical and historical interpretation of the Bible. Historical critics pursue the history of and behind religious texts, but cannot contribute to knowledge of religious truth per se. We can only orient ourselves toward such truth through a philosophy of practical reason.

Kant develops these ideas in part in *Religion within the Limits of Mere Reason*, a work that Strauss names in the introduction to the *Life of Jesus* as a major contribution to the field of biblical criticism. As the title suggests, Kant sets out to conceive the truths of Christianity without transgressing the limits of reason. In the Bible, he claims, we only find symbols of moral truths. Strauss cites his response to Michaelis's interpretation of Ps 59 as an example of this symbolic, moral interpretation. Kant first notes that the psalm goes to terrifying extremes in its petition for divine vengeance.

Taken in its literal sense, it stands in discomfiting tension with our—inherent in Kant's view—drive toward morality. Michaelis had argued that the psalms were inspired and therefore authoritative: "if in them punishment is prayed for," he wrote, "it cannot be wrong, and we must have no higher morality than the Bible."[64] For Kant, this claim confuses the facts of the text with its religious truth. A philosophical interpreter will approach it instead from the grounds of rational morality. From this perspective, the psalm cannot refer to actual enemies. It refers to symbolic enemies: an individual's own inclinations toward evil.

His interpretation of Jesus proceeds in a similar fashion: Jesus is as an archetype of the idea of moral perfection, an idea toward which our moral reasoning tends ineluctably. Various biblical descriptions of Jesus—as the son of God, as the one who descends from heaven, et cetera—emerge from our idea of the possibility of moral perfection. Nevertheless, we by no means require an empirical person to assure us of this possibility;[65] on the contrary, if we were simply to assert Jesus's existence as the positive divine-human or if we were to demand empirical proof of historical miracles, we would relinquish our rational autonomy. Our decision to adopt moral maxims would depend on a determinate empirical reality rather than on the transcendental exercise of our will.

Kant leaves questions of what the Bible in fact meant, whether it was inspired, who said it, et cetera aside altogether. As a historical document of positive religion, Scripture is a mere "dead" object: "Historical faith 'is dead, being alone'; that is, of itself, regarded as a creed, it contains nothing, and leads to nothing, which could have any moral value for us."[66] The Bible comes to life only as a rational, philosophical interpreter reconciles it to the universal moral truth that inheres in human consciousness. There is consequently nothing we can say about the Bible's intrinsic value. It is only serendipitous if it happens to contain "perfectible" representations: symbols which are uniquely amenable to the aspirations of universal truth and reason. And in fact this is what we find when we read it philosophically. Although Kant separates between historical and philosophical faith, the Bible's status as an object of theological reflection remains intact.

In the introduction to the *Life of Jesus*, Strauss presents Kant's model of interpretation in an ambivalent light. Like Origen's allegorical and mythi-

---

64. Kant, *Religion and Rational Theology*, 142 n. *.
65. Ibid., 119.
66. Ibid., 143.

cal interpretation, the moral view leaves aside positive, historical truths and seeks absolute truths in the gospels. In this respect it improves on aspects of the work of Paulus and others. But Kant seeks these ideas from the perspective of individual consciousness, where they become subjective rational postulates about God, Jesus, et cetera. As such, he and Origen diverge equally from the mythical interpretation. "The allegorical interpreter," he explains,

> as well as the moral, may with the most unrestrained arbitrariness separate from the history every thought he deems to be worthy of God, as constituting its inherent meaning; whilst the mythical interpreter, on the contrary, in searching out the ideas which are embodied in the narrative, is controlled by regard to conformity with the spirit and modes of thought of the people and of the age.[67]

For all of his antipathy to positive historical faith, Strauss keeps his mythical approach tethered to history. But by "history," he means the history of cultures and consciousness, not of specific events.

In the later response to his Hegelian critics, Strauss traces his opposition to Kant to the speculative philosophies of Hegel and Schelling. He reiterates the romantic generation's familiar critique of Kant as a subjective idealist. Kant's attempts to reconcile human consciousness to eternal truth had exacerbated the fragmenting tendencies of the Enlightenment; he sustained a dualistic worldview. Strauss explains that when he separates things-in-themselves from the phenomena of consciousness, Kant makes the world and all that is in it, including the Bible, appear as dead objects in opposition to the living consciousness of the subject who conceives them. Fichte would eventually take this view to its culmination—"the Fichtean 'I,'" he writes, "took reality standing over against it to be a dead mass into which the subject had to import form and understanding through its own activity"; but Kant's idealism already presses in this direction.[68] Strauss cites, for example, "Kant's view that purpose in organisms is a rationality merely imported by the subject into nature."[69] Kant refrains from granting that beings in nature and history have a palpable share in spirit.

---

67. *LJ* 1835, 1:52; *LJ* 1892, 65.
68. Strauss, *In Defense of My Life of Jesus*, 9.
69. Ibid.

3. MYTH AND THE NOCTURNAL SIDE OF NATURE   131

As a consequence, his view fails to rise to the level of speculative philosophical science. He can only claim what objects in the world should or might be from the universal vantage of subjective reason. But he cannot discern what it is in itself—his "ought" stands opposed to whatever "is" as to something distant and fixed in place. Kant and Fichte are like the deists or Descartes in that they fail to conceive the "absolute," the unity of spirit and nature. Strauss draws on Hegel and claims that they set the "actual," existent world in opposition to the "rational," subjective ego: "The philosophical systems immediately preceding Hegel's view knew only the tautological proposition, 'the rational is rational; the actual is actual.' They could unite both sides only in the form 'the rational should also be actual, the actual should also be rational.'"[70] Kant's moral, symbolic interpretation exemplifies this abstractly negative relation to actual religious objects. The interpreter does not access its truth as such; he or she only reimagines its meaning and tells us what it should say within the dictates of reason.

Hegel and Schelling, on the other hand, unite subject and substance, God and nature, spirit and matter, et cetera into a universal totality. Spirit pervades everything. Hegel proposes accordingly that "the actual is rational and the rational is actual."[71] If spirit is inscribed in the objective world, subjective reason cannot oppose the existent as if it were extrinsic and dead. It must instead grapple with "objective spirit," an actual historical universe, infused with rationality, of which it is part in turn.[72]

The consequences of Hegel's and Schelling's view for biblical interpretation align with those of Schelling's and Herder's views on myth: no existing reality, even an ancient text like the Bible, can lack its own, native spiritual meaning and truth. This conception pushes back at once against rationalism and the moral interpretation. Of course Kant stood directly opposed, along with Lessing and Reimarus, to Eichhorn or Paulus: he separated religious truth from biblical history. But Strauss claims they share a rationalistic conceit in common: they all treat Christianity as "perfectible," to use Kant's terminology. They use critique as a means of separating the eternal core of Christian—historical or philosophical—truth from its supernaturalistic narrative husk. For Semler, this meant that Christian historical revelation is real, but only where it corresponds to the grounds of

---

70. Ibid., 8. Strauss draws directly on Hegel here (Hegel, *Encyclopaedia Logic*, 28–30 [§6]).
71. Strauss, *In Defense of My Life of Jesus*, 8.
72. Ibid., 8–9.

modern reason. For Paulus and, to an extent, for Schleiermacher, it meant that we have to find the unique, semidivine Christ in the historical Jesus. For Kant, it meant that Christian truth had to be liberated from positive faith altogether. Strauss groups these views together and levels Hegel against them:

> We are even beyond considering the Christian religion as one in which the best element is "perfectibility" and as one which is to be the first to be led back through a "censorship" of the thinking subject into the "limits of reason" and purified as a "religion of the mature and of the more perfect." Rationality and truth exist in all reality in general, and thus particularly in religion, the highest spiritual reality, and, in the deepest sense, in the Christian religion as the absolute religion. A critique which makes a move to excise a mass of untruths and unhistorical assertions in Christianity draws from the beginning the accusation that it has not yet been raised to the Hegelian point of view.[73]

Yet again, an affirmation of speculative philosophy coalesces with his affirmation of the essential truth of Christianity. The effect is to spread the reach of science into the entire realm of Christian thought and doctrine. This movement enables Strauss to theorize explicitly the view that appears in his critiques of Olshausen's account of demons and Schleiermacher's reading of the resurrection. It is impossible to expose Christianity's innate perfection by separating a rational core from the irrational husk. There is no irrational husk. Even the most strange, superstitious regions of religious thought are expressions of spirit, which emerge as humans in history strive to make sense of their world with the cognitive tools at hand. Consequently, science must focus on even those areas where the Bible breaks overtly with modern thought, where traces remain of pre-modern superstition and irrationalism. The speculative view of a God who is coextensive with the universe of history, nature, and living and dying natural beings underpins an objection to rationalistic critique in all of its manifestations—Kantian, deist, or rationalist.

At this point, Strauss admits that it would seem that, with Hegel and Schelling, he had done away with Kant and Fichte's critical emphasis altogether. One could use Hegel's philosophy to affirm the intrinsic rationality, and therefore legitimacy and truth, of whatever is actual. The existing

---

73. Ibid., 9.

3. MYTH AND THE NOCTURNAL SIDE OF NATURE

world, including the Bible, has no need of being critiqued: they are manifestations of the rational, objective spirit in history. Politically conservative Hegelian thinkers drew on this view to justify the established social and political order.[74] Theologically conservative Hegelians drew it into the service of orthodox belief: they argued that every conceptual truth in the Bible must also have been an historical reality. For example, if the idea of divinity and humanity united is true, then a unique divine-human must truly have existed.[75]

But Strauss takes a second, crucial step, one that distills the essence of his interpretation of Hegel's philosophy. He draws a series of distinctions, namely, between Hegel and Schelling based on the preface to Hegel's *Phenomenology of Spirit*.[76] Like Schelling, Hegel sets finite forms of natural, historical life within a dynamic system of interlocking mediations—they intersect with, shape, and transform one another constantly. But Hegel insists more firmly on the negative side of the absolute. For Schelling, Strauss explains, we grasp the absolute immediately, at once, through intuition.[77] For Hegel, we can conceive it only through the ongoing stages of its evolution in human thought and collective life. In fact, this succession constitutes absolute spirit, which comes to recognize itself in the course of history. Distinct modes of culture and consciousness emerge one after the other. "Mediated" worldviews gradually inform and transform "immediate" modes.[78] In modern, mediated worldviews, people learn to recognize how consciousness and the world intersect. This process leads to dawning self-consciousness, where human spirit recognizes its freedom and involvement in its own—social, political, natural—life and world. People become rational and self-conscious as they cease to take objects of all types as fixed, transcendent, or eternal realities over and against them.[79]

It is plausible that with these distinctions Strauss and Hegel both elide aspects of Schelling's thought; however, they enable Strauss to define Hegel's thought in a way that determines the conceptual framework for his methods of critique: Schelling's philosophy, he says, does in fact suppress critique in the name of the absolute, objective spirit, but Hegel's only

---

74. Toews, *Hegelianism*, 93–97.
75. Strauss, *In Defense of My Life of Jesus*, 14.
76. Ibid., 9–10.
77. Ibid., 10.
78. Ibid., 11.
79. Ibid.

appears to do so. In the *Phenomenology of Spirit*, he inscribes critique back into history. Hegel historicizes Kantian critique. He moves the limits that Kant identified between subjective reason and the objective world, namely, into the heart of the monist and organic cosmology of Schelling. The limits do not appear between subjects and the world, but between stages in historical evolution. If both Hegel and Schelling had a dynamic account of the movement of spirit in history, Hegel alone made this into a critique of collective social and historical consciousness, that is, of cultural mentalities. Both have a hierarchy of culture, but Hegel alone gives Strauss the resources to show where modern thought must break once and for all with and reject the ancient mentalities from which it sprang. His philosophy provides resources to draw critical lines between ancient and modern modes of thought.

Of crucial importance for Strauss to that end is the distinction that Hegel draws between modern, philosophical "concepts" (*Begriffe*) and the "representations" (*Vorstellungen*) of religious mentalities. Hegel uses the category of "representation" to connote imagistic forms of religious ideation, distinct from the concepts of philosophy and critique. Representational thought looks for truth, namely, in positive, external objects, persons, and events. It does not conceive them as mediated through history and culture. This is the view of the evangelists, who set their conceptions of God and spirit to rest on the person of Jesus and the particular events of his life. In the representation of Jesus's incarnation, for example, the idea of the absolute takes a sensuous, historical form. In philosophical concepts, thought achieves a rationally- and historically-mediated perspective on religious truth. This is the point at which thought turns back from the historical events to the historical modes of consciousness that had conceived them. With the rise of modern forms of self-consciousness, the former begin to dominate over the latter.

The distinction between representational and conceptual thought has an ambivalently secularizing, modernizing tendency. Like Schleiermacher or Schelling, Hegel believed he had reconciled faith and science. The conceptual view justified and completed representations even as it transcended them. Christian ideas about the incarnation or kingdom of God, for example, in which God and humanity were united, expressed in a primitive, other-worldly form what modernity would bring about on earth. At the end of spirit's long development from Greco-Roman antiquity through Judaism, early Christianity, the Middle Ages, and the Reformation, the modern enlightened subject and state finally instantiated

3. MYTH AND THE NOCTURNAL SIDE OF NATURE   135

religious ideas in terrestrial and rational forms. Concepts completed the *Verweltlichung*, the "making-worldly," of religious concepts.

Hegel's followers disagreed on how this secularization of religious self-consciousness should be understood, however: as a final liquidation of Christianity, for example, as its perfection, or as a transfer of its dogmas into a postdogmatic idiom.[80] The question preoccupied Strauss in the early 1830s, when he and his friends at the Tübingen Stift first discovered Hegel. They welcomed the distinction between representations and concepts as a means of navigating the breach that the Enlightenment had opened between faith and science. But they struggled with how far to take its critical implications: could the conceptual kernel stand without its representational husk? And in the modern age could representations be reduced to concepts?[81]

Strauss answers yes on both counts. He does so most famously in the concluding dissertation to the *Life of Jesus*, in which he cites Hegel explicitly. Here he argues that Christian representations are premodern, limited expressions of human self-consciousness. They represent an "early stage" of faith, in which it "is governed by the senses and therefore contemplates a temporal history; what [it] holds to be true is the external, ordinary

---

80. In the end of *In Defense of My Life of Jesus* (38–66), Strauss divides Hegelians into those of the "Right," "Left," and "Center" according to their position on the implications of Hegel's philosophy for the gospel history. The more orthodox, "Right" Hegelians include Carl Göschel (*Aphorismen über Nichtwissen und absolutes Wissen im Verhältnis zur christlichen Glaubenserkenntnis* [Berlin: Franklin, 1829]) and Bruno Bauer (review of *Das Leben Jesu, kritisch bearbeitet*, by David Friedrich Strauss, *JWK* Dec. 1835, 110:881–88; Dec. 1835, 111:889–94; Dec. 1835, 112:897–904; Dec. 1835, 113:905–12; review of *Das Leben Jesu, kritisch bearbeitet 2*, by David Friedrich Strauss, *JWK* May 1836, 86:681–88; May 1836, 87:689–94; May 1836, 88:697–704). Bauer later shifted to a critical stance and theology that placed him to the "left" of Strauss. Karl Rosenkranz (*Encyclopädie der theologischen Wissenschaft* [Halle: Schwetschke, 1831]; *Kritik der Schleiermacherschen Glaubenslehre* [Königsberg: Gebrüder Bornträger, 1836]) occupies the more ambivalent and ambiguous "center" position. Strauss places himself alone in the third, "left" category, which is characterized by his commitment to historical critical investigation as the means of liberating the truth of the gospel history (66). Toews, *Hegelianism*, 203–16, argues that Strauss's division applies well to the Hegelianism of the late 1830s that his work also helped to shape.

81. "In a short time, the most important question about this for us became how the concept related to the historical components of the Bible, especially the gospels: whether the historical character belongs to the content, which since it is the same for both representation and concept, thus demands recognition by the latter; or whether the historical character is to be considered as mere form to which conceptual thought, therefore, is not bound?" (Strauss, *In Defense of My Life of Jesus*, 3).

event."[82] First-century followers of Jesus concretized their idea of divine and human unity in an external reality: the "Divine-Human" Christ. These ancient people grasped human spirit—Strauss's version of Hegel's absolute spirit—but they confused this primitive insight with an actual individual human being. It is therefore the task of the modern critique of dogma to elevate these representations into philosophical concepts—to show, for example, the humanistic ideals that ancient people struggled to grasp in the incarnation or resurrection.

The later essay clarifies the critical application of myth. In the religious field, Strauss explains, the representational mode of thought takes the standpoint of "believing certainty," that is, belief locates truth in the sensuous, historical reality of particular religious objects and events. Believing certainty corresponds to the standpoint of "sense certainty," one of the first stages in Hegel's *Phenomenology of Spirit*: "Sense certainty is demonstrated in the process of the *Phenomenology* to be the poorest and emptiest mode of knowing, and thus, believing certainty, the retaining of the indicated 'this,' 'this' miracle, 'this' person, in general 'this' excision from the rest of history and reality, must be recognized to be a relatively lacking form of religious life."[83] Strauss's attack on the gospel miracle expands to encompass the entire mode of historical consciousness on which these narratives rest. Belief in miracle is only a species of that ancient mentality which looks for truth in particular, positive historical representations. Modern thought and culture begin as positive belief falls away.

Consequently, the conceptual view does not only seek ideas to replace representations; it also drags them into view so that we can better understand the whole process of history and the movement of spirit. When we see truths presented as immediate realities, we know we are in the presence of ancient thought. We return as such to the first part of the *Life of Jesus*, to myth and the critique of miracles. Here Strauss does not cite Hegel explicitly, but he brings myth under the heading of "representations." For example, when he appeals to Schelling to articulate the "unartificial and spontaneous origin of myths in general," he renders this argument according to Hegel's distinction: "The sages of antiquity," he explains, did not only speak in historical forms for the sake of their ancient audiences, but also for their own: "in order to illuminate what

---

82. *LJ* 1836, 2:737; *LJ* 1892, 780.

83. Strauss, *In Defense of My Life of Jesus*, 15; see Hegel, *Phenomenology of Spirit*, trans. Arnold V. Miller (Oxford: Oxford University Press, 1977), 149-60.

3. MYTH AND THE NOCTURNAL SIDE OF NATURE 137

was obscure in their representation [*Vorstellung*] in a sensuous portrayal, because of their lack of abstract concepts [*Begriffe*] and expressions."[84] In later editions he adds further passages to make the connection clear. He writes, for example,

> If religion be defined as the perception of truth, not in the form of an idea [*Begriff*], which is the philosophic perception, but invested with imagery [*Vorstellung*]; it is easy to see that the mythical element can be wanting only when religion either falls short of, or goes beyond, its peculiar province, and that in the proper religious sphere it must necessarily exist.[85]

At times he revises key passages to bring myth under the heading of representations. Where in the first edition he claims that for mythical and allegorical interpretation the historical element in the narratives served as "the mere shell of a transcendent truth or meaning,"[86] he later describes it as "the mere shell of an idea [*Ideellen*], of a religious representation [*Vorstellung*]."[87] He clarifies in this way the breach between ancient and modern thought. If the concluding dissertation translates mythical narratives more directly into stories, the long historical-critical portion of the *Life of Jesus* serves to let us know where precisely the lines between ancient and modern culture and consciousness are to be drawn.

Because the lines between these regions mark divisions in a one-sidedly progressive evolution, moreover, they define a clear hierarchy of *Bildung*, as much as Strauss's account of ghost sightings at the Weinsberg prison. We learn through the course of the *Life of Jesus* to see how modern culture has advanced beyond ancient thought—and where it still clings to it or covers over the breach. And once again, the same task reappears in analogous forms at all levels of culture. It determines a labor of *Volksaufklärung*. At the end of the *Life of Jesus*, Strauss urges preachers to do what they can to lead their unlearned congregations in the direction of humanistic theology. He grants that most will not be prepared for the full impact of modern scientific and critical thought. But preachers could highlight those representations that pressed most actively in its direction. A theologian preacher should "adhere to the

---

84. *LJ* 1835, 1:31.
85. *LJ* 1840, 1:84–85; *LJ* 1892, 80.
86. *LJ* 1835, 1:52.
87. *LJ* 1840, 1:54–55; *LJ* 1892, 65.

forms of the popular representations [*Vorstellungen*], but ... exhibit their spiritual significance, which to him constitutes their sole truth, and thus prepare—though such a result is only to be thought of as an unending progress—the resolution of those forms into their original ideas in the consciousness of the community also."[88] Furthermore, with this historicized, critical view of consciousness, Strauss opens wide the field of social and political adaptations of Hegel's philosophy, including his own. By the 1840s, he would claim that the shift to an immanent conception of spirit was the last, crucial step toward a new, modern age, in which the educated, philosophical class would rule. He would call for a future, postreligious "humanity state" (*Humanitätstaat*). In the *Glaubenslehre*, he claims that a society grounded in principles of immanence will be the most just society:

> Just as revelation is not to be grasped as inspiration from outside, nor as an individual act in time, but rather as one with the history of human generations ... so is this earth no longer a vale of tears, whose wanderings have their goal outside of themselves in a future heavenly state of being, but rather it is valid here to take up the treasure of divine lifeforce, which every moment of earthly life nurtures in its womb.[89]

Conclusion

Strauss's practice of myth interpretation and Hegelian account of the same recapitulate the movement that I have traced throughout the previous chapters. Here once more, Strauss takes up aspects of romantic thought and draws on his experience with the nocturnal side of nature. In the process, he defines a scientific and demystifying approach to religion. This approach mirrors both his account of his early *Bildung* and his scientific critiques of ancient miracles and modern demons. He draws near to and takes seriously the strange, discomfiting regions of religious thought. He illuminates and grapples head-on with nonmodern mentalities. In his treatment of myth, Strauss draws this movement into the service of a new critical task: To sever ancient and modern culture. This project would enable him to conceive a Hegelian critique of social, historical conscious-

---

88. *LJ* 1836, 2:742; *LJ* 1892, 783, translation modified.
89. Strauss, *Glaubenslehre* 1:68.

ness. It would serve in addition, like his writings on demoniacs and ghost seers, to define a hierarchy of *Bildung*.

We might be inclined at this point to consider Strauss's repeated claims to do justice to the gospels' intentions and Christian faith to be hypocritical, if not disingenuous. There is evidently an ironic dimension to his protests against the violence that rationalists do to the Bible. Strauss rejects these views and favors a pious or romantic affirmation of the plain sense of narratives, but he uses this plain sense as leverage against positive religion. He harnesses the manifest alien, ancient qualities of the narratives to liberate a critical, scientific modern world from its attachment to the Bible.

Nevertheless, if Strauss takes an ironic approach to religious matters, he does not cast them aside; rather, he works sincerely through their own internal movement. As we think through representations, we are led inexorably to modern, philosophical concepts. As such, Strauss's critical approach keeps the Bible firmly at the heart of modern culture. The gospels are key texts by which modern people know who they are and what they are not. They have this function as central documents of Christian faith. The Bible is the socially and religiously authoritative text *par excellence*. It is consequently the most certain testing ground on which to liberate Christian modernity from its past. If any document risks stirring up lingering confusions about antiquity and modernity or religious representations and philosophical concepts, it will be this one. Strauss contributes therefore to the rise of universities and academics, in the place of churches and religious leaders, as the guardians of expertise on spiritual matters.

Furthermore, as in other modes of critique, Strauss's efforts to establish limits also set lines of contact between the divided regions. These are needed to secure the historical foundations for modernity and modern reason—especially after he makes it clear that they did not lie in the gospels or Jesus. In the next chapter, I will consider the points at which Strauss connects modernity and the work of critical science explicitly to Christian faith. These links shed further light on the strange piety that underlies Strauss's vision of science, as well as on its points of contact with models of esoteric religious belief, practice, and experience. I begin from the point of his most radical breach with historical faith and affirmation of a modern, secularizing critique of religion: his account of the historical Jesus.

4
The Nocturnal Side of Christian and Modern Origins

In this chapter I turn to Strauss's account of the historical Jesus and Christian and modern origins. When Strauss turns to the person of Jesus, he breaks decisively with previous mythical interpretations of the Bible. He outlines Jesus's messianic self-consciousness in light of his age and context. Normally, mythical analysis leads Strauss to argue that elements of the gospels are unhistorical. But here it leads him to the opposite conclusion. He authenticates a number of Jesus's apocalyptic sayings—passages that modern interpreters had, with the notable exception of Reimarus, tended to ignore. His Jesus is a Jewish apocalyptic thinker with a full-fledged messianic self-conception. This image proved unsettling for theologians in his day. The Jesus of Strauss's *Life of Jesus* was not a figure on whom they could set their faith. Strauss's method in this arena follows the familiar ironic movement that we have seen in each of the previous chapters. He takes the unsettling, alien elements of Jesus's sayings seriously and brings them fully into view. Where orthodox interpreters might have tried to redeem some of these elements, Strauss uses them to demonstrate the insuperable breach that had opened between the ancient and modern worlds.

With the figure of Jesus, however, this negative exercise in cultural critique takes on new dimensions. It underwrites an alternative account of Christian origins, one that reflects Strauss's distinct vision of the progress of modernity and science. Strauss undertakes a critique of modernity: he establishes the origins, conditions, and boundaries of modern rational and critical thought. The limiting work that Strauss carried out on miracles and mentalities in the gospels now confines ancient and modern historical individuals, including modern theologians, to their respective contexts. Strauss takes aim in particular at interpreters in his day who tried to modernize Jesus. For Strauss, such interpretations lift Jesus beyond the bounds of his mortal existence as surely as stories about his resurrection. They make him into a ghost. He conceives of cultural and historiographical anachronisms, like eschatological beliefs, as subject to the inexorable mortality of people and cultures. The theologians who indulge in these anachronisms—even critical theologians like Schleiermacher, for example, de Wette, and Paulus—put their status as modern critics in question.

As he sets limits on modernity, however, Strauss also attempts to determine and secure its foundations. Once he had divided the ancient and modern worlds, he had to account for the historical passage between them. Early nineteenth-century German theologians and philosophers widely regarded Christianity as the necessary foundation of enlightened modernity. To be authentically modern was to grasp the inner truth of Christianity; to grasp Christianity's inner truth, in turn, was to become modern. For many of these scholars, Jesus was the historical originator of a modern, rational worldview. He had surpassed the philosophical and religious wisdom of his day, for example, had comprehended and expressed the absolute with singular clarity, and had set a unique example of enlightened ethical thought and conduct. Strauss removed this foundation when he insisted that Jesus could only be conceived as an ancient apocalyptic thinker. Thus he created a conundrum, not only for Christian faith, but for modern reason. To divest history of the protomodern Jesus was to root out the standard mechanism by which antiquity was supposed to give way to the modern age. Strauss's critique could seem as such to risk the legitimacy of its own operations, that is, of a thoroughly modern, humanistic vision of the progress and method of science.

Consequently, Strauss had to offer an alternative point of origin, and here again his work on the nocturnal side of nature played an important role. In the final sections of the *Life of Jesus*, Strauss posits that the "resurrection event" was the primary motor of spirit in Christian history. To understand this event, he turns to analogies from the realm of paranormal experience. Strauss argues that the disciples, devastated by the crucifixion of the Messiah, were pitched into a state of religious enthusiasm in which they hallucinated that they saw the spirit of Jesus. The women in particular believed that they had seen his ghost. This strange experience was the point at which Christianity as such began. It was the event on the basis of which Christians conceived their most important beliefs and practices. Furthermore, he argues that belief in the resurrection was the driving force behind Christian theology and ritual as they evolved into the early modern period, when they mutated into rational, conceptual thought. Strictly speaking, the resurrection event was the historical crux of the advent of the modern age.

The whole edifice of Christianity and modernity rests as such on an experience that resembles the ghost seeing of Hauffe, Grombach, and the Weinsberg prisoners in Kerner's case studies. Strauss's historical Jesus and critique of modern reason bring the demystifying aspect of his work to new heights. Yet here, at the apex of his critical project, he appeals again to the nocturnal regions of religious belief. This appeal has an ambivalent effect. On the one hand, it appears to secure the triumph of critical, rational science over religious mystification. Where previous interpreters rejected or ignored the troubling, irrational elements of human religious thought and experience, Strauss turns them to the profit of his vision of modernity and reason. To do so, however, he must entangle himself in a more intimate fashion with the nocturnal side of spirit. This entanglement troubles in turn the economy of modern reason in which he aims to secure it.

Throughout the chapter I contrast Strauss's approach to the resurrection event and image of the historical Jesus with de Wette's Kantian, rationalist account of Jesus as the foundation of Christian and modern origins. In many respects, Strauss and de Wette's approaches to the Bible resemble one another. But Strauss opposes de Wette directly on this issue. Their argument illuminates the radical features of Strauss's account of modernity and Christianity as well as the difficulties into which it leads him.

Strauss on Jesus's Messianic Self-Consciousness

In his treatment of the historical Jesus, Strauss puts the mythical interpretation to a distinct use. He makes Jesus's consciousness an object of analysis alongside that of the gospel writers. Mythical interpretation tended to show that where a narrative corresponded to first-century ideas, it was not likely historical. When applied to the historical Jesus's sayings, however, it leads to the opposite conclusion. A saying is likely to be genuine precisely when it reflects an ancient apocalyptic *Weltanschauung*. If we are to accept the division between ancient, Biblical and modern rational thought, then the words and thoughts of Jesus must also be considered strictly in the light of first-century Jewish messianism. Strauss grants the eschatological sayings pride of place among the remainders by which one might reconstruct who Jesus was.

The results of this analysis make Jesus an unfamiliar ancient thinker, one who stands at a far remove from the protomodern, ethical religious innovator conceived by liberal theology. Strauss's Jesus embraced wholesale the demonology of first-century Judaism, for example. His many direct references to demons in gospel sayings had been "a source of offense for those whose *Bildung* does not brook such a belief in demon possession."[1] Not only Olshausen, but also his more liberal, rationalist contemporaries sought to avoid this pitfall and read the sayings as symbols of the struggles of faith. For Strauss, there is nothing figurative in Jesus's expressions. He cites Matt 12:25–30 (Mark 3:23–28 // Luke 11:17–23) and Luke 10:18–20 as prime examples.[2] In the passage from Matthew, Jesus frames his exorcisms as part of an apocalyptic confrontation between the kingdoms of God and Satan—"If it is by the Spirit of God that I cast out demons," he says, "then the kingdom of God has come upon you" (Matt 12:28). In Luke 10:18–20, Jesus states that the successes of his disciples as exorcists show their authority over the "power of the enemy," their capacity to bring the evil spirits into submission (10:19); it manifests a shift in the apocalyptic cosmos, Satan's "fall from heaven, like lightning" (Luke 10:18).

Nor does the apocalyptic worldview only frame particular aspects of Jesus's life and character for Strauss. It constitutes the central features of his self-conception and teaching. Jesus believed he was the Messiah. The discourses on his second coming, future kingdom, and return in clouds of glory express his most characteristic thoughts about his destiny, duty, and identity:

> Wherever he speaks of coming in his messianic glory, he depicts himself surrounded by angels and heavenly powers (Mt 16:27, 14:30, 25:30 ff.; Jn 1:52); before the majesty of the Son of Man, coming in the clouds of heaven, all nations are to bow without the coercion of the sword, and at the sound of the angel's trumpet, are to present themselves, with the awakened dead, before the judgment-seat of the Messiah and his twelve apostles. All this Jesus would not bring to pass of his own will, but he waited for a signal from his heavenly Father, who alone knew the appropriate time for this catastrophe (Mk 13:32), and he apparently was not disconcerted when his end approached without his having received the expected intimation.[3]

---

1. *LJ* 1836, 2:10; *LJ* 1892, 417, translation modified.
2. *LJ* 1836, 2:9; *LJ* 1892, 417.
3. *LJ* 1835, 1:493–94; *LJ* 1892, 296.

4. CHRISTIAN AND MODERN ORIGINS

Strauss's Jesus is a first-century Jewish messianist with delusions of grandeur whose predictions proved untrue. Strauss judges authentic, for example, the main portion of Mark 13 and its parallels (Luke 21; Matt 24), in which Jesus places the imminent destruction of Jerusalem in connection with the approaching apocalyptic catastrophe and return of the Son of Man. He concedes that details of the discourse may have been added later, but it is likely that both the apostles and Jesus believed the parousia would occur in their lifetimes. The notion that the Messiah would return soon at the right hand of God to judge the living and dead stood ready to hand in contemporary thought. It appears plainly in the seventh chapter of Daniel, one of the later books of the Hebrew Bible. It was therefore likely that Jesus, "so soon as he held himself to be the Messiah," made this image part of his self-conception.[4] Of course, we know that the parousia did not follow the destruction of the temple in the late first century: "it will soon be eighteen centuries since the destruction of Jerusalem, and an equally long period since the generation contemporary with Jesus disappeared from the earth … the announcement of Jesus appears so far to have been erroneous."[5]

The image of a misguided apocalyptic Jesus contrasts with the rational aspirations of the modern age. By the beginning of the nineteenth century, apocalyptic beliefs had fallen into disrepute in the German theological establishment. They continued to enjoy some popularity among the broad sweep of German Christians, with the influence of figures like Bengel and Hans Jung-Stillung still palpable in Pietist circles. Nevertheless, they were rare in the established churches and universities. Schleiermacher presented the consensus view when he asserted that Christian faith rested on Jesus's character and God consciousness, not on his second coming or resurrection.[6] Theologians who inclined to apocalyptic rhetoric retained it only in a spiritualizing, individualist reconfiguration. Conservative Pietists and orthodox Christians writing in the 1830s stripped biblical apocalyptic discourse of its mystical revelations, images of divine irruptions in the mundane order, and appeals for a transformed material world; in their place they set the afterlife and the fate of the soul. Even the fiery Krummacher, for example, drew on the gospels' images of the last judgment only to urge his listeners to repent. In an infamous sermon on Matt 25, he reminded his congregation that they would all one day face

---

4. *LJ* 1835, 2:360; *LJ* 1892, 596.
5. *LJ* 1836, 2:344; *LJ* 1895, 591.
6. Schleiermacher, *Christian Faith*, 417 (§99).

death and judgment; those who renounced sacred history to follow the philosophers—he names Kant, Fichte, Hegel, and Strauss—also gave up their entry fee into heaven.[7]

As such, Strauss's account of Jesus's messianic consciousness forecloses any attempt to make Jesus modern. Along with his negative view of the historical authenticity of the stories and treatment of the gospels as myths, it appeared to sever the link between Christian origins and rational, modern thought. Strauss updates in a postromantic idiom the position of Reimarus, whose writings fifty years prior had described Jesus as a disappointed political messianist. Recall that for Lessing, Reimarus's Jesus was sure proof that we should not seek religious truth in the realm of historical contingencies. Strauss only aggravates this effect. He removes Reimarus's this-worldly, humanizing emphasis on Jesus's political ambitions.[8] Strauss's Jesus is caught up in a world of angels, demons, and grand cosmic struggles between good and evil.

This was also the point at which Strauss broke with de Wette and led mythical interpretation onto wholly new terrain. De Wette's critical studies of the Hebrew Bible, and specifically his adaption of romantic myth theory to this region, influenced Strauss's approach to the gospels. Even more, de Wette had suggested before Strauss that there were mythical elements in the New Testament. In his *On Religion and Theology*, which appeared twenty years before the *Life of Jesus*, he claims we must consider that the evangelical history reflects the worldview of a period after Jesus and the disciples. These are not individual eye-witness writings, in other words, but myths; they are collective and unconscious compositions, "the work of an entire era or a sect."[9] Nevertheless, he refuses to bring this view to bear in his analysis of the historical Jesus. In his 1816 *Biblical Dogmatics*, he rejects outright the possibility that many of Jesus's apocalyptic sayings were authentic. These sayings are too "*Schwärmerisch*," he says, that is, too

---

7. Krummacher, "The Last Judgment," in *The Foreign Protestant Pulpit* (London: Dickinson, 1870), 181–94.

8. *LJ* 1835, 1:491–94; *LJ* 1892, 295–96.

9. De Wette, *Ueber Religion und Theologie: Erläuterungen zu seinem Lehrbuche der Dogmatik* (Berlin: Reimer, 1815), 154. Hereafter cited as *Ueber Religion*. Thomas Howard finds it telling that Strauss neglected to mention this passage from de Wette, even though he had read *Ueber Religion*. Strauss's history of myth interpretation forms part of a "self-aggrandizing" introduction to previous interpretation of the New Testament (Thomas Howard, *Religion and the Rise of Historicism* [Cambridge: Cambridge University Press, 2000], 96).

fanatical: they contrast "with the clarity of spirit [*Geistesklarheit*] that did not abandon [Jesus] in his death, and which is incompatible with fanaticism [*Schwärmerei*]."[10] For de Wette, Jesus was thoroughly rational and remained so even in the face of crucifixion. His account directly opposes Reimarus's, in which Jesus's final words in Mark and Matthew—"my God, my God, why have you forsaken me?"—show the disappointment that he and his disciples must have felt at his failed messianic project (Matt 27:46, Mark 15:34).

After Strauss lays out the essential features of Jesus's messianic self-consciousness,[11] he confronts de Wette on this point. He cites the passage from the *Biblical Dogmatics* and writes,

> Those who shrink away from Jesus' messianic ideas merely because they would make him look like a fanatic [*Schwärmer*][12] should consider how these hopes corresponded to the long-cherished expectations of the Jews. In the supernaturalistic soil of that time and in the closed-off circles of the Jewish nation, an extravagant national representation [*Nationalvorstellung*] which offered some portion of truth and excellence might draw in even a reasonable man [*einen besonnenen Mann*].[13]

The citation plays on the contrast that de Wette's reading of the apocalyptic sayings provides to the mythical mode of interpretation he had developed: de Wette's aversion—his "shrinking away"—at the thought of Jesus's fanaticism blinds him to the messianic heart of first-century Jewish national identity—a stunning oversight for the person who taught Strauss to attend to "national representations" (*Nationalvorstellung*). Strauss turns myth analysis back against his teacher. A scientific mythical interpretation must grapple seriously with Jesus's claims and the cultural, national worldview on which they rested. It has to recognize their relative legitimacy, namely, that they appear "reasonable" or "sound" within the bounds of their particular historical and psychosocial milieu—as much as Hauffe and Grombach's visions of dead souls or the gospel representations of demons. And as we face these representations, we learn just how far we stand from that milieu. We come untethered from Jesus and his world.

---

10. De Wette, *Biblische Dogmatik*, 190.
11. *LJ* 1835, 1:493–94; *LJ* 1892, 296.
12. Here he cites the passage from de Wette, *Biblische Dogmatik*.
13. *LJ* 1835, 1:494; *LJ* 1892, 296.

The familiar ironic movement appears here again, with romantic myth theory playing a leading role. Strauss faces and takes seriously an unsettling piece of Christian tradition; he exacerbates the feelings of aversion that ensue; and he drives a wedge in the process between the ancient and modern worlds. He shows de Wette where he had fallen short of the scientific potential behind his own method. But there is more at stake here than the security of modern faith. De Wette's analysis of the sayings and Strauss's response comprise distinct views of the origins of Christianity; behind these accounts of origins lie divergent visions of religion, critique, and modernity. Their points of disagreement consequently deserve careful consideration.

Fanaticism, Religion, and the Origins of Christianity

The exchange between de Wette and Strauss falls within a long history of Enlightenment and modern discourse on apocalypticism, fanaticism, and religion. Writings on apocalyptic heresy extend back to ancient Christianity. In the early modern era, however, these polemics took a distinct turn in German Protestant thought when they were coupled to the emerging discourse on *Schwärmerei*, a feminine noun that can variously mean enthusiasm, rapture, ecstasy, or fanaticism. In the 1520s, Martin Luther developed the modern connotation of *Schwärmerei*, from the verb *schwärmen* ("to swarm," like insects or animals), as a caricature of the spiritual and political agitations of his theological opponents. He used it to designate those individuals who, he believed, sought revelation or interpreted the Bible in ways that could not be legitimated in a public realm. Luther's rhetoric served to shore up forms of Christian orthodoxy as well as civil authority against religious threats.[14] In succeeding centuries, the term passed from theology to philosophy and medicine. Kant, Herder, and others used it to caricature the positions of their theological and philosophical opponents, whether these were orthodox or Pietist, romantic or rationalist. The uses to which they put the term varied widely. It could signify the overly calculated system-building of a rational philosopher as much as the

---

14. Dominique Colas, *Civil Society and Fanaticism: Conjoined Histories*, trans. Amy Jacobs (Stanford: Stanford University Press, 1997); William Cavanaugh, "The Invention of Fanaticism," *Modern Theology* 27 (2011): 226–37.

4. CHRISTIAN AND MODERN ORIGINS 149

excesses of religious and mystical feeling.[15] Herder leveled it against the abstractions of French *Philosophism and Fanaticism*,[16] for example, where Kant brought it to bear on the mesmerist Cagliostro.[17] By the time of the *Vormärz*, the term took on an increasingly secular, psychological cast. It had become a standard, if flexible, diagnosis for a number of "religious madnesses" (*religiose Wahnsinnen*)—Teufelswahn, Demonomania, and so on—spiritual disorders whose names appeared in registers of asylums in Europe.[18] Apocalyptic beliefs, which had been, since Luther, heretical forms of *Schwärmerei*, now began to be classed among psychopathological species of the same disorder. Throughout the period, the term continued to serve key discursive functions—that, in particular, of marking out legitimate and illegitimate or sound and unsound forms of thought, belief, and action. Discourses on *Schwärmerei* outlined in reverse their authors' distinct visions of the public sphere, rationality, and civil authority. With Kant, for example, discussions of fanaticism served as a natural corollary to the work of critique. It was Kant's conception of fanaticism in particular that stood behind de Wette's analysis.[19]

Kant wrote extensively on *Schwärmerei*. His reflections on the topic surveyed a variety of mental states.[20] In an early essay "On the Sicknesses of the Head" (1764),[21] he diagnoses as *Schwärmern* those individuals who claim immediate inspiration or special intimacy with God. In later

---

15. The uncertainty and widespread use of the term was such that Christoph Weiland asked in 1775 that writers try to stabilize its meaning ("Enthusiasmus und Schwärmerei," in *Sammtliche Werke* [Leipzig: Göschen, 1840], 35:134–37). La Vopa considers Wieland's challenge and the various responses that followed from Herder, Kant, and others in "Philosopher and the 'Schwärmer.'"
16. Johann Gottfried Herder, "Philosophei und Schwärmerei, zwo Schwestern" in *Sammtliche Werke*, ed. Bernard Suphan, 33 vols. (Berlin: Weidmann, 1877–1913), 9:501–4.
17. Immanuel Kant, "On Exaltation and the Remedy for It," in *Raising the Tone of Philosophy*, ed. Peter Fenves (Baltimore: Johns Hopkins University Press, 1993), 107–8.
18. Goldberg, *Sex, Religion, and the Making of Modern Madness*, 137–41.
19. De Wette identified as a Kantian theologian and biblical critic. For a discussion of his close adherence to Fries's Kantian defense of faith, see Howard, *Religion and the Rise of Historicism*, 43–50.
20. La Vopa writes that between 1772 and 1798, "we find Kant clarifying the term *Schwärmerei* repeatedly." It served for him "as a kind of diagnostic catch-all, with ample room for madness, melancholy, mysticism, biblical literalism, excessive introspection, traditional metaphysics, and 'lazy-free thinking'" ("Philosopher and the 'Schwärmer,'" 105).
21. In Immanuel Kant, *Observations on the Feeling of the Beautiful and Sublime and Other Writings*, ed. Patrick Frierson and Paul Guyer (Cambridge: Cambridge University Press, 2011), 203–18.

writings, the term's pathologizing usage provides a natural complement to his visions of critique, reason, and the public sphere. Like Strauss, Kant posits that once we recognize subjective limits, we have to account for a given subject's failure to take them seriously. For Strauss, this leads to disordered psychophysical states and cultural psychologies. For Kant, it leads to subjective delusion (*Wahn*), of which *Schwärmerei* would represent a privileged species. For example, he often uses the term to connote actions and ideas that fail to meet rigorous standards of mediated rational discourse in the public sphere. In the piece on Cagliostro, for example, he names the educated classes' "mania for reading," their failure to read scientific works with care and discipline, as the root of their fanatical inclination toward strange medical cures;[22] they will be cured of their delusion, he says, when they cease skimming so many works and begin to read only a few well.[23] In other instances, he uses *Schwärmerei* to signify overreaching the critical limits that reason sets on its own operation. In a 1786 essay, "What Does It Mean to Orient Oneself in Thought?" he suggests that fanaticism names "the maxim that reason's superior lawgiving is invalid."[24] In his 1788 *Critique of Practical Reason*, he suggests in a similar vein that "in the most general meaning," one may consider *Schwärmerei* "an overstepping of the bounds of human reason undertaken according to principles."[25] It differs as such from madness (*Wahnsinn*), strictly speaking. In the *Critique of Judgment*, he explains that fanaticism is not a "passing accident," like madness, which might afflict a person of sound understanding at random. It is rather a mania (*Wahnwitz*) and can be circumscribed by the proper use of the understanding. It takes hold only where we seek to visualize or grasp an abstract, nonsensible idea of reason as such: *Schwärmerei* is "the delusion [*Wahn*] of wanting to *see* something beyond all bounds of sensibility."[26] An abstract idea of freedom, for example, can liberate our imagination

---

22. Kant, "On Exaltation and the Remedy for It," 107.

23. Ibid., 108.

24. Immanuel Kant, "What Does It Mean to Orient Oneself in Thinking?" in Wood and Giovanni, *Religion and Rational Theology*, 13 (translation modified); trans. of "Was heisst: Sich im Denken orientiren?" in Kant's *Sammtliche Werke*, ed. Karl Rosenkranz and Friedrich W. Schubert [Leipzig: Voss, 1838], 1:388).

25. Immanuel Kant, *Critique of Practical Reason*, trans. Werner Pluhar (Indianapolis: Hackett, 2002), 110.

26. Immanuel Kant, *Critique of Judgment*, trans. Werner Pluhar (Indianapolis: Hackett, 1987), 135. He compares this limit of reason to biblical proscriptions against idolatry.

4. CHRISTIAN AND MODERN ORIGINS 151

and free action, but we cannot make it visible to ourselves. To attempt to do so must lead to a derangement of the understanding.[27]

In a late essay, "On the End of All Things" (1794), Kant names apocalyptic thinking as a particular species of thought in which fanaticism can take hold. He takes as a guiding example the passage from the tenth chapter of John's Apocalypse in which an angel declares "henceforth time shall be no more."[28] Here John tries, he argues, to reflect on and transcend the basic condition of our life in time: the constancy of alteration. John opposes this temporal condition to an absolute, posttemporal timelessness. The effort is doomed to fail, however, leading only to Revelation's grotesque images of a static heaven or hell where people endlessly praise God or weep and wail.[29] The hideousness of these images speaks to the contradictory logic at work in them. It is impossible to think a "time" *after* time in a way that would not put this "new time" within the framework of succession and alteration—that is, one cannot think of this *new* time as both *after* and also eternal or infinite. As such, the notion must violate the theoretical limits on reason. Anyone who lingers too long on it will "fall into mysticism ... where reason does not understand either itself or what it wants, but prefers to indulge in fanaticism [*lieber schwärmt*] rather than—as seems fitting for an intellectual inhabitant of the sensible world—to limit itself within the bounds of the latter."[30]

In the *Biblical Dogmatics*, de Wette draws directly on this pathology of apocalyptic *Schwärmerei*. He locates its roots in the dualistic view of history that Kant outlines in his essay. Certain sayings manifest a basic "misunderstanding of the relation between the eternal and temporal"; if

---

27. Ibid.

28. Immanuel Kant, "Das Ende der Alle Dinge," in *Immanuel Kants Schriften zur Philosophie der Religion*, ed. Gustav Hartenstein (Leipzig: Modes & Baumann, 1839), 391–408; translated as "The End of All Things," in Wood and Giovanni, *Religion and Rational Theology*, 221–28. Kant follows Luther's translation when writes "henceforth time shall be no more" ("Dass hinfort keine zeit mehr sein soll," "Ende der Alle Dinge," 400; idem, "End of All Things," 226). Recent translators have preferred instead "there shall be no more delay" (NRSV 10:6), emphasizing imminence rather than a dualistic concept of time and eternality. Kant's reliance on this translation of the verse speaks to the core elements of his modernizing discourse on apocalyptic thought: "Henceforth there shall be no more time" highlights with precision the problem of dualism, the opposition between two modes of temporality, one finite and one infinite, even if this was not in fact the concern of the author of Rev 10:5–6.

29. Kant, "Das Ende der Alle Dinge," 402; idem, "End of All Things," 227.

30. Kant, "End of All Things," 228.

Jesus held such views, they "would have produced *Schwärmerei* in him."³¹ Kant's view stands behind Strauss's account as well. Alongside the passages on the second coming in the Synoptics, Strauss raises the question of Jesus's fanaticism in reference to sayings on his "preexistence," in the Gospel of John. In both sets of passages Jesus appears to hold a radically dualistic conception of time. He distinguishes his present, mortal life from a past or future "time" outside of time. In fact, the Johannine passages present the more dramatic examples. A saying like John 8:28, "Very truly I tell you, before Abraham was, I am," implies that Jesus experienced the kind of radical disjunction between memory and experience with which Strauss was familiar from his psychological writings on "derangements of consciousness." If authentic it would suffice, he says, "to ruin [Jesus's] healthy consciousness and expose him to a fanaticism of which he otherwise shows himself free."³²

Both de Wette and Strauss reject the possibility that Jesus is a fanatic, however. For de Wette, the sayings are inconsistent with Jesus's *Geistesklarheit*. For Strauss, the Johannine sayings clash with first-century Jewish thought. The apocalyptic sayings are more likely historical; however, these do not prove either that Jesus was a fanatic. Faced with the possibility, Strauss equivocates. Either Jesus is a *Schwärmer*, but nevertheless a relatively *besonnen*—"thoughtful," "level-headed," or "reasonable"—one or else he does not qualify as a *Schwärmer* at all. What would be fanaticism for us is a live option for the most reasonable first-century messianic Jewish thinker. Strauss applies to de Wette's analysis the reasoning that mythical interpreters had leveled against deists in defense of Christian narratives. Ancient mythical mentalities are distinct from modern rationality, but also from individual disorders. This reasoning displaces the question of Jesus's fanaticism on historical grounds and creates a new ambiguity in the process: Jesus, as an apocalyptic thinker in the ancient world, appears at once reasonable and fanatical to our modern eyes, a sort of reasonable fanatic.

---

31. De Wette, *Biblische Dogmatik*, 191 n. c.

32. *LJ* 1835, 1:484. In the *New Life of Jesus*, he argues that it would pitch him beyond the realm of sanity altogether: "He who thinks he remembers his former existence anterior to his birth ... which no other human being remembers, nor he himself either, is in our opinion nothing but a madman [*ein Verrückter*]. He who expects to come again after his death, as no human being ever has done, is in our opinion not exactly a madman, because in reference to the future imagination is more possible, but still an arrant enthusiast [*Schwärmer*]" (*NLJ* 1865, 323).

4. CHRISTIAN AND MODERN ORIGINS 153

It appears that in this way Strauss protects Jesus from those who would bring Reimarus together with Kant or de Wette to question his psychological well-being.³³ But this appearance elides the essential role that Jesus's ambivalent mental status plays in Strauss's analysis. The ambiguity is stubborn enough that Schweitzer, paraphrasing Strauss's portrait of Jesus eighty years later, restates it without comment: "the Nazarene, even though *that fanatical idea had gripped him*, can be considered, nonetheless, as *one in full possession of his faculties*, partly because of the fact that his expectation has its roots in the general conceptions of late [sic] Judaism."³⁴ In fact, although he does not call Jesus delusional, Strauss's equivocal rhetoric serves as a secularizing challenge in its own right. When Strauss displaces the Kantian pathology of *Schwärmerei* from the person of Jesus, he also sets the terms of a distinct underlying account of reason, religion, and modernity.

In order to trace these effects, we have first to move from the question of a diagnosis to consider the functions that the discourse of *Schwärmerei* has in de Wette and Strauss's respective accounts. Neither theologian sets out primarily to decide whether Jesus is a *Schwärmer* or not per se. Although it had begun to make its way into medical discourse, the term remained relatively ambivalent and its meanings contested throughout the modern period. It did not lend itself readily to concrete medical applications. It was this same ambivalence, however, that made it useful for those who wished to draw lines between legitimate and illegitimate forms of thought, belief, and action. Here Kant set the stage for Strauss and de Wette once again.

When Kant locates fanaticism as a capacity within reason, he turns it into a rhetorical wedge by which to shore up the legitimacy of forms of rational thought and moral action. This operation plays an especially important role in his account of practical reason—his attempt to set ethics

---

33. Strauss rejects Reimarus's interpretation, because he does not believe that Jesus's words evince revolutionary political ambitions. The sayings are still chiliastic, however; Jesus only waits on God to bring about the imminent transformation of the world. He does not look forward to a political revolution or a spiritual regeneration, but to the miraculous resurrection of the dead. This Jesus is thus *more* alienating and ancient even than Reimarus's, although Strauss claims that he represents a midpoint between the political millenarian reading of Jesus among "opponents of Christianity" and the personal, spiritualizing turn of orthodox Christianity (*LJ* 1835, 1:492–94 ; *LJ* 1892, 295–96).

34. *The Psychiatric Study of Jesus*, trans. Charles R. Joy (Boston: Beacon, 1948), 35, emphasis added.

and values on rational grounds. Kant's conundrum here is simple enough: If there is such a thing as free moral action, it cannot be determined by the phenomenal world. Otherwise, it would only be a function of that world, a reflexive response to an existing set of conditions, and therefore not genuinely autonomous. But it cannot be grounded in anything transcendent either, any supersensible object, for example, since this would vault reason beyond its own horizon. The subject's appeal to supersensible objects would determine its action just as thoroughly from the other, transcendent side. If I do something "good" out of my loyalty to God, subjection to the word of the Bible, or a desire to go to heaven, my actions remain heteronomous—I am only responding to my notion of God, et cetera, yet another feature of the phenomenal realm. Kant needs to find a nontranscendent universal. Kant therefore distinguishes the universality of the "law of duty," to which the moral actor appeals, from the "moral *Schwärmer*'s" appeal to immediate revelation, divine inspiration, or some other source of his or her freedom. To locate the source of one's action anywhere other than in the law of duty is to risk fanaticism.[35] But at the same time, this hypothetical *Schwärmer* gives some sense of security to the ambiguous "law of duty." The unconditional nature of this law of duty in Kant's account places the moral actor in proximity to a fanaticism against which the term functions as a ward. The imagined fanatic reassures the rational moral actor that the free pursuit of a good action is not merely reflexive and that it does not cross the bounds of reason.[36]

A related discourse on *Schwärmerei* appears in Kant's meditations on progress in history. In this region he draws a distinction between "fanaticism" and "enthusiasm" (*Begeisterung*). When the term *Schwärmerei* appears for the first time in "On the Sicknesses of the Head," it serves an ostensibly diagnostic function. But it diagnoses the imaginative leap beyond the present that a "fanatic" would take, in opposition to that of the more sober "enthusiast," who helps to bring about real change in history. The distinction crops up again in a famous passage in "An Old Question Raised Again: is the Human Race Constantly Progressing?" Here

---

35. Kant, *Critique of Practical Reason*, 110.
36. Fenves, "The Scale of Enthusiasm," 123–35, considers how tenuous this distinction is and the consequences that follow from this uncertainty. See also Fenves's introduction, "The Topicality of Tone," to idem, *Raising the Tone of Philosophy*, 1–49, and in the same volume Jacques Derrida, "On a Newly Risen Apocalyptic Tone in Philosophy," 117–72.

4. CHRISTIAN AND MODERN ORIGINS 155

Kant responds to Edmund Burke's polemics against the "fanaticism" of the French Revolutionaries and the philosophers who inspired them. In response, Kant defends the enthusiasm of the German spectators—the readerly public sphere—across the Rhine.[37] For these learned spectators, the French Revolution is a "sign" of progress, mediated through thought and culture. This symbol of progress, like the symbolic Jesus in *Religion within the Limits of Mere Reason*, signals an idea and a possibility; it does not represent an immediate reality we could grasp. The distinction between fanaticism and enthusiasm helps as such to outline historical progress in the nonrevolutionary public sphere.

These two functions of Kant's discourse on *Schwärmerei*—to secure the space of free, rational action and to establish the grounds of progress in history—move explicitly into the field of religion in de Wette's historical Jesus and Christology. De Wette's Jesus is a Kantian moral actor. In the place of any objective revolutionary or messianic goal, this Jesus had a longing and a presentiment of a higher truth. He only acted *as if* a better world were possible, *as if* he could transcend the bounds of his mortal life and apprehend God. But Jesus claimed no firm evidence to that effect. Otherwise he would be a *Schwärmer*. If he anticipated an imminent transformation in the world, as in Reimarus's account, for example, this would negate the freedom of his action. The significance of his death is "separate," accordingly, "from any goal which he might have wished to accomplish through the same."[38] He did not have any doctrine of atonement, for example. He acted in response to "sin" only in a symbolic sense and sacrificed himself to "the evil of [his] opponents, the dishonest ethos of his confessors, and the dominance of evil in people's earthly nature."[39] Nor did Jesus submit to his ordained duty out of blind faith. Ancient Jewish people, de Wette claims, already submitted to God's law reflexively; their submission formed part of their national identity. Jesus, in contrast, was a free moral individual who responded to universal interests. In his semi-autobiographical novel, *Theodore*, de Wette explains that Jesus's motto was "all or nothing": he knew that his attempt to bring the "infinite and perfect" into the world would be impossible, strictly speaking; he therefore "satisfied himself by sealing with his death the idea and recognition of

---

37. Kant, *Religion and Rational Theology*, 297–309.
38. De Wette, *Über Religion*, 163.
39. Ibid.

them, the faith in them."[40] To say that he takes up his duty and his cross with *Geistesklarheit* is to say that he knew the bounds of human thought and action.

This resigned death forms the crux of de Wette's Kantian Christology. De Wette insists on Kant's boundary between the phenomenal and noumenal, subjective experience and the reality of "things-in-themselves" in order to secure a space for legitimate Christian belief. For de Wette as for Kant, subject and object do not cohere in any immediate way, but he follows Jakob Fries and argues that a subject can still experience their union tenuously in religious *Ahnung*—perception, intuition, or aesthetic feeling—independently of rational inquiry. Thus when a rational Christian sees Christ's death, he or she can still feel his resignation as something sublime. Because Jesus submits to God in spite of pervasive and realistic forms of evil, he tempers his death with hope, and resignation opens thereby unto a second category of religious feeling, *Andacht*, reverence or worship.[41] Jesus manifests reverence when he sees the infinite at work through the thick of his ultimately lethal, mortal relationships and experiences. When a modern Christian contemplates this story, he or she experiences reverence as well.[42] The modern rational person still has this intuitive access to Christ.

De Wette follows as such the lead of Kant's *Religion within the Limits of Mere Reason*. The Jesus of history is obscure; in fact, he is shrouded precisely in the mythical thought of his contemporaries. But we can encounter the Christ of faith in a mediated, subjective form, as a symbol.[43] More than Kant, however, he uses this symbolic reading to shore up an image of the historical person of Jesus.[44] The stories about Jesus's resurrection are not historical, for example, but they reflect real experience by early Christians of an extraordinary individual who gravitated toward the true and universal. Here de Wette draws on another category of religious feeling, one that is familiar from Kant's discourses on fanati-

---

40. De Wette, *Theodore: Or the Skeptic's Conversion*, trans. James F. Clarke (Boston: Munroe, 1856), 2:354.

41. De Wette, *Ueber Religion*, 163.

42. Ibid., 164.

43. Strauss groups Kant and de Wette's Christologies together as "symbolical" interpretations in his reflections on dogma in the conclusion to the *Life of Jesus* (*LJ* 1836, 2:720; *LJ* 1892, 773).

44. De Wette posits *Ahnung* as the category by which we grasp these symbols. He thereby put a stronger emphasis than Kant on the work of faith.

4. CHRISTIAN AND MODERN ORIGINS 157

cism: *enthusiasm* (*Begeisterung*). This is the inspiration that ancient and modern Christians feel when they reflect on the epic character of the gospel narrative—imagining Jesus standing strong against naysayers and enemies, for example, or taking firm steps toward his inevitable death.[45] As in Kant's account of the French Revolution, this good enthusiasm is distinct from the bad fanaticism of a millenarian. It does not lead to radical action, but ends in the sympathetic intuition of a spectator. In faithful contemplation of Jesus, a Christian intuits the absolute—the reconciliation of the finite and infinite—as a *possibility*, where the fanatic would claim it as an objective reality.

To say Jesus is a symbol is not to dismiss the historical importance of his life and death. De Wette still offers a concrete, realized eschatology: Jesus actually reconciled the divine and human in history. But this reconciliation was not miraculous or immediate, as supernaturalists—those orthodox and Pietist interpreters who still defended the historicity of the gospel miracles—argued. Rather, Jesus changed religious consciousness when he submitted to the infinite in clear-sighted recognition of natural, human finitude. He opened thereby a new, more rational mode of faith in the ancient world. In spite of his obscure historical origins, Christ was the "initiator of a spiritual metamorphosis, not just for his nation, but for all of humanity."[46] For de Wette, Judaism had perfected the feeling of *Andacht*, reverence, while paganism had perfected *Begeisterung*, enthusiasm. Christianity brought these together with *resignation*. He believed this new constellation made distinctly modern forms of subjectivity possible.

Indeed, de Wette held that Jesus Christ inaugurated modernity: in a letter to Fries in 1817, he writes, "Christ is for me the anticipation of educated reason [*Verstandbildung*] that has brought about the whole modern period; he is the first free point from which our free life has developed."[47] When Jesus intuited God in his human relationships, he grasped the universality of humanity in a new way. He was a humanist *avant la lettre*. This is nowhere more evident than when we envision his death: "Christ on the cross is the image [*Bild*] of humanity purified by self-sacrifice."[48]

---

45. De Wette, *Ueber Religion*, 163.
46. Ibid., 162.
47. Henke, "Berliner Briefe," 104, quoted and translated in John W. Rogerson, *W. M. L De Wette: Founder of Modern Biblical Criticism: An Intellectual Biography* (Sheffield: JSOT Press, 1992), 136–37.
48. De Wette, *Ueber Religion*, 163–64.

The image makes modern people's humanism possible. Christ provides the symbolic *and historical* prototype for a rational, free moral subject.

De Wette shared with many of his contemporaries the view that through Christ, Christianity begins and anchors modernity and rationality; enlightened European thought is the culmination of Christian truth. In controversies over historical science and belief, such an argument could cut both ways. On the one hand, it might push back against the deistic separation between history and belief. In contrast to Reimarus, the gospel history is still an object of faith for de Wette. Indeed, this faith has precisely to be cordoned off from the work of empirical testing. It rests on the mediation of a rational or feeling subject. In German idealism, the historical Jesus reemerges from the crucible of criticism in a transfigured form: he is a symbol, image, or ideal of modern rational *Bildung*. As in older Christian figural readings of the Old Testament, the "history" presages a later truth that transcends its referents.[49] On the other hand, they set the terms of what counts as legitimate faith in more or less scientific terms. To say one can access Christ only in subjective faith delegitimizes both rationalist theological metaphysics and orthodox dogma. It underwrites a shift from Protestant to modernizing triumphalism: the truth of early Christianity crystallized in the reformation; it would perfect itself in modern philosophy or theology.

With de Wette, this two-sided approach to the historical content of the New Testament takes a Kantian shape. De Wette means to save faith by limiting the incursions of rationalist or empiricist reason: the symbol is safe from history. But he also affirms that reason has the power to set these limits in a radical way. He strikes out in this way against orthodox and Pietist supernaturalism and positive religion and defines a modern hierarchy of spirit in which rational religion stands at the apex. If Jesus Christ marks the advent of modern, humanistic rationalism, this does not only mean that rationalistic Christianity is defensible; it is the *most* legiti-

---

49. Howard, *Religion and the Rise of Historicism*, 93–94. Howard argues that in this way German idealism drew back, albeit in a highly rationalized fashion, from Enlightenment empiricism's objection to figural or typological modes of interpretation. Protestant theologians and philosophers accepted that the older typology, which looked to the historical images of the Hebrew Bible for types of Christ, was defunct. Nevertheless, they transplanted this model onto a new field. Strauss makes a similar claim when he states that mythical and "moral" or symbolic interpretation (i.e., Kant and de Wette) follow the lead of ancient allegorical interpretation in the vein of Origen. All three sacrifice a strict focus on the positive, historical kernel to the underlying religious truth (*LJ* 1835, 1:52; *LJ* 1892, 65).

mate form of faith. When de Wette opens the possibility that Jesus was a *Schwärmer*, he brings its illegitimate others into relief. After he acknowledges that some of the kingdom of God sayings appear fanatical, he adds, "the typical supernaturalist can say nothing against that, since his belief in the literal truth of these promises would rest on the same misunderstanding of the relation between the eternal and the temporal which would have brought forth fanaticism in Jesus' case."[50] He delegitimizes supernaturalism by conflating it with apocalyptic *Schwärmerei*. Orthodox or Pietist interpreters would have bristled at this claim. They would object to being called *Schwärmeren*, of course. But de Wette's suggestion goes further. He conflates "typical," milder forms of apocalyptic and miraculous thinking with full-fledged millenarianism—even though he knows very well that early nineteenth-century supernaturalists by no means embraced the latter.

Strauss's rebuttal to de Wette strikes back at this rationalist etiology of Christianity. It does so in two regions in particular: de Wette's underlying conception of modernity and his corresponding vision of religion and critique. He develops, to begin, a distinct account of origins of modern consciousness and the modern age. For Strauss, unlike de Wette, modernity does not build on or extend Christianity; it repeats it. Christian and modern origins are distinct but isomorphic. Both movements opposed the cultures in which they emerged. Unlike Judaism or Greek religion, which brought a civilizing process to primitive antiquity, Christianity came into an advanced civilization and therefore "a distinction manifested itself from the first."[51] In previous religions, the development of culture had led interpreters to rework old traditions. But with the advent of Christianity, a new religion sprang up against its native civilization. Early Christianity was at once reactionary and progressive: in its reaction it developed a "new principle" that challenged the cultural world around it. When the Roman Empire adopted Christianity, religion and culture coalesced again, and this more or less harmonious union lasted for fifteen hundred years—until the Reformation manifested a first disturbance: "The Reformation ... was the first vital expression of a culture, which had now in the heart of Christendom itself, as formerly in relation to Paganism and Judaism, acquired strength and independence sufficient to create a reaction against the soil of

---

50. De Wette, *Biblische Dogmatik*, 191 n. c. (§216).
51. *LJ* 1840, 1:10–11; *LJ* 1892, 44.

its birth, the prevailing religion."[52] Once again, a new principle opposed an old world. But in its first stirrings, modernity struck back against the very religion whose origins it was repeating. This reaction against Christianity would become the characteristic feature of the modern age. It led from the Reformation to criticism: deism, rationalism, and speculative philosophy. Modernity begins with Luther, not with Christ. Strauss transposes de Wette's mythical analysis from one stage of history to another. De Wette had focused the attention of his contemporaries on the difference between modern historical thought and the mythical view of the Old Testament "histories." Strauss insists on the same rupture between modernity and early Christianity.

As Strauss extends the boundaries of the mythical age into the world of early Christianity, he also reshapes the critical architecture behind de Wette's Christology. Their disagreement does not only concern the advent of modernity, but its shape. They disagree, above all, about the nature of religion and modern reason. Apocalyptic fanaticism serves in de Wette's account to mark the old territory against which the rational, modern Jesus emerges on the scene of history. Myth and fanaticism intertwine. Both oppose equally the modern, rational faith that he hopes to preserve and augment. Within this framework, reason is not opposed to religion. Rather, a critic can distinguish within religion between legitimate, rational and illegitimate, "fanatical" modes consciousness. A person may be a fanatic or a rational person; nonetheless, he or she is still religious.

Strauss reorders this network of mentalities. Where de Wette links myth variously with both religion and fanaticism, Strauss brings myth together with religion under the auspices of Hegel's concept of "representation" (*Vorstellung*) in opposition to modern concepts. Religion is "defined as the perception of truth, not in the form of a concept [*Begriff*], which is the philosophic perception, but as a representation [*Vorstellung*]"; consequently, "the mythical element can be wanting only when religion either falls short of, or goes beyond, its peculiar province, and ... in the proper religious sphere it must necessarily exist."[53] This view defines a comparative and critical approach to religion as such, including ancient and modern Christianity. Strauss refutes the prevailing theological view, namely, "that which distinguishes Christianity from the heathen religions

---

52. *LJ* 1840, 1:10–11; *LJ* 1892, 44.
53. *LJ* 1840, 1:84–85; *LJ* 1892, 80; translation modified.

is this, they are mythical, it is historical."[54] All religions can be compared on the basis of their mythical elements, and all religions are forms of representational thought. With this view, we no longer draw lines between fanatical and rational religion. Religion is set in opposition, along with fanaticism, to modern reason.

Strauss's Critique of Modern Reason, Part 1: The Limits of the Modern Spirit

The nature and task of critique changes accordingly. The *Life of Jesus* operates in effect as a critique of modern reason. It defines the limits and conditions of the modern age and modern, rational thought. For Kant or de Wette, the process of critique and progress in the religious field is subjective in origin. It crops up wherever a rational person in any culture tries to bring religion within the limits of reason. In the *Life of Jesus*, Strauss paraphrases a passage from *Religion within the Limits of Mere Reason* as an example of this view: "in all religions old and new which are partly comprised in sacred books, intelligent and well-meaning teachers of the people have continued to explain them, until they have brought their actual contents into agreement with the universal doctrines of morality."[55] Greek and Roman philosophers, for example, perfected their religious narratives by interpreting the most dubious popular narratives about the gods according to their "mystical sense." Ultimately, they integrated their diverse pantheon into a single, rational god. Teachers of Judaism, Christianity, Islam, and Hinduism all developed similar means of transforming popular narratives into increasingly universal ideas.

For Strauss, on the other hand, critique demands an internal reckoning in the spirit of a whole age or culture. In order for progress to take place, it must confront its own calcified, outmoded or contradictory ideas and mentalities. It is not a question of individuals emerging on the scene to make the world more rational, but of an age taking its own old representations utterly seriously in order to press itself into the future. The *Life of Jesus* and Strauss's writings on the nocturnal side of nature form contributions to such an effort. In these works, he not only shows that ancient and unlearned people are mistaken; he also shows his readers where their own conceptions and beliefs linger in the realms of

---

54. *LJ* 1840, 1:61; *LJ* 1892, 69.
55. *LJ* 1835, 1:7–8; *LJ* 1892, 51.

these ancient and uncultured modes of thought. As he enters the *camera obscura* of ancient thought, he also reflects a critical light back up into the modern age.

When de Wette rejects the authenticity of the apocalyptic sayings, he also draws an analogy between orthodox supernaturalists and ancient apocalyptic thinkers. In his rebuttal to de Wette, Strauss does the same thing, in effect, to de Wette—as well as to Schleiermacher, Paulus, and Olshausen. We have seen two reasons already that he rejected other interpreters' accounts of Jesus. First, they did not recognize the clear violations of the immanent world in the gospels. Second, they obscured the fact that Jesus and the gospel writers belonged to an ancient, alien world. We can now add a third: for Strauss, these authors also violated the limits of spirit in their own right. When they made Jesus a unique, modern figure, they breached the limits on bodies and souls. They affirmed a singular exception to the immanent limits of nature, and they brought the soul of Jesus beyond its embodied context into the modern world.

Strauss recognized that interpreters who sought this modern and rational Jesus had not so much done away with "miracle" as recuperated it in a new idiom. For these figures as for supernaturalists like Neander or Tholuck, historical facticity and revelation were still bound up together, but now in the fact of Jesus's uniquely exemplary, personal character. Many of them reflected explicitly on this shift. Krummacher wrote in his autobiography that when he visited Paulus and accused him of treating Jesus as a "mere man," Paulus angrily shot back,

> That is an unjust statement which people are not weary of repeating against me! Believe me, that I never look up to the Holy One on the cross, without sinking in deep devotion before Him. No, He is not a mere man as other men. He was an extraordinary phenomenon, altogether peculiar in His character, elevated high above the whole human race, to be admired, yea, to be adored.[56]

With Schleiermacher, the rationalists, and other defenders of the positivity of Jesus's person, questions about miracle had simply shifted onto new terrain.[57] As Strauss puts it, the rationalists, "in a certain sense retained for

---

56. Krummacher, *Autobiography*, 187.
57. Hans Frei claims that as such the quest for positive revelation endured in a natural idiom. "Positivity thus became anchored in 'miracles' not of a physical but of a pecu-

Jesus the character of a divine manifestation," presenting him as "the greatest man who ever trod the earth—a hero, in whose fate providence is in the highest degree personified."[58] Theological interpreters found a naturalist refuge for miracle and set the stage for the ethical, modern Jesus who has dominated liberal theology ever since.

In the conclusion to the *Life of Jesus*, Strauss cites Schleiermacher's notion of Jesus's unique God-consciousness as a prime example of this view in the field of theology. Strauss follows Heinrich Schmid and asserts that even to presume, like Schleiermacher had, that in Jesus's consciousness of God, "the ideal was manifested in a single historical individual, involves the violation of the laws of nature by a miracle." In fact, Schleiermacher acknowledged this, with some caveats. "It is true," as Strauss notes, that "he limits the miraculous to the first introduction of Christ into the series of existence and allows the whole of his further development to have been subject to all the conditions of finite existence." Schleiermacher distinguished between this "relative miracle" and the kind of "absolute" miracle that would be impossible in an immanent theology, "but this concession cannot repair the breach, which the supposition of only one miracle makes in the scientific theory of the world."[59] Schleiermacher's distinction between an "absolute miracle" and the "relative miracle" of Christ's person remains spurious.

Furthermore, Strauss claims that a modern thinker like Schleiermacher can remain mired in eschatological dualism. His Christ had a soul—a timeless essence—that went beyond the limits of his bodily existence: "the limitation, the imperfection of the relations of Christ, the language in which he expressed himself, the nationality within which he was placed, modified his thoughts and actions, but in their form alone; their essence remained nevertheless the perfect ideal."[60] Schleiermacher set out expressly, in fact, in his lectures on the life of Jesus to distinguish the time-conditioned appearance of Jesus's particular actions from his underlying, divine character. He posited that Christian thinkers had accessed this soul more and more over time. Schleiermacher's view encapsulates the standard view of Christianity's "perfectibility": theolo-

---

liarly historical, inward, or moral sort, perhaps one should say miracles of character" (Frei, *Eclipse of Biblical Narrative*, 58).

58. *LJ* 1836, 2:708; *LJ* 1892, 767.
59. *LJ* 1836, 2:715; *LJ* 1892, 771.
60. *LJ* 1836, 2:715; *LJ* 1892, 771.

gians slough off its historically-conditioned husk to access its timeless core. But in the process he violated the limits of a human life in history, albeit in a different sense than particular eschatological representations of resurrections or apocalyptic transformations. When he turns to critique modern thinkers' images of Jesus, Strauss transposes the psychological and physiological limits on spirit from the individual to the collective sphere. He frames Jesus's embodied, historical consciousness within a social psychology.

> As Schmid has satisfactorily shown, an historical individual is that which appears of him, and no more; his internal nature is known by his words and actions, the condition of his age and nation are a part of his individuality, and what lies beneath this phenomenal existence as the essence, is not the nature of this individual, but the human nature in general, which in particular beings operates only under the limitations of their individuality, of time, and of circumstances. Thus to surpass the historical appearance of Christ, is to rise nearer, not to his nature, but to the idea of humanity in general.[61]

Schleiermacher separated Jesus's person and actions, his essential inner being and the physical form to which he was limited. Consequently, he repeated the basic dualistic logic of bodies and souls. In this case, however, these conditions no longer concerned the individual, mortal body, but nationality, context, and history.

In the passage from psychological to historical criticism, Strauss moves from one mode of embodiment to another, from the sympathetic and ganglionic systems to the phenomenal world of social and historical life. The "soul" is the collection of an individual's appearances in the world, all of which belong to a particular cultural matrix. Anything beyond that is only an expression of the highest-order social totality, that is, of humanity per se. In this earliest edition of the *Life of Jesus*, at least, he rejects the romantic search for an eternal inner person as firmly as he had rejected Hauffe's nerve-spirit. This search reproduces the ancient error of separating a soul out from an individual body. It repeats, in other words, the logic of resurrection and eschatology in general. The image of resurrection is only the most basic form of reification, of a soul abstracted and sustained beyond its natural, living regions. And as such Schleierm-

---

61. Ibid.

acher's claims about Christ's person were not a far cry from the modern ideas about personal immortality that he rejected. In effect, Strauss claims, interpreters like Schleiermacher, de Wette, and Paulus make Jesus into a *ghost*:

> What spectres and doppelgangers must Moses and Jesus have been if they mixed with their contemporaries without any real participation in their opinions and weaknesses, their joys and griefs: if, mentally dwelling apart from their age and nation, they conformed to these relations only externally and by accommodation, while, internally and according to their nature, they stood among the foremost ranks of the enlightened in modern times.[62]

Representational, religious mentalities remain trapped in resurrective, ghost-seeing thought.

Once more, as in the writings on the nocturnal side of nature, we resolve these ghosts by entering fully into the mentalities that conceived them—by granting them room to speak. Modern concepts do not simply reject representations. We must encounter them intimately in a process that mirrors Strauss's youthful *Bildung* and his inverted image of "exorcism": the critic mirrors the exorcist who enters into a possessed person's *idées fixes*, leads them to confess and, in the process, unravels their contradictory internal thoughts—that is, who inaugurates "the psychological dissolution of the sick person's demonic delusion."[63] The critic of religion draws similarly close to the religious object and takes it utterly seriously in order to learn where its mortal limits lie and, in doing so, to call modern culture to confess its internal contradictions.

The modern historical critic helps spirit come to know itself as mortal. Strauss interprets Hegel's philosophy of history and consciousness accordingly, through the disorienting material terms of the emerging science of romantic medicine. At each stage of spirit's evolution, it sets calcified thought forms—those that take historical entities strictly as objects of the senses, for example—into a process of transformation. The *Phenomenology of Spirit* traces the progress of spirit through a series of historical and epistemological mediations, culminating in absolute knowledge, the perspective from which Hegel's philosophy begins. In

---

62. *LJ* 1835, 1:620; *LJ* 1892, 359.
63. Strauss, *Charateristiken und Kritiken*, 316.

the preface to the work, Hegel identifies this process as "a way of doubt and despair"; in the final lines he designates absolute knowing, the last stage of self-consciousness and the point from which his own philosophy begins, the "Calvary of Absolute Spirit." Modern absolute knowing would recapitulate what Christianity had already formulated in the primitive, prephilosophical form of a crucified God-human: absolute spirit dies. The progress of self-consciousness that he traces is the process of spirit coming to take death more and more seriously: "The life of spirit," he writes in the preface to the work, "is not the life that shrinks from death and keeps itself untouched by devastation, but rather the life that endures it and maintains itself in it."[64]

Strauss concretizes this Hegelian account of spirit in two ways: he brings it directly into the field of early Christian history, and he centers it on the limits of the human body as defined by natural science. If modernity marked the last stage in the progress of spirit, then this stage was defined by a strictly psychophysical reckoning with death. In history, society, and consciousness, *Bildung*, education or the development of culture, takes place as spirit comes to know its mortal limits in history. Culture advances through a critical pedagogy of death. Thus Strauss would set his own youthful experience, beginning with his affinities with mystical religious thought and ending with the insight that there was "nothing to" the resurrection, as the standard of historical criticism.

The Critique of Modern Reason, Part 2: The Condition of Modernity

As the process of critique sets limits on the modern spirit, it drives the age toward its culmination. Strauss did not only redefine the task of critique, however. He also tore up the grounds on which theologians set the origins of both Christianity and the modern age. De Wette's conception of those grounds—that is, the unique and uniquely rational person of Jesus—resembled many other contemporary accounts. Schleiermacher needed his Jesus to represent a "relative miracle" on the historical field, for example, so he could account for the world-transformation that came about with Christian origins. Even if critique works through Christianity and religion

---

64. Hegel, *Phenomenology of Spirit*, 19 (§32). The negative movement of critique transforms, for Strauss, into a resource from which the modern spirit can profit. It draws what appears to stand outside of reason—ancient religion, fanaticism, ghost seeing, etc.—into a process of mediation.

to reach modernity, then, it would appear that Strauss had torn Christianity's history away from modernity altogether. If critique emerges in the reformation to inaugurate the modern world, where exactly does it begin? How do we get from the apocalyptic Jesus to modern faith and from there to modern reason? When Strauss moves the origins of the modern world from Jesus to the reformation and defines the limits of modern philosophical reason over and against religion, he appears to sever once and for all the links between Christianity and modernity. He acknowledges as much in the concluding section of the *Life of Jesus*:

> The results of the inquiry we have now brought to a close, have apparently annihilated the greatest and most valuable part of that which the Christian has been wont to believe concerning his Saviour Jesus, have uprooted all the animating motives which he has gathered from his faith, and withered all his consolations. The boundless store of truth and life which for eighteen centuries has been the aliment of humanity seems irretrievably dissipated; the most sublime levelled with the dust, God divested of grace, man of his dignity, and the tie between heaven and earth broken.[65]

But this bleak picture was not the end of the story for Strauss. In his view, his work, for all of its critical results, had not so much ended belief as shifted its grounds: from the history of historical individuals to the history of the idea of humanity.

The conclusion to the *Life of Jesus* accordingly sets out, as he says, "to re-establish dogmatically that which has been destroyed critically."[66] This short section consists of an essay on the "Dogmatic Import of the Life of Jesus," in which he argues that with the loss of the positivity of the historical narratives, the Christian dogma of the "God-human" still remains true. But it is true only inasmuch as it is translated into its philosophical form, that is, when it is conceived as a representation of universal humanity. This concept supplants the representational view, as such, which still sees the God-human as a singular historical object. Modern concepts of humanity follow suit. For Strauss, each of the major components of the Christian story—Jesus's divine-human parentship, his miracles, his death, and his resurrection—signify something about the comingling of human and divine natures in the course of human existence. Miracles, for example,

---

65. *LJ* 1836, 2:686; *LJ* 1892, 757.
66. *LJ* 1836, 2:686; *LJ* 1892, 757.

symbolize "the miracles of intellectual and moral life belonging to the history of the world ... the almost incredible dominion of man over nature ... [and] the irresistible force of ideas."[67] Faced with such tangible, this-worldly wonders, Strauss asks, how could one possibly compare "the cure of some sick people in Galilee?"[68] The Jesus Christ of the gospels is the representation of the human species as such. The religious representation of him is the faltering step by which ancient people moved toward modern humanistic thought.

Most theological and historical-critical commentators have seen this as an unsatisfactory answer to the problem he raised. Strauss's humanistic revision of Christian ideas feels arbitrary; it would soon be surpassed by more capable interpreters—notably Feuerbach in his 1841 *Essence of Christianity*. The consensus among Strauss's readers has been that his true contribution was to sever and thereby liberate historical criticism and theology. He had accomplished in a more effective manner what Kant set out to do: to make the search for religious truths separate from historical investigation. His effort to bridge the two in the concluding dissertation failed, but the shambles that it left had a certain value.[69]

The same criticism would apply to his account of the breach that had opened up between the ancient and modern world in general. When he submerges the historical Jesus into his context, he cuts off a singular point of access between ancient Christianity and modernity. The comparison with de Wette demonstrates that this would not only be an issue for faith. It would concern modern reason as well. Where, precisely, do the foundations of modern reason lie in Strauss's account, if not with this—now utterly ancient and apocalyptic—Jesus? It was this question in part that drove him, in his later *New Life of Jesus for the German People*, to fall back again to the Kantian-de Wettian model of Jesus as a supremely rational religious innovator. In this later work, he abandons the image of Jesus as an apocalyptic thinker. He uses the Sermon on the Mount to show that Jesus was a humanist before his time, one who came into a world rife with fanaticism and single-handedly rationalized it. The work represents a radical departure from the first *Life of Jesus*.

---

67. *LJ* 1836, 2:737; *LJ* 1892, 781.
68. *LJ* 1836, 2:737; *LJ* 1892, 781.
69. Thus, e.g., Hans Frei, "David Friedrich Strauss"; Robert Morgan, "Straussian Question to New Testament Theology."

4. CHRISTIAN AND MODERN ORIGINS

But in fact, Strauss has an account of the origins of Christianity in the first *Life of Jesus*. Furthermore, like Kant and de Wette, he distinguishes in this account between the good enthusiasm that moves through history and the fanaticism that fails to operate. Commentators tend to elide this account in favor of the negative historical-critical and philosophical elements of the *Life of Jesus*. But it is a historical account, one that establishes a passage between the ancient and modern world through a process of concrete social and historical development.

Strauss traces the beginning of Christianity, namely, to the resurrection event—the first disciples' experience of Jesus's return from death. The importance of this event for early Christian believers is attested by the entire New Testament, from the gospels and Acts to Paul's letters.[70] Strauss turns to these sources to argue that among his earliest followers, Jesus's suffering and death had lent a new urgency to the question of his messiahship. After the crucifixion, the anxious disciples came to believe that Jesus's death must have led to his resurrection and ascension to the right hand of God. From there, the entire Christian dogma unfolded inevitably. The doctrine of atonement, the future resurrection and kingdom of God, Jesus's supernatural generation, his preexistence with God and cosmic rulership, et cetera, all followed suit from the combined ideas of Jesus's human death, resurrection, and heavenly ascension. The resurrection was as such the "foundation stone, without which the Christian church could not have been built."[71] Standing at the end of the historicizing narratives in the gospels, the resurrection event marks the beginning of Christianity per se.

The disciples would not have arrived at this conception, however, without a concrete, historical experience to justify it. At this crucial moment in Strauss's account of Christian and modern origins, he must pivot as such in the direction of orthodox interpreters, who insisted on the facticity of the resurrection. But for Strauss the event could not have been the kind of literal event these interpreters imagined. We have seen that resurrection represented a limit case for him on the field of history. The idea of a soul reentering its body, returning life to dead matter, is the most clear and direct contravention possible of the immanent limits of history. And yet, the disciples' *experience* of Jesus's resurrection turns out, for Strauss, to be the actual, historical hinge on which the origin of Christianity—and, by

---

70. *LJ* 1836, 2:690–91; *LJ* 1892, 758–59.
71. *LJ* 1836, 2:718; *LJ* 1892, 772.

extension, modernity—turns. It is the only thread that connects the world his critiques of myth and miracle had torn apart.

What, then, was the nature of this event? Strauss hypothesizes that it was a collective hallucination in the aftermath of Jesus's ignominious crucifixion. He draws here on an analogy from the nocturnal side of natural science. He knew firsthand that people could have convincing visionary experiences of dead souls. He turns for evidence of this view from the gospels to Paul's letters, specifically to the fifteenth chapter of Paul's first letter to the Corinthians. There Paul describes how, after his death, Christ appeared to Peter, James, the twelve, five hundred others, and, finally, to him "as to someone untimely born" (1 Cor 15:1-8).[72] The passage poses a dilemma: either Paul claimed he encountered Jesus in a physical, earthly form, as in the stories in John or Luke, or else he assumed that Peter, James, the twelve, and others had the same kind of experience of Christ resurrected that he had: "For aught that [Paul] knew, those earlier appearances were of the same nature with the one experienced by himself."[73] If we agree that Paul's vision was only subjective, it stands to reason that the other resurrection experiences were as well. Paul presents the experience in terms that suggest this was the case. Even apologetic theologians in Strauss's time were reluctant to imagine that Paul had actually seen Jesus. Neander, for example, for all of his insistence on the physicality of Jesus's resurrection in the gospels, did not "positively dare to maintain more than an internal influence of Christ on the mind of Paul."[74]

The hypothesis poses some difficulties for a historical critic. Strauss acknowledges that it is hard to see how the disciples would arrive at the idea that Jesus had come back from the dead. When Paul had his vision, he had heard the story of the resurrection from the sect whom he was persecuting; he had only to "vivify it in his imagination until it became his own experience."[75] The disciples, on the other hand, had to make the much more audacious leap of imaginatively dragging their crucified leader out of the grave in the first place. To account for this surprising act of imagi-

---

72. He mentions this revelation two other times in his letters (1 Cor 9:1; Gal 1:11-16). He also similarly states that he traveled into the "third heaven" to receive "visions and revelations of the lord" in 2 Cor 12, and in Acts 9, Luke uses it as the basis for his account of Paul's conversion on the road to Damascus.
73. *LJ* 1836, 2:656; *LJ* 1892, 740.
74. *LJ* 1838, 2:688; *LJ* 1892, 741 (added to third edition).
75. *LJ* 1836, 2:656; *LJ* 1892, 741.

nation, Strauss puts himself in their shoes: "we must transport ourselves yet more completely into the situation and frame of mind into which the disciples were thrown after his death."[76] This interpretive choice is, in Strauss's case, stunning. We have seen Paulus, Eichhorn, Olshausen, and others transplant themselves onto the theater of early Christian history in order to reconstruct particular events. But it is nearly without precedent in Strauss's interpretative work in the *Life of Jesus*. When he turns to other narratives that might be explained as hallucinations—the appearance of an angel to Zacharias in the temple, for example, in the opening of Luke—he rejects similar visionary hypotheses, opting instead to read these stories as myths. He could easily imagine that early Jesus followers would add familiar apocalyptic elements—angels, visions, et cetera—to stories as they transmitted them. But mythical modes of consciousness shaped the stories as they were passed along, not as they were experienced.

At this pivotal scene in the origins of Christianity, however, he develops a highly speculative account of the event itself. He strings his narrative together with a medley of references to the gospels. He begins with the cognitive dissonance and despondency that must have followed the crucifixion. The disciples, accustomed to thinking of Jesus as the Messiah, were faced with a crisis: how could this semidivine figure, who was supposed to usher in the kingdom of God, have died? This "first shock" soon passed, however, and led to the "psychological necessity of solving the contradiction," that is, "of adopting into their idea of the Messiah the characteristics of suffering and death."[77] They turned to the Scriptures and found precedents for a suffering and dying Messiah in passages from the Psalms and Isaiah. The fact that these interpretations were tenuous at best only convinced them that they had unlocked the hidden secret of the texts. Their enthusiasm redoubled, and they came to believe that Jesus had "entered into glory," remaining with them as a spiritual presence—"by his death he had only entered into his messianic glory (Lk 24:26) in which he was invisibly *with them always, even unto the end of the world* (Mt 28:20)."[78] With this reassurance, however, a new expectation followed suit: that the glorified Savior would manifest himself to them directly. At this moment in Strauss's account, the disciples had reached a height of "enthusiasm":

---

76. *LJ* 1836, 2:656; *LJ* 1892, 742.
77. *LJ* 1836, 2:659; *LJ* 1892, 742.
78. *LJ* 1836, 2:659; *LJ* 1892, 742.

> But how could [Christ] fail, out of this glory, in which he lived, to give tidings of himself to his followers? and how could they, when their mind was opened to the hitherto hidden doctrine of a dying Messiah contained in the scriptures, and when in moments of unwonted enthusiasm [*Begeisterung*] their hearts burned within them (Luke 24:32),—how could they avoid conceiving this to be an influence shed on them by their glorified Christ, an opening of their understanding by him (24:45), nay, an actual conversing with him?[79]

The longed-for event would soon follow:

> How conceivable is it that in individuals, especially women, these impressions were heightened, in a purely subjective manner, into actual vision; that on others, even on whole assemblies, something or other of an objective nature, visible or audible, sometimes perhaps the sight of an unknown person, created the impression of a revelation or appearance of Jesus: a height of pious enthusiasm [*Enthusiasmus*] which is wont to appear elsewhere in religious societies peculiarly oppressed and persecuted.[80]

Here we have Strauss's image of the founding of Christianity. The death of the Messiah posed the question of the divine and human in a new way. It might have extinguished the disciples' eschatological hope; however, the sight of the crucified Messiah escalated their enthusiasm. That enthusiasm soon reached such an elevated pitch that his followers, the women in particular, hallucinated that Jesus appeared to them.

With this dramatic reconstruction Strauss has led us back to the nocturnal side of nature. The ghost-seeing disciples recall the clairvoyants and possessed people with whom he was familiar from his writings on Hauffe, Grombach, and others. Gender and class inform this account of Christian origins, just as they had shaped his analysis of the prisoners at Weinsberg. In both cases, it is a question of "education," *Bildung*, for Strauss. The *ungebildete* prisoners are like the people who have not yet attained modern culture, specifically, the "correct opinion of the relation of bodies to souls." In both cases, this lack of *Bildung* leads people to see ghosts. Strauss traces these appearances of spirits detached from their mortal bodies back to the vexed modes of consciousness that generated them. The breakdown of the

---

79. *LJ* 1836, 2:659–60; *LJ* 1892, 742.
80. *LJ* 1836, 2:660; *LJ* 1892, 742.

psychophysical subject negatively defines the limits of spirit on the field of history; positively, it unfolds the space of spiritual thought and experience. As a critic, he accordingly shifts our focus from the demons and apparitions—the resurrected Jesus, the ghosts of the Weinsberg prison, the spirits inhabiting a man in ancient Gadara or a woman in modern Württemburg—to their roots in consciousness.

We might suspect that this account forms part of Strauss's repellant portrait of early Christianity. When he makes the disciples out to be a group of enthusiasts, he distances theology still further from early Christian history and modern consciousness from its ancient precursors. However, Strauss also makes the resurrection event the actual, historical mechanism by which spirit moves through history. His account of this first experience mirrors and inverts his conception of science and critique, namely, as a work of coronership that begins with a "sharp, but not unbelieving" embrace of the ghosts of religious thought. For the first Christians, the death of the Messiah condenses and clarifies the limits of spirit: the Messiah is supposed to initiate a new age, a new heaven and earth; his death—ignominious, in this case, and criminal, as much a matter of contingency as his messiahship—marks the impossibility of any such rupture in the course of history and nature. The tragic event provokes an emotive response in those who witness it, however, one which that culminates in real transformations in the life of spirit. It sets a new mode of consciousness in motion.

In the final, "concluding dissertation" of the *Life of Jesus*, Strauss argues that since the time of its origins the progress of Christian consciousness has taken place as believers ritually internalized the death and resurrection of the "God-human" as the experience of the community and, eventually, of their own individual egos:

> The God-Man, who during his life stood before his contemporaries as an individual distinct from themselves, and perceptible by the senses, is by death taken out of their sight: he enters into their imagination and memory: the unity of the divine and human in him, becomes a part of the general consciousness; and the church must repeat spiritually, in the souls of its members, those events of his life which he experienced externally. The believer, finding himself environed with the conditions of nature, must, like Christ, die to nature—but only inwardly, as Christ did outwardly—must spiritually crucify himself and be buried with Christ, that by the virtual suppression of his own sensible existence, he may

become, in so far as he is a spirit, identical with himself, and participate in the bliss and glory of Christ.[81]

In the place of the objective, sensible, and historical Christ, the believers come to identify God and humanity's unity with their own subjective existence. They spiritually participate in Jesus's death and resurrection, and, in the process, learn to feel their communion in the history of spirit. In its discourse and practice of religion, the Christian community begins to experience itself as a form of relative universality. Over time, these experiences lead its members to contemplate a more and more universal, human, and immanent idea of divinity. The concept of "humanity" consequently emerges, Strauss argues, as the latent truth of Christian representations, in which a single, particular human, Christ, was supposed to incarnate universal interests. This universalization would culminate in the modern era with the rise of the secular state and speculative philosophy.

The resurrection event serves, as such, as the necessary lynchpin in Strauss's Hegelian account of modern origins. If the idea, not the fact, of the God-human is the motor of history, then the experience of the resurrection event is the vehicle through which this idea passes into the ancient disciples' consciousness. Eventually, it leads to modern humanism. The impression made by Jesus's teachings and person, especially his eschatological ideas, prepared the disciples for the resurrection event. But even Jesus was ultimately incidental to the protohumanist doctrine he represented. Rather, it is the resurrection event that unites theology and history as well as the two parts of the *Life of Jesus*. The disciples' confrontation with the death of the Messiah leads, historically speaking, to the next stage in the history of spirit. Strauss's mythical interpretation, in the historical critical section, ends with the resurrection and ascension; his Hegelian account of representations turning into concepts, in the dogmatic conclusion, begins with them.

This entire movement of spirit through history begins as such with a group of ancient religious people's encounter with a ghost. In his final, alternative account of the origins of Christianity, Strauss brings us back to the world of Hauffe and Grombach. He breaks with Enlightenment rationalism; he refuses to expel the dark, irrational side of spirit from the history of modernity. He aims rather to secure and stabilize it as a necessary moment within an economy of ascendant reason and developing culture.

---

81. *LJ* 1836, 2:732; *LJ* 1892, 778.

His account of the resurrection event mirrors his concept of science as well as his later recollection of his first encounter with Hauffe. In each case, Strauss sets out toward a direct vision of the divine realm only to confront confused ghost seers. Where he looked for other-worldly transcendence, he found only human embodied, mortal life. The first disciples experienced something similar when they saw the Messiah crucified. But in each instance this seemingly failed vision turns out to be a necessary moment in the evolution of *Bildung*. Strauss follows the lead of romantic thinkers and posits that what enlightened theologians might reject as irrational—an emotional, collective, enthusiastic experience of an impossible event—is in fact essential for science and reason. In his ironic reworking of romanticism, however, this rejected moment bears the seeds of its own disenchantment and transformation. Where previous Enlightenment rationalism turned away in revulsion from what is nocturnal or irrational in human thought and life, Strauss follows Hegel and insists that we must confront it. The negative, critical movement in which we learn to see the limits of bodies, souls, and spirit press us onward toward a more fully humanistic culture. The irrational, nocturnal elements of spirit are sublated as necessary moments in the economy of modernity and reason.

Once again we can see how inexorably Strauss's approach functions to secure a hierarchical vision of the triumph of modern culture. But the modernity on which the operation rests becomes more tenuous where he attempts to fix it in place. If Hauffe or the disciples serve as foils for modernizing *Bildung*, Strauss's vision of history brings him back into a difficult proximity with them. He has to resort to an atypical—illegitimate, from his usual perspective—series of reconstructive, imaginative exegetical manoeuvers in order to watch the event unfold. For his account of history to work, Strauss needs to visualize the alien moment in which spirit transforms and a new age begins. He is constrained to raise up the dead Jesus and his specters in order to consign them to the past.

Conclusion

In this chapter, I have considered two points at which, in contrast to his typical approach, Strauss reconstructs positive historical elements behind the gospel narratives: Jesus's apocalyptic self-consciousness and the disciples' collective vision at the resurrection event. Both recall the labor of critical *Bildung* that runs throughout his work. As he grapples with the historical Jesus, he exposes the unfamiliar heart of ancient, biblical thought.

He means to break critique, modernity, and rationality away from religion in the process. Religion and fanaticism come to form two distinct antitheses to modern reason. Strauss sets out to expel the ghosts of Jesus once and for all from modern thought and to press the age on to its culmination. He demonstrates the divisions between the ancient, biblical and modern, rational worlds and defines the contours of the modern age. But he still needs to account for the passage between these divided territories, for the bridge that leads from antiquity to modernity. Here, at this crux of his account of spirit, he turns back to the nocturnal side of religious belief and experience. The consequent image of the resurrection event resembles one of Kerner's case studies of possessed or clairvoyant individuals. Christianity, modernity, and science begin with ghost seeing and enthusiasm.

Conclusion
Strauss's Visions of Modernity and Historical Science

Strauss's account of the resurrection event epitomizes the ambivalent quality of his scientific approach to the gospels and Christian religion. He rejects supernaturalist accounts of an actual resurrection along with rationalist attempts to save Jesus by other, natural means from death on the cross. He reconstructs the event as a mere subjective vision. And yet, he declares with orthodox theologians that this experience was the necessary foundation of Christian faith. Even more, it was the historical mechanism by which spirit and culture evolved. The disciples' enthusiastic vision of Jesus's resurrection led to their enthusiastic composition of mythical narratives about him. In these stories they developed the core dogmas of Christian faith: the incarnation, ministry, death, resurrection, and ascension of Jesus, the historical "God-human." Over the long course of the centuries to follow, this representation of a singular divine human would transform, in the ritual life of Christian communities, into the modern concept of "humanity." Strauss claims in the final pages of the *Life of Jesus* that this shifting view returns, albeit "by an inverted path," to Christian orthodoxy:

> For while there, the truth of the conceptions of the church concerning Christ is deduced from the correctness of the evangelical history; here, the veracity of the history is deduced from the truth of those conceptions. That which is rational is also real; the idea is not merely the moral imperative of Kant, but also an actuality. Proved to be an idea of reason, the unity of the divine and human nature must also have an historical existence.[1]

Orthodox Christians sought the truth of Christianity in the stories about Jesus recorded in the gospels. Modern humanism would locate it in the

---

1. *LJ* 1836, 2:732–33; *LJ* 1892, 779.

idea of divine-human unity that gave shape to these stories. The orthodox view correctly asserted that this idea exists in history. But its existence could not be reduced to any singular historical individual. Rather, it comprises the totality of human consciousness and culture as it evolves in the natural world. In the modern era, this humanistic idea supersedes theological representations of Jesus Christ. It shapes the modern critical and scientific reaction to the Christian world in which it originated. Nevertheless, it bears repeating that here, just as in Strauss's account of his own early *Bildung* in the German countryside, modern science only begins after a detour through the esoteric regions of pious religious faith. Historically speaking, modern philosophical, theological, and historical science depend,[2] as much as Christianity, on the paranormal visionary experience of a group of apocalyptic enthusiasts and ghost seers. Strauss's account of the resurrection confirms Nast's suggestion that his infamous skepticism shared more in common than it might appear, at first glance, with his early affinity for religious esoterica. It illustrates the irreducibly wayward route of modern disenchantment.

Strauss's lesser-known studies and early experiences in the realms of the nocturnal side of nature shed light on this difficult movement in the *Life of Jesus*. We have seen that his critical writings in the 1830s emerged in a context where speculative idealism and romanticism still converged with popular religious belief to shape scientific discourses and methods. Scholars of the nocturnal side of natural science, figures like Kerner and Schubert, framed their objects of study within an antidualistic philosophy of the universe; they remained assiduously open to religious beliefs that their enlightened contemporaries dismissed; and they sought to confirm the reality of paranormal experiences through rigorous empirical testing. Strauss developed an affinity for this field of research at an early age. He published a series of his own critical writings on the topics of ghost seeing, clairvoyance, and possession. Over the previous four chapters, I have considered how his work in this region sheds light on his better-known

---

2. We can take this dependence in two senses. On the one hand, Strauss means to follow Hegel and secure the nocturnal or irrational elements of nature, consciousness, and history as necessary moments within an economy of modern reason. This attempt underwrites much of the strikingly modern, even contemporary aspects of his work. It sets him apart from the more straightforward, rationalist Enlightenment criticism of religion that still dominated in his context. On the other hand, this dependence troubles this economy. It opens questions about the fragile status of the modernity Strauss would appear to represent.

5. CONCLUSION

contributions to the critical, scientific study of history and theology. In the first chapter, I outlined the main features of his critical approach to demon possession and ghost seeing. I turned in the subsequent chapters to examine three well-known aspects of his 1835 *Life of Jesus*: his critique of miracle narratives, his interpretation of the stories as myths, and his account of the historical Jesus and origins of Christianity.

The Results: The Nocturnal Side of Strauss's Vision of Historical and Theological Science

The results of this analysis fall into three major categories. First, we have seen a series of instances in which Strauss's experiences with the nocturnal side of nature informed his analysis of the gospels directly. They furnished natural analogies for "miracles" in ancient texts. He knew that stories about exorcisms and miraculous healings could be based on real events. Ancient consciousness could be compared, in turn, to that of contemporary people who lacked education or suffered from psychophysical disorders. They grasped religious truth differently than their enlightened, modern counterparts. Strauss used psychological explanations, at times in opposition to his usual negative tendency, to authenticate portions of Jesus's biography and the history of early Christianity. He acknowledged the possibility that Jesus could have performed "exorcisms" and magnetic healings, for instance. The most remarkable example of this analysis appears in his account of the resurrection event, in which he imaginatively transports himself into the minds of the disciples after the crucifixion. Furthermore, Strauss believed ancient poets and modern demoniacs could craft realistic narratives unconsciously from the fabric of their cultural experience. If the resurrection event resembled the ghost seeing of Esslinger, the composition of the gospels resembled Anna U's spontaneous confessions in the voice of her sixteenth-century possessor. In these instances, Strauss granted a relative legitimacy to myths and paranormal experiences. Their subjects were not insane, stupid, or disingenuous. He agreed with Kerner and Schubert that their stories deserved to be taken seriously. Science should shed light on the cultures and mentalities at work within them.

Second, he drew on romantic medicine and natural philosophy to set firm limits against their supernatural elements. Kerner had demonstrated that empirical analysis could marshal evidence in favor of demons and ghosts. To critique his arguments and the gospel miracle stories, Strauss had to turn back to the terrain of ontology and theology. The immanent, organic worldview of Schelling played a consequential role in this effort, along with romantic physicians' conceptions of unitary, embodied subjects. Here as in the wide sweep of romantic thought, the microcosm of the human subject mirrored the macrocosm of the universe. God and nature, spirit and matter, and bodies and souls were all bound up together. They could not be separated or reunited in particular, discrete instances. Kerner and theologians like Olshausen and Tholuck used this immanent view to validate the reality of religious beliefs about "supernatural" entities. They reduced dualistic views of spirit and matter to a natural frame in order to retain them—the world of spirits was concealed or diffused in the order of nature. Strauss carried this immanentizing movement a step further. Souls were utterly coextensive with human bodies, just as God was coextensive with nature. He thereby set radical limits against the same phenomena—demons, the nerve-spirit, ghosts, the resurrection of Jesus—that Kerner and Olshausen meant to validate. Furthermore, he turned these limits against anachronistic rationalist conceptions of the historical Jesus. If souls are limited to the mortal lives of individual subjects, then ancient people cannot exceed the historical milieu in which they lived and died. Jesus cannot have been a modern, rational person before his time. To suggest otherwise is to make him into a mere specter.

Finally, we have seen that Strauss adapted speculative romantic and idealist views of the dynamic evolution of the world-spirit in both the psychological writings and the *Life of Jesus*. Schubert, Schelling, and Kerner believed that humanity had fallen away from its ancient, primitive unity with God. Humans evolved into fully rational beings at the cost of that unity. The Enlightenment had brought the disjunction to its apex, but it also opened new means of reconciliation. Modern natural philosophy, studies of myth, and romantic medicine seemed destined to reunite reason with religion and humanity with the divine. They would make evident the unity of the cosmos and development of the world-spirit. The words of ancient poets and modern somnambulists could open dull modern ears to the obscure voice of God in nature. Strauss adapted the basic terms of this account to a one-sidedly progressive, critical, and humanist vision. He too rejected the dualistic tendencies of Enlightenment criticism and conceived history in terms of the overarching progress of spirit. However, the world-spirit was the spirit of humanity, and the dualism of ancient thought, in which God intervened immediately in the natural order, appeared less satisfactory even than the subjective, critical dualism of the deists or Descartes. Ancient representations grasped real truths, but these

5. CONCLUSION

truths only came into the full light of day under the auspices of modern concepts. He interpreted Hegel's *Phenomenology of Spirit* as a critique of consciousness. Hegel made critique into a driving force within history. Historical and philosophical criticism articulated the self-consciousness of objective spirit.

This critical adaptation of speculative thought captures Strauss's vision of the scientific method. Science does not arrive *ex nihilo* on the scene of history to correct false beliefs. It evolves out of religious representations. The scientific study of history and psychology cannot, as such, merely discard or cut away the false husk from the rational core of religion. It must take beliefs seriously and remain open to the experiences they describe. Critique gives voice to somnambulists, demoniacs, and ancient stories about apocalyptic events and miracles. But it enables them to speak only within an immanent frame that it has defined in advance. To take the evangelists or demoniacs seriously is to expose the latent rationality at work in their most alienating expressions. This process transforms them irrevocably.

The work of science mirrors the operation by which Strauss explains the efficacy of "exorcisms" in Kerner's *Accounts of the Modern Possessed*. The exorcists in Kerner's reports did not expel any actual demons; rather, they entered into the *camera obscura* of people's disordered psyches. When they appeared to compel the "demons" to confess, they in fact gave the demoniacs room to articulate and resolve the contradictory internal presuppositions of their *idées fixes*. Exorcism was only "the psychological dissolution of the sick person's demonic delusion."[3] The criticism of religion operates in the same manner. Strauss expresses the plain sense of the gospel narratives in a strictly human and this-worldly idiom, that is, he reads them as myths. In the process, the internal contradictions of these representations appear in the light of day along with their latent, conceptual truth. Demystification recapitulates in an "inverted" form the work of exorcism. It expels the ghosts of the Bible and German countryside when it compels them to speak. Strauss substitutes rationalistic and immanent explanations for supernaturalist alternatives; he articulates a humanistic worldview; and he sets historical-critical science at the vanguard of modern culture. Still, these skeptical elements of Strauss's work shared a foundation with his early affinity for mysticism and religious eso-

---

3. Strauss, *Charakteristiken und Kritiken*, 316.

terica. He was of course not a romantic religious thinker in the vein of Kerner or an orthodox theologian like Olshausen. But neither were his claims to share crucial affinities with these thinkers disingenuous. Strauss conceives the process of scientific critique and historical progress in terms that mirror his inverted mystical initiation into the mysterious worlds of Böhme, Kerner, and Hauffe. We become modern as we engage earnestly and articulate in full self-consciousness the nature and truth of religion, even in its most pious, mystical, or esoteric regions.

Strauss as a Historian and Student of the Nocturnal Side of Natural Science

The results of this analysis complicate the common image of the *Life of Jesus* as a strictly negative, rationalistic account of the gospel history and Christian religion. Orthodox critics in Strauss's day first developed this view of the work. Hengstenberg accused him of reverting to the deist view of myths as false beliefs. Conservative Hegelians claimed he had broken with Hegel and Schelling's "objective spirit" in favor of a subjective approach to critique. Modern commentators have tended to repeat elements of this characterization.[4] Strauss followed Kant, Reimarus, and Lessing, for example and divided the critical study of history from the philosophical pursuit of truth.[5] He failed to reconcile historical-critical and philosophical *Wissenschaft*. The first, historical-critical portion of the *Life of Jesus* exemplifies a subjective, rationalist, and empiricist model of science. His sole aim here is to separate fact from fiction.[6] The analysis does not produce any truth; rather, it demolishes the historical foundations of

---

4. The main features of the characterization that follows appear in the majority of works on Strauss as a theologian and historical critic. They appear for example, in Frei, "David Friedrich Strauss"; Morgan, "Straussian Question to New Testament Theology"; Hodgson, introduction; and in Zachhuber, *Theology as Science in Nineteenth-Century Germany*. Most commentators focus on the question of how Strauss's historical and theological work related to his Hegelianism. The standard view of his Hegelianism follows Sandberger, *David Friedrich Strauss*. Strauss's appeal to Hegel was sincere and had real effects on his work; however, his attempted synthesis of speculative and historical science diverged from Hegel (Sandberger). The standard account of his historical contribution tends to follow Van Harvey ("Strauss's Life of Jesus Revisited"): it was equally legitimate apart from its Hegelian tendency, but lacked hermeneutical sophistication.

5. Frei, "David Friedrich Strauss."
6. Ibid., 233.

5. CONCLUSION

faith. Only at the end of the work, when he turns to Hegelian speculative philosophy, does Strauss attempt to reconstruct the true meaning of Christianity out of the rubble of historical critique. Furthermore, theologians from Strauss's time onward have found his reconstruction of the "eternal truths of Christianity" totally inadequate. It served only to illustrate how inexorably historical science had broken with theology. In fact, in this view, this is where the *Life of Jesus*'s true value lies. Strauss may be seen, for example, to have liberated historical criticism from theology, as well as theology from historical criticism.[7] He showed that they comprise totally different arenas of the scientific pursuit of truth. Strauss defined a theological problem of lasting significance, in particular, when he demonstrated the incommensurable divide between the "Jesus of history and the Christ of faith." The distinction between the two can be traced to Strauss's 1865 work of that title, in which he responded to the published edition of Schleiermacher's lectures on the life of Jesus. In spite of an early and serious engagement with Hegel, Strauss's contribution to theology should be measured accordingly in his ongoing confrontation with Schleiermacher's approach to historical criticism.[8]

Elements of this characterization are certainly correct. Strauss does in fact claim, often in terms that echo Kant, that the truths of Christianity are independent of the results of historical-critical judgments on the facticity of particular events. He sets out to undertake a scientific pursuit of history, free from dogmatic presuppositions, and he establishes criteria by which to test the authenticity of the gospel stories. His image of the historical Jesus defined a lasting problem and focal point for subsequent theological and historical-critical inquiry. Still, this view emphasizes certain aspects of his work at the expense of others. Accounts of his treatment of the resurrection event exemplify this tendency. Strauss is widely recognized as the author of the "subjective vision hypothesis."[9] But commentators have not taken seriously the central importance he attaches to this event or the role that he grants it in the history of ancient faith and modern reason. It appears rather, ironically, as one among the many points at which Strauss liberated Christian faith from history.[10]

---

7. Morgan, "A Straussian Question to New Testament Theology."
8. Frei, "David Friedrich Strauss"; Lange, *Historischer Jesus oder mythischer Christus*.
9. E.g., Hodgson, introduction, 794–95, editor's note, 795 §140.
10. Or they ignore it altogether, e.g., Frei, "David Friedrich Strauss," and Schweitzer, *Quest of the Historical Jesus*.

Strauss rejected the view that he had severed historical-critical and philosophical science. The roots of his vision of the task and meaning of historical critique lay, as much as his humanistic reconstruction of the dogmatic truth of Christianity, in the realm of speculative romanticism and idealism. He makes the point clear in his 1837 response to his Hegelian critics. He draws on Hegel and argues that critique is part of the evolution of absolute spirit. It is inscribed in the historical life of cultures and societies, and it reflects objective spirit becoming self-conscious. The most rudimentary historical criticism, in Strauss's view, is the product of a process of spiritual evolution, a process which brings modernity to its culmination. This evolution and the resulting critique did not rest in subjective empirical research, but in shifting ontologies. Even the historical "freedom from presuppositions," which rejects miracles and sets history on a flat, even plane, begins from speculative claims about the nature and shape of divine action in the cosmos. Strauss did not undertake historical criticism as a preliminary, limiting attempt to shift faith onto other grounds. He sought to trace and drive onward the movement of spirit through history.

Nor did Strauss approach the work of science as a subjective rationalist who takes religion, texts, and historical entities as external, dead objects. Critique was not, as in de Wette's view of Christian and modern origins, a subjective rational capacity that an individual—Jesus or a modern theologian—could access. The very possibility of this subjective rationalism emerges, rather, from the immanent history of spirit. The task of critical science differs accordingly. External critiques of religious objects contrast dramatically with Strauss's ironic rapprochement with the esoteric and marginal regions of religion. The critic does not simply stand back and test the veracity of religious and historical facts. Nor does he or she try to slough off untruths in search of a rational historical core. Rather, critique engages religious representations and takes them on their own terms, until they unravel and transform.

When we claim that Strauss's only contribution was to have severed the Jesus of history from the Christ of faith, we miss major hermeneutic insights in his work.[11] In the *Life of Jesus*, he rejects positivism and defines

---

11. Jens Schröter, by contrast, has emphasized certain elements of Strauss's hermeneutical contribution that correspond to the account that follows ("New Testament Science beyond Historicism," in *From Jesus to the New Testament: Early Christian Theology and the Origin of the New Testament Canon*, trans. Wayne Coppins (Waco, TX: Baylor University Press, 2013), 9–21.

5. CONCLUSION

a robust approach to historical and theological *Wissenschaft*. Strauss conceives of ancient culture, consciousness, religious experience, and narrative composition as part of history. He does not only argue that the historical Jesus cannot be the end goal of theological inquiry. History cannot be reduced to a positive record of events. It also consists in the movement and exchange of ideas and culture, what people believed and experienced, and how they grappled with their world. Historiography in general should not fixate on momentous events or the actions of great individuals. To do so is to sustain the ancient search for miracles in the immanent cosmos. Schleiermacher, Paulus, and de Wette's images of Jesus present a case in point.

In fact, we have no direct access to events or individuals except through the mediation of culture and consciousness. The biblical historian will not arrive at pure facts. It is not impossible to gauge the likelihood of events behind the records, but these cannot be extricated one-by-one from the legendary form in which they appear. Nor should they be. The legend deserves historiographical attention in its own right. Strauss recognized the place of historical imagination in ancient narratives. The visionary "enthusiasm" of the first disciples, when they hallucinated Jesus's return from the dead, repeats in the "enthusiasm" by which they compose and hand on narratives about him. Ghost seeing and unconscious invention are part of history as much as the events they conceive and represent. For Strauss, events cannot be separated in any neat way from the social and psychological worlds and experiences they represent. These worlds and experience, in turn, are part of the conceptual truth of history. Thus whereas Kant turned back, in Strauss's view, from history to the idea to search for the truth of Christianity, Strauss turned to the "idea in reality," that is, the historical consciousness and culture of ancient people.

Furthermore, he calls attention to the positionality of the modern scientific historian. His work functions as a critique of modern reason. Each image of ancient mythical thought serves to outline in reverse the boundaries of modern consciousness. With certain notable exceptions,[12] commentators have tended to neglect his inquiry into the origins, conditions, and limits of modern science and critique. Strauss shared with his German Protestant contemporaries the conceit that modernity emerged out of Christianity. Only he altered the nature of this generational transformation. For de Wette, Schleiermacher, and others, modern reason began with

---

12. See especially Blanton, *Displacing Christian Origins*; Massey, *Christ Unmasked*; and Toews, *Hegelianism*.

Jesus. He stood astride history and inaugurated the rational transformation of the world. Reason and science bring Christianity to its culmination when they oppose and cut away false ideas about ghost seeing, apocalypticism, and demon possession. For Strauss, on the other hand, these elements are essential to the historical emergence of modern reason and science. We must experience them intimately in order to begin to conceive them.

Strauss's account raised his contemporaries' anxieties in part because it challenged positive faith. But he also gave a disorienting account of the foundations of modern science, reason, and criticism. Ancient stories and modern historiography are equally mediated, for Strauss, by consciousness and culture. The only historical Jesus whom we encounter is conceived through historical imagination. At a certain point it becomes difficult to disentangle the enthusiastic visions and fictional compositions of ancient disciples from positive historical representations. This insight defines the radical antipositivism of Strauss's work. The *Life of Jesus* did not only appear to his contemporaries to threaten the theological, historical foundation of positive religion, but also the positive study of history. Tholuck complained that Strauss "volatilized history." In 1838, Johann Friedrich Wurm wrote a satirical *Life of Martin Luther* in response to the *Life of Jesus*. He presented the text as the composition of a Hegelian critic writing from Mexico in the year 2838. Wurm's satire takes events from contemporary accounts of Luther's life and argues that they were contrived for other reasons.[13] For example, Luther's father was a miner, because "the statement suggested a symbol of the vocation of the son—namely, to bring forth to the light of day the jewel of pure doctrine, out of the pit in which it was concealed";[14] Luther was born in 1483, because that would make him thirty-four when he began his ministry—he was a year older than the age at which Jesus finished his.[15] In an 1840 essay on Strauss, the American transcendentalist Theodore Parker complained that a dedicated critic could "dissolve any given historical event in a mythical solution."[16] One

---

13. Johann Friedrich Wurm, "Extracts from the Life of Luther: Mexico, 2838," in *Voices of the Church in Reply to Strauss's 'Leben Jesu,'* ed. J. R. Beard (London: Simpkin & Marshall, 1845), 324–44.

14. Ibid., 328

15. Ibid.

16. Theodore Parker, "Strauss's Life of Jesus," in *The Critical and Miscellaneous Writings of Theodore Parker* (Boston: Munroe, 1843), 248–308 (299). Parker's account is nevertheless appreciative overall. He calls the *Life of Jesus* a work of "profound theological significance" (248).

could call the whole history of the United States, for example, "a tissue of mythical stories, borrowed in part from the Old Testament, in part from the Apocalypse, and in part from fancy."[17] We could reduce important historical dates and events in American history to their numerological significance or resemblance to incidents in the book of Revelation.

But in fact Parker and Wurm's remarks come close to describing real features of the mythologization of Luther and America. Parker suggests among other things that "the British government oppressing the puritans could be read as the "great 'red dragon' of the Revelation."[18] The suggestion conveys an unintended insight. The British government's oppression of Puritans may have been real, but American accounts of it then and now are informed by the apocalyptic self-conception of Puritan settlers in the seventeenth-century. Strauss's volatilization of history activates critical vigilance about our accounts of national and religious origins.

Ultimately, Wurm and Parker speak to a subversive tendency in Strauss's work. He exposes his own culture and consciousness, along with ancient mentalities, to critical scrutiny and, as such, opens it to transformation. Strauss's contemporaries believed the *Life of Jesus* had radical social and political implications. It began with what appeared to be firmly established in history and dissolved it back into the mediated, historical, and immanent sphere of collective life.[19] In the late 1830s and early 1840s, figures like Bauer and Marx would carry this approach further and argue that all established institutions carry the seeds of their own dissolution. To say the "real is rational" means, in that sense, that no "given," including forms of scholarly, clerical, or governmental authority, stand over and against the living process of spirit. Bauer and Marx conceived the idealist-critical rejection of historical empiricism and positivism as an active manifestation of antipathy to the established order. Positivist historiography rests on a conservative veneration for traditions; it affirms the past as an inheritance of cultural treasures and a firm foundation for the present. Hegelian critique as Strauss had begun to conceive it, on the

---

17. Ibid., 300.
18. Ibid.
19. Massey argues that Strauss's contemporaries identified this "ironic structure" of his account of positive religion with Young German literary irony and criticism of the restoration state.

other hand, set loose and revolutionized whatever takes on an appearance of fixed inevitability.[20]

Strauss's 1864 *New Life of Jesus* and 1872 *Old Faith and the New* and the Genealogy of Historical-Critical Science

In the eyes of the reading public of the German *Vormärz*, Strauss's *Life of Jesus* placed him firmly among the critics who had begun to challenge the authority of the church and state. His name became associated with those of Feuerbach and Bauer. But Strauss did not remain long in this company. He never embraced openly the democratic political implications of his work. When he was elected by liberals to a government post in 1849, he surprised his constituency and took a staunch monarchist position. At the same time, from the 1840s onward, he abandoned the speculative idealist and romantic elements of his early work. In his later writings on the historical Jesus, he embraced historical positivism and the secular bourgeois culture that came over the course of the century to dominate in the German public sphere.

In his 1864 *New Life of Jesus*, he takes a positive empirical approach to historical critique.[21] His last work, the 1872 *Old Faith and the New*, celebrates the postreligious habits and beliefs of the modern bourgeoisie; it places empiricist historical criticism at the head of the representative sciences of the new "faith" of those individuals who, liberated by capital from governmental and religious authority, could no longer rest content with Christianity.[22] These two works present two distinct, alternative accounts of Christian and modern origins, each of which breaks with the first *Life of Jesus*'s image of the resurrection event as the historical axis on which Christian spirit turned. Furthermore, they represent a defensive movement against the field of critique he had opened inadvertently with the

---

20. E.g., Bauer, *Trumpet of the Last Judgment against Hegel the Atheist and Antichrist*, trans. Lawrence Stepelevich (Lewiston, NY: Mellen, 1989), 205–6; Marx, "The Philosophical Manifesto of the Historical School of Law," in "Writings of the Young Marx," 96–105. The continuity between Strauss, Bauer, and the young Marx on this point points up the inadequacy of caricatures of "Young Hegelian" works on religion as part of a mere objectivist "criticism of religion," as opposed to the more radical social "critique" embraced by Marx. In these texts from the late 1830s and early 1840s, they conceived critique explicitly as an inquiry into the grounds of contemporary social and political life.

21. *NLJ* 1865.
22. *OFN* 1872 and *OFN* 1873.

1835 *Life of Jesus*. They foreclose or obscure those elements that enmesh demystifying critique actively in esoteric fields of religious belief and experience. We have seen repeatedly that Strauss used his critical writings on psychology and history to define a hierarchy of culture. The later writings secure this hierarchy against every countervailing tendency of his own early work.

Strauss composed the *New Life of Jesus for the German People* in 1864, thirty years after the first *Life of Jesus*. Here he sets out to produce a strictly positive, objective image of Jesus, in contrast to the infamously negative portrait in the previous work. He reverts, surprisingly, to the kind of unique, semidivine Jesus conceived by de Wette and Schleiermacher, along with a similar model of empirical and rationalist historical *Wissenschaft*.[23] In the preface to the work, he declares his intention to sift through the canon for its most authentic parts: "We have to distinguish between that part of it which is true and valid for all time, and that which, depending on casual and temporary circumstances, has now become useless or pernicious."[24] This approach clashes with his declaration in 1837 that "a critique which makes a move to excise a mass of untruths and unhistorical assertions in Christianity draws from the beginning the accusation that it has not yet been raised to the Hegelian point of view."[25] Strauss falls back to rationalism. He uses historical criticism to bring Christianity in line with reason.

His portrait of Jesus mirrors Schleiermacher's. Jesus is a uniquely moral person endowed with a heightened "God-consciousness." Strauss bases this figure on the synoptic account of the Sermon on the Mount.[26] In the 1835 *Life of Jesus*, he had argued that this passage exemplified the apocalyptic discourse of Jesus's age. It offered a list of "conditions of par-

---

23. A year later, in his 1865 "The Christ of Faith and Jesus of History," Strauss would challenge Schleiermacher's recently-published lectures on Jesus's life. But he only attacks particular historical results. In particular, he rejects Schleiermacher's appeal to the Gospel of John.

24. *NLJ* 1865, xiv.

25. Strauss, *In Defense of My Life of Jesus*, 9.

26. And its parallel in Luke 6, the Sermon on the Plain. Strauss held to the view that Matthew was the first, more authentic Gospel. He believed that Luke's version included many of Jesus's original sayings, especially in the Beatitudes, but Matthew captured their correct, more original meaning. Schleiermacher relied on John's Gospel for his image of Jesus. Strauss relied on the Sermon on the Mount. But the basic image that they devised as a consequence was very similar.

ticipation in the kingdom of heaven,"[27] ethical injunctions which were colored throughout by Jesus's messianic and eschatological self-conception.[28] Historically speaking, it was likely authentic, but no more than any other messianic sayings. In 1864, on the other hand, the apocalyptic element falls into the background and he treats it as the most authentic of Jesus's speeches. "The Sermon on the Mount has always been, and rightly so, regarded as the nucleus of the synoptic speeches," he writes, and, in a footnote, adds "Keim calls it the most genuine of all that is genuine."[29] He argues that the apocalyptic elements of the sermon are incidental to its universalizing notions of human brotherhood, as exemplified by famous sayings like Matt 7:3, "Why do you look at the speck of sawdust in your brother's eye and pay no attention to the plank in your own eye?" and the Golden Rule of 7:12, "So in everything, do to others what you would have them do to you, for this sums up the Law and the Prophets."

In 1835, Strauss argued that any attempt to separate out Jesus's "inner person" from his time-conditioned thoughts and actions would only expose his underlying humanity, which all people share. In 1864, he claims that Jesus's ability to access this inner humanity marks him off from everyone around him. Jesus reconciled God and humanity in his own mind, perceiving the divinity of humanity itself, and this notion flowed from "the innermost principle of Jesus' *own* heart."[30] This Jesus is a full-fledged humanist *avant la lettre*. He stands opposed to the apocalyptic Jesus of the first work and the apocalyptic worldview of his ancient context.

Commentators have long questioned Strauss's failure to grapple rigorously in the *New Life of Jesus* with the apocalyptic Jesus whom he had done so much to illuminate. Reviews of the work in his day already raised the question. In a letter to Wilhelm Lang in 1864, Strauss offers the following response:

> I have continually recited to myself that we are not permitted to carry our occidental views into the oriental world to which the New Testament personalities still belonged; but I could not bring myself to swallow the hard nut of his second coming. I find in the earlier speeches of Jesus, namely the Sermon on the Mount, such a rational disposition, that I

---

27. *LJ* 1835, 1:495; *LJ* 1892, 297.
28. *LJ* 1835, 1:492; *LJ* 1892, 293.
29. *NLJ* 1865, 276 n. 2.
30. Ibid., 280.

cannot rightly believe him capable of that idea, which in my eyes stands so near to madness [*Wahnsinn*].[31]

Strauss acknowledges the imperative to attend, as he had before, to the world of the first century. At the same time, he wishes to keep Jesus safe from the fanaticism to which he had exposed him in the first *Life of Jesus*. It is plausible that Strauss hoped thereby to stave off the disturbing implications of his first *Life of Jesus* for Christian faith. But it bears considering that this was not from any sense of piety, strictly speaking. The explanation to Lang suggests he was more concerned to safeguard the rationalist disposition that he found in the Sermon on the Mount than he was to retain the historical Jesus as an object of religious devotion. "The rational disposition" in Jesus's speeches on brotherhood risks contamination by apocalyptic thought, which "stands so near to madness."

The 1864 image of the historical Jesus does not only preserve a historical object of faith. It anchors and stabilizes positive historical science and rational humanism. By 1864, this singular, subjective, and rational humanist appeared to Strauss to be more secure of a foundation than the enthusiastic disciples who grappled with the death of the Messiah and hallucinated his return. As in de Wette's account of many years earlier, Strauss presses the foundations of Christian faith and modern reason back to the person of Jesus. The ethics of the Sermon on the Mount show how "the *peculiar* moral principle of Christianity" opposed and catalyzed transformations in the existing Jewish and Greco-Roman worlds. Its universalizing tendency brought a reformative impulse to Judaism in keeping with the "true essence of religion."[32] From the mere externality of the law, Jesus turned inward to the deeper, more universal laws of reason. In a conventional and opprobrious example of Enlightenment Protestant conceptions of Judaism, Strauss makes Jesus's opposition to the religion of his contemporaries exemplify both the essential newness of Christianity and the process by which autonomous rationality overcomes the particularism of existing religious forms in general. Jesus's famous antithetical statements in the Sermon—"you have heard it said ... but I have come to tell you"—model the ways in which a "new principle" opposes itself to what already exists. It does not proceed through the evolution of objective spirit. It emerges where individuals embrace their inner rationality.

---

31. Quoted in Ziegler, *David Friedrich Strauss*, 609.
32. *NLJ* 1865, 277.

This shift from the *Life of Jesus* of 1835 to the *New Life of Jesus* of 1864 corresponds with shifts in Strauss's social and political self-conception. In 1835, he was at odds with his culture. He believed he stood on the cusp of an incipient bourgeois modernity, holding fast against the regressive tendencies of the German state and church. In 1864, on the other hand, he could point to the adequate liberalism of the German constitutional monarchy and the relative political security of the middle classes. The *Humanitätstaat* that he prophesied in 1840 felt more like a reality, with only residues of age-old superstition and dogma remaining to be wiped away. He directs the *New Life of Jesus* to the increasingly triumphant bourgeoisie—it is *"für das Deutsche Volk,"* as the subtitle says. He only expected theologians to read the first work; here, he devises a history of Jesus that would be appropriate for all "educated laymen." He dedicates the work to his brother, as their representative. His brother can afford, socially and politically, to have a controversial work dedicated to him, he says, because he is "independent—exempted by the privilege of commercial pursuits from any solicitude as to the favor or displeasure of spiritual or lay superiors." Consequently,

> I consider him as a representative of the people [*das Volk*], believing that among the German people, for whom the book is destined, there are many like himself; many who find their best solace after a day of toil in serious reading; many possessing the exceptional courage to disregard the beaten track of conventional and ecclesiastical routine, and to think for themselves on the most important objects of human concernment; I may add—the still rarer capacity of seeing that there is no security in Germany, at least, for political liberty and progress, until the public mind has been emancipated from superstition, and initiated in a purely human culture.[33]

The *Volk* who will read the work do not include every German person. They are the kind of people who read theologically controversial works for edification in their leisure time. Strauss had come to see himself as the great author whose task it was to give voice to the German reading public.

In 1872, he would move further in this direction. In his final major work, *The Old Faith and the New: A Confession* (1872), he abandons the effort to secure the foundations of historical criticism and modern

---

33. *NLJ* 1865, iv.

5. CONCLUSION

reason. Rather, he takes their triumph for granted. In its totality, the work offers a paean to quietist bourgeois secularism and modern scientific thought. He juxtaposes the negative results of the modern historical criticism of Christianity with an account of the "new faith" of the modern age. Modern people adhere to Darwin's view of human origins, for example, appreciate the constitutional monarchy, and are wary of the first international. They read the newspapers and enjoy political discussion. They love the great figures of literature and music, but without any excess of devotion. Nietzsche, in the first of his *Untimely Meditations* (1873), and Franz Overbeck, in "How Christian is our Present day Theology?" (1873), criticized this work as the epitome of the nineteenth-century bourgeoisie's self-satisfaction and exhaustion.[34] Strauss gathers up the scientific, philosophical, and literary "geniuses" of the modern era—Darwin, Goethe, and Lessing, among others—and sets himself at their head. But he eschews the radicalism of each of their projects in turn, along with that of his own early work. Their writings become treasures in the collection of the bourgeois reader.

Strauss had once struck out on a treacherous course. In the *Old Faith and the New*, he presents himself as a literary genius and founder of a "new faith." He takes as evidence of his greatness the fact that he and his bourgeois readership can still scandalize a few orthodox theologians. The source of the scandal lay in his conclusion, namely, that he and his readers were no longer Christian. He based this verdict on an image of Christian origins that appears, at first glance and in a surprising reversal from the *New Life of Jesus*, to revert to positions he developed in the first *Life of Jesus*. He lays out the most severe results of historical criticism and insists on the divergence between ancient and modern culture. He concludes first that we have almost no information on which to base faith in Jesus: "the Jesus of history, of science, is only a problem; but a problem cannot be an object of worship, or a pattern by which to shape our lives."[35] He secures this result with the few positive remainders that he finds credible in the gospels. These consist in Jesus's familiar apocalyptic speeches on his messiahship: the angels, the second coming, the presentiment of death and judgment. Strauss concludes that, if Jesus was in fact the son of God, then such beliefs are legitimate on his part. But no modern person can accept

---

34. Nietzsche, *David Friedrich Strauss*; Franz Overbeck, *How Christian Is Our Present-Day Theology?* ed. Martin Henry (London: T&T Clark, 2005).

35. *OFN* 1872, 81; *OFN* 1873, 91.

this kind of supernaturalistic figure. Consequently, "there is no help for it; according to our conceptions he was a *Schwärmer*."[36] Here, finally, he metes out the diagnosis that he had brushed aside with romantic myth interpretation and rationalism in the *Life of Jesus* and *New Life of Jesus*, respectively: Jesus was an apocalyptic fanatic.

Nor does the resurrection event fare any better. His subjective vision hypothesis remains the same. The disciples, the women in particular, were devastated after the crucifixion. They experienced "spiritual conflicts which, in Oriental and especially female natures of an unbalanced religious and fantastical development, easily turned into ecstasies and visions."[37] There was nothing disingenuous about the disciples' account of their own experience: "It was no case of pious deception, but all the more of self-deception; embellishment and legend, of course, although possibly still in good faith, soon became intermingled with it."[38] But it was an illusion all the same. At this point, however, Strauss's account changes. He divests the resurrection of its historical significance. It was still the root of Christian faith, the event that kept Jesus's name and teachings from being erased from human memory—otherwise he would only have been one fanatic in a sea of contemporary apocalyptic believers. But the significance of the event for Christian faith and modern culture changes altogether. Strauss explains that although he had already given a "thorough investigation" of the event in the first *Life of Jesus*, he still considered it a "duty and a right to express without any reserve" the "consequence" [*Ergebnis*] of that analysis:[39]

> Taken historically, i.e., comparing the immense effect of this belief with its absolute baselessness, the story of the resurrection of Jesus can only be called world-historical humbug. It may be humiliating to human pride, but nevertheless the fact remains: Jesus might still have taught and embodied in his life all that is true and good, as well as what is one-sided and harsh—the latter after all always producing the strongest impression on the masses; nevertheless, his teachings would have been blown away and scattered like solitary leaves by the wind, had these leaves not been

---

36. *OFN* 1872, 80; *OFN* 1873, 92.
37. *OFN* 1872, 71; *OFN* 1873, 80–81.
38. OFN 1872, 71; *OFN* 1873, 80–81.
39. *OFN* 1872, 72; *OFN* 1873, 83, translation modified.

held together and thus preserved, as if with a stout tangible binding, by a delusional belief [*Wahnglauben*] in his resurrection.[40]

The event is no longer the mechanism, in other words, through which spirit moves through history. On the contrary, it is precisely the opposite: a mere contingency, on the one hand, and a piece of "world-historical humbug," on the other; a "delusional belief" that steered people wrong for centuries.

Here Strauss delivers the verdict that commentators have attributed to the first *Life of Jesus*: The Jesus of history is a fanatic who opposes the Christ of faith. The foundation of Christian belief is a collective delusion that must be abandoned. Modernity and antiquity, faith and reason, are severed once and for all. This crucial alteration of his view of Christian origins epitomizes Strauss's shift to a secular scientific worldview, one that is unmoored from speculative idealism and romanticism. There is no question of truth arising in the experience of the resurrection event, or of historical science beginning in the realm of an assiduous faith. To an extent, this account seems to augment or confirm the radical elements of the first *Life of Jesus* as a critique of religion. But it abandons the critique of modern consciousness that formed an integral part of that earlier work. Strauss reserves his critical energies strictly for religion and the ancient world. In the first *Life of Jesus*, he still had to carve out a space against which to articulate modern thought over and against religion. The effort involved certain risks. It put scientific demystification in a complex proximity with esoteric religious thought and practice. In the *Old Faith and the New*, on the other hand, he occludes the complexities in which his early work involved him. Disenchantment appears as an inevitable, natural process.

Nietzsche's critique of the later work captures this transformation. He asserts that Strauss's "new faith" manifests the complacency and disingenuousness of modern "philistine" culture and its faux-transgressive "scientific men." The rejoinder anticipates key elements of Nietzsche's later genealogical works. It presages his later genealogical accounts of the base origins of religious and scientific morality and truth. In his 1887 *Genealogy of Morals*, Nietzsche argues, among other things, that the scientific quest for knowledge can recapitulate aspects of religious asceticism. A petty, disingenuous will to power fuels both. Strauss was likely one of the scientific ascetics whom Nietzsche still had in mind. In 1872, he argues

---

40. *OFN* 1872, 72–73; *OFN* 1873, 83.

that where Strauss claims to eschew political power in pursuit of literature and science, his true, covert aim is to neutralize all challenges to the ease and contentment that he derives from the established order. Strauss dedicates himself as such to the "deification of success."[41] His historical methods short circuit their own unsettling possibilities in favor of collecting edifying, entertaining facts. Strauss exemplifies the fate of historical *Wissenschaft* that Nietzsche would lament in this and his second *Untimely Meditation*, "On the Use and Abuse of History for Life." Strauss exemplifies the exhaustion of modern science. In general, Nietzsche claims, "a true paradox lies in the nature of the scientific man," namely,

> he behaves like the proudest idler of fortune: as if existence were not an unholy and precarious matter, but rather a firmly-held possession, secure for eternity. He feels permitted to waste his life on questions whose answer could only have importance for those to whom eternity is guaranteed. On the earth for a brief moment, he is surrounded by terrifying precipices, so that every step should remind him to ask, "Whither? Whence? Why?" But his soul is warmed by the task of counting stamens on a flower or breaking up stones on the road, and he plunges the whole weight of his absorption, passion, strength, and pleasure into this work.[42]

In the contemporary historical science exemplified by Strauss's *Old Faith and the New*, this situation has reached a nadir. Here, Nietzsche claims, the assiduous pursuit of facts and details had begun to feel like a necessity, a kind of enslavement. Scientific scholars have become exhausted laborers, who have neither the time nor energy to consider the threatening territory beside which they tread.[43] Strauss showed some audacity and rigor at least in his early work[44] In the *Old Faith and the New*, he gives himself over to quiescent bourgeois cultural apologetics and self-congratulation.

Nietzsche claims in addition that Strauss's *Old Faith and the New* is underwritten throughout by his vision of a *healthy* modern subject. He "invents for his habits, modes of thinking, favor and disapproval the general formula 'healthiness' [*Gesundheit*], and disposes of every discomfiting troublemaker as being sick and neurotic."[45] He stands among the many

---

41. Nietzsche, *David Friedrich Strauss*, 14.
42. Ibid., 53–54.
43. Ibid., 54.
44. Ibid., 74.
45. Ibid., 15.

5. CONCLUSION

nineteenth-century historians who "profess to hate fanaticism and intolerance in every form," but "in fact hate the dominating genius and tyranny of the real demands of culture, and therefore turn all their power to paralyzing, dulling and dissolving every ground on which a fresh and powerful movement is expected to appear."[46] And historical consciousness is the means by which people like Strauss "save themselves from enthusiasm."[47] This scientific irenicism converges in turn with Strauss's quietist politics. Strauss complains, for example, that the social democrats' attack on hereditary property undermines the "indispensable basis of morality, as well as of culture."[48]

We have seen how the elementary materials of such a cultural pathology appear in Strauss's work in the 1830s. There he determines the limits and conditions of modern reason in a radical fashion. Where earlier Enlightenment critics had rejected fanaticism and false beliefs, Strauss brings them under the auspices of a regime of corrective cultural education. He sets the nocturnal, irrational side of human spirit within a hierarchy and an economy of modern reason. But the negative movement of the first *Life of Jesus* includes countervailing elements as well. We can think of this negativity in two senses, both of which are distinct from his negative, limiting critique of supernatural phenomena. First, there is the sense in which Strauss is a critical Hegelian. He appeals to the rationality of the actual in a way that opens culture to infinite transformation and reevaluation. The negative capacity of human thought, the ability to think in opposition to what already exists, opens the endless work of social critique. At a certain point, this critique would have to fall back on the modern order and its attendant institutions. Tendencies in this direction develop in the late 1830s and early 1840s, in the critical writings of figures like Arnold Ruge, Max Stirner, Mikael Bakunin, Bauer, and the young Marx. Second, there is a more difficult sense in which negativity remains irreducible in Strauss's account. His clumsy attempt to reconstruct the resurrection event as the concrete historical foundation of spirit's progress captures this aspect of his work. An imaginative account of an ancient hallucination serves as the fragile heart of his vision of modern reason and critical, humanist culture. His struggle to determine this foundation illustrates the uncertain status of science and critique. He has to resort to

---

46. Ibid., 14.
47. Ibid., 13.
48. *OFN* 1872, 278; *OFN* 1873, 324.

the kinds of interpretive maneuvers that he otherwise rejects emphatically. Demystification and progressive *Bildung* take place, for Strauss, in intimate encounters with ghost seeing, apocalypticism, and demonomania. But they become entangled with these modes of consciousness in the process. The difficulty should activate our critical vigilance in the face of the tendency of Strauss's later work. It disturbs any assurance that historical positivism and secular criticism are the sure possessions and guarantees of a new, modern and secular faith.

Works Cited

Bahrdt, Karl Friedrich. *Briefe über die Bibel im Volkston: Eine Wochenschrift von einem Prediger auf dem Lande.* Halle: Dost, 1782.
Baier, Karl. *Meditation und Moderne: Zur Genese eines Kernbereichs moderner Spiritualität in der Wechselwirkung zwischen Westeuropa, Nordamerika und Asien.* 2 vols. Würzburg: Könighausen & Neumann, 2009.
Bauer, Bruno. *Feldzüge der Reinen Kritik.* Frankfurt: Suhrkamp, 1968.
———. *Kritik der Evangelischen Geschichte der Synoptiker.* 3 vols. Leipzig: Wigand, 1841–1842.
———. Review of *Das Leben Jesu, kritisch bearbeitet*, by David Friedrich Strauss. *JWK* Dec 1835, 109:879–80; 110:881–88; 111:889–94; 112:897–904; 113:905–12.
———. Review of *Das Jeben Jesu, kritisch bearbeitet 2*, by David Friedrich Strauss. *JWK* May 1836, 86:681–88; 87:689–94; 88:697–704.
———. *Trumpet of the Last Judgment against Hegel the Atheist and Antichrist.* Translated by Lawrence Stepelevich. Lewiston, NY: Mellen, 1989.
Baur, Ferdinand C. *Paulus, der Apostel Jesu Christi: Sein Leben und Wirken, seine Briefe und seine Lehre: Ein Beitrag zu einer kritischen Geschichte des Urchristenthums.* Stuttgart: Becher & Müller, 1845.
Bell, Matthew. *The German Tradition of Psychology in Literature and Thought 1700–1840.* Cambridge: Cambridge University Press, 2005.
Benz, Ernst. *The Mystical Sources of German Romantic Philosophy.* Allison Park, PA: Pickwick, 1983.
Blackwell, Jeannine. "Controlling the Demonic: The Possession of Anna Elisabeth Lohmann." Pages 425–42 in *Impure Reason: Dialectic of Enlightenment in German.* Edited by Daniel Wilson and Robert Holub. Detroit: Wayne State University Press, 1993.
Blanton, Ward. *Displacing Christian Origins: Philosophy, Secularity, and the New Testament.* Chicago: University of Chicago Press, 2007.

Boddy, Janice. "Spirit Possession Revisited: Beyond Instrumentality." *Annual Review of Anthropology* 23 (1994): 407–34.
Bourguignon, Erika. "Suffering and Healing, Subordination and Power." *Ethos* 32 (2004): 557–74.
Brazill, William. *The Young Hegelians*. New Haven: Yale University Press, 1970.
Brecht, Martin. *Martin Luther: Shaping and Defining the Reformation, 1521–1523*. Translated by James Schaaf. Minneapolis: Fortress, 1990.
Breckman, Warren. *Marx, the Young Hegelians, and the Origins of Radical Social Theory: Dethroning the Self.* Cambridge: Cambridge University Press, 1999.
Cavanaugh, William. "The Invention of Fanaticism." *Modern Theology* 27 (2011): 226–37.
Colas, Dominique. *Civil Society and Fanaticism: Conjoined Histories*. Translated by Amy Jacobs. Stanford: Stanford University Press, 1997.
Crabtree, Adam. *From Mesmer to Freud: Magnetic Sleep and the Roots of Psychological Healing*. New Haven: Yale University Press, 1993.
Derrida, Jacques. "On a Newly Risen Apocalyptic Tone in Philosophy." Pages 117–72 in *Raising the Tone of Philosophy*. Edited by Peter Fenves. Baltimore: Johns Hopkins University Press, 1993.
Eichhorn, Johann Gottfried. "Uebrige Ungedruckte Werke des Wolfenbüttlischen Fragmentisten." Pages 3–90 in *Allgemeine Bibliothek der biblischen Litteratur*. Vol. 1. Leipzig: Weidmann, 1787.
———. *Urgeschichte*. Edited by Johann Philip Gabler. Vol. 3. Altdorf bei Nürnberg: Monath & Kussler, 1793.
Ellenberger, Henri. *The Discovery of the Unconscious: The History and Evolution of Dynamic Psychotherapy*. New York: Basic Books, 1970.
Fenves, Peter. "The Scale of Enthusiasm." *HLQ* 60 (1997): 117–52.
———. "The Topicality of Tone." Pages 1–49 in *Raising the Tone of Philosophy*. Edited by Peter Fenves. Baltimore: Johns Hopkins University Press, 1993.
Feuerbach, Ludwig. *The Essence of Christianity*. Translated by George Eliot. New York: Harper, 1957.
Fichte, Johann Gottlieb. *The Science of Knowledge, with the First and Second Introductions*. Translated by Peter Lauchlan Heath and John Lachs. Cambridge: Cambridge University Press, 1982.
Foucault, Michel. *Madness and Civilization: A History of Insanity in the Age of Reason*. New York: Pantheon, 1965.

Frei, Hans. "David Friedrich Strauss." Pages 215–60 in vol. 1 of *Nineteenth Century Religious Thought in the West*. Edited by Ninian Smart, John Clayton, Steven Katz, and Patrick Sherry. 3 vols. Cambridge: Cambridge University Press, 1985.

———. *The Eclipse of Biblical Narrative: A Study in Eighteenth and Nineteenth Century Hermeneutics*. New Haven: Yale, 1977.

Goldberg, Ann. *Sex, Religion, and the Making of Modern Madness: The Eberbach Asylum and German Society, 1815–1849*. Oxford: Oxford University Press, 1999.

Gregory, Frederick. "Gotthilf Heinrich Schubert and the Dark Side of Natural Science." *NTM* 3 (1995): 255–69.

———. *Nature Lost? Natural Science and the German Theological Traditions of the Nineteenth Century*. Cambridge: Harvard University Press, 1992.

Göschel, Karl. *Aphorismen über Nichtwissen und absolutes Wissen im Verhältnis zur christlichen Glaubenserkenntnis*. Berlin: Franklin, 1829.

Hanegraaff, Wouter. *Esotericism and the Academy: Rejected Knowledge in Western Culture*. Cambridge: Cambridge University Press, 2012.

———. "A Woman Alone." Pages 211–47 in *Women and Miracle Stories*. Edited by Anne-Marie Korte. Leiden: Brill, 2001.

Harris, Horton. *David Friedrich Strauss and His Theology*. Cambridge: Cambridge University Press, 1973.

Harrison, Peter. *"Religion" and the Religions in the English Enlightenment*. Cambridge: Cambridge University Press, 1990.

Hartlich, Christian, and Walter Sachs. *Der Ursprung des Mythosbegriffes in der modernen Bibelwissenschaft*. Tübingen: Mohr Siebeck, 1952.

Harvey, Van A. "D. F. Strauss's Life of Jesus Revisited." *CH* 30 (1961): 191–211.

Hegel, Georg Wilhelm Friedrich. *The Encyclopaedia Logic, with the Zusätze*. Vol. 1 of *The Encyclopaedia of Philosophical Sciences with the Zusätze*. Translated by Theodore F. Geraets, W. A. Suchting, H. S. Harris. Indianapolis: Hackett, 1991.

———. *Lectures on the Philosophy of Religion*. Edited by Peter Crafts Hodgson. Berkeley: University of California Press, 1987.

———. *Phenomenology of Spirit*. Translated by Arnold V. Miller. Oxford: Oxford University Press, 1977.

Hengstenberg, Ernst Wilhelm. *Evangelische Kirchen-Zeitung*, June 1836, no. 48.

Herder, Johann Gottfried. *Another Philosophy of History and Selected Political Writings*. Indianapolis: Hackett, 2004.

———. *Maran Atha oder das Buch von der Zukunft des Herrn*. Riga: Hartknock, 1779.

———. *Philosophical Writings*. Translated and edited by Michael N. Forster. Cambridge: Cambridge University Press, 2002.

———. *Sammtliche Werke*. Edited by Bernard Suphan, Reinhold Steid, Carl Christian Redlich, Otto Hoffman, and Jakob Balde. 33 vols. Berlin: Weidmann, 1877–1913.

———. *Vom Geist der Ebräischen Poesie: Eine Anleitung für die Liebhaber derselben, und der ältesten Geschichte des menschlichen Geistes*. 2 vols. Desau, 1782–1783.

Heyne, C. G. *Apollodori Atheniensis Bibliothecae Libri Tres et Fragmenta*. 2nd ed. Göttingen: Dietrich.

Hodgson, Peter. Introduction to *The Life of Jesus: Critically Examined*, by David Friedrich Strauss. Edited by Peter Hodgson. Translated by George Eliot. Philadelphia: Fortress, 1972.

Howard, Thomas. *Religion and the Rise of Historicism*. Cambridge: Cambridge University Press, 2000.

Hume, David. *An Enquiry Concerning Human Understanding and Other Writings*. Edited by Stephen Buckle. Cambridge: Cambridge University Press, 2007.

Kant, Immanuel. *Critique of Judgment*. Translated by Werner Pluhar. Indianapolis: Hackett, 1987.

———. *Critique of Practical Reason*. Translated and edited by Werner Pluhar. Indianapolis: Hackett, 2002.

———. *Critique of Pure Reason*. Edited and translated by Paul Guyer and Allen W. Wood. Cambridge: Cambridge University Press, 1998.

———. "Das Ende der Alle Dinge." Pages 391–408 in *Immanuel Kants Schriften zur Philosophie der Religion*. Edited by Gustav Hartenstein. Leipzig: Modes & Baumann, 1839.

———. *Metaphysical Foundations of Natural Science*. Translated by Michael Friedman. Cambridge: Cambridge University Press, 2004.

———. *Observations on the Feeling of the Beautiful and Sublime and Other Writings*. Edited by Patrick Frierson and Paul Guyer. Cambridge: Cambridge University Press, 2011.

———. "On Exaltation and the Remedy for It." Pages 107–8 in *Raising the Tone of Philosophy*. Edited by Peter Fenves. Baltimore: Johns Hopkins University Press, 1993.

———. *Prolegomena to Any Future Metaphysics that Will Be Able to Come Forward as Science with Selections from the Critique of Pure Reason*. Translated by Gary Hatfield. Cambridge: Cambridge University Press, 1997.

———. *Religion and Rational Theology*. Translated and edited by Allen Wood and George di Giovanni. Cambridge: Cambridge University Press, 1996.

———. *Sammtliche Werke*. Edited by Karl Rosenkranz and Friedrich W. Schubert. Vol. 1. Leipzig: Voss, 1838.

Keck, Leander E. Introduction to *The Christ of Faith and the Jesus of History: A Critique of Schleiermacher's Life of Jesus*, by David Friedrich Strauss. Translated and edited by Leander E. Keck. Philadelphia: Fortress, 1977.

Keller, Mary. *The Hammer and the Flute: Women, Power, and Spirit Possession*. Baltimore: Johns Hopkins University Press, 2002.

Kerner, Justinus. *Eine Erscheinung aus dem Nachtgebiete der Natur: Durch eine Reihe von Zeugen bestätigt und dem Naturforschern zum Bedenken mitgetheilt*. Stuttgart: Cotta, 1836.

———. *Franz Anton Mesmer aus Schwaben, Entdecker des thierischen Magnetismus: Erinnerungen an denselben, nebst Nachrichten von den letzten Jahren seines Lebens zu Meersburg am Bodensee*. Frankfurt am Main: Literarische Anstalt, 1856.

———. *Die Seherin von Prevorst: Eröffnungen über das innere Leben des Menschen und über das Hereinragen einer Geisterwelt in die Unsere*. Stuttgart: Cotta, 1829.

Kerner, Justinus, and Carl August von Eschenmayer. *Geschichten Besessener neuerer Zeit: Beobachtungen aus dem Gebiete kakodaemonisch-magnetischer Erscheinungen nebst Reflexionen über Bessessenseyn und Zauber*. Stuttgart: Wachendorf, 1834.

Kluge, Carl Alexander Ferdinand. *Versuch einer Darstellung des animalischen Magnetismus als Heilmittel*. Vienna: Franz Haas, 1815.

Knudsen, Jonathan B. *What is Enlightenment? Eighteenth-Century Answers and Twentieth-Century Questions*. Edited by James Schmidt. Los Angeles: University of California Press, 1996.

Krummacher, Friedrich Wilhelm. *An Autobiography*. Translated by M. G. Easton. New York: Carter & Brothers, 1869. Translation of *Eine Selbstbiographie*. Berlin: Wiegandt & Grieben, 1869.

———. "The Last Judgment." Pages 181–94 in *The Foreign Protestant Pulpit*. London: Dickinson, 1870.

Lange, Dietz. *Historischer Jesus oder mythischer Christus: Untersuchungen zu dem Gegensatz zwischen Friedrich Schleiermacher und David Friedrich Strauss.* Gütersloh: Gütersloher Verlaghaus, 1975.

La Vopa, Anthony. "The Philosopher and the 'Schwärmer': On the Career of a German Epithet from Luther to Kant." *HLQ* 60 (1997): 85–115.

Legaspi, Michael. *The Death of Scripture and the Rise of Biblical Studies.* Oxford: Oxford University Press, 2010.

Lessing, Gotthold. *Lessing's Theological Writings.* Translated by Henry Chadwick. Stanford: Stanford University Press, 1957.

Lowth, Robert. *De Sacra poesi Hebraeorum.* Edited and annotated by Johann David Michaelis. Göttingen: Dietrich, 1770.

Magee, Glenn Alexander. *Hegel and the Hermetic Tradition.* Ithaca, NY: Cornell University Press, 2001.

Marx, Karl. *Writings of the Young Marx on Philosophy and Society.* Translated and edited by Loyd David Easton and Kurt H. Guddat. Indianapolis: Hackett, 1997.

Massey, Marilyn. *Christ Unmasked: The Meaning of the Life of Jesus in German Politics.* Chapel Hill: University of North Carolina Press, 1983.

———. "David Friedrich Strauss and His Hegelian Critics." *JR* 57 (1977): 341–62.

———. Introduction to *In Defense of My Life of Jesus against the Hegelians*, by David Friedrich Strauss. Translated and edited by Marilyn Chapin Massey. Hamden, CT: Archon, 1983.

———. "The Literature of Young Germany and D.F. Strauss's Life of Jesus." *JR* 59 (1979): 298–323.

Mee, Jon. *Romanticism, Enthusiasm, and Regulation: Poetics and the Policing of Culture in the Romantic Period.* Oxford: Oxford University Press, 2005.

Mesmer, Franz Anton. *Abhandlung über die Entdeckung des thierischen Magnetismus: Aus dem Französischen übersetzt.* Carlsruhe: Macklot, 1781. Translation of *Mémoire sur la découverte du magnetisme animal.* Paris: Didot le jeune, 1779.

———. *Mesmerism.* Translated and compiled by Georg Bloch. Los Altos, CA: Kaufmann, 1980.

Midelfort, H. C. Erik. *Exorcism and Enlightenment: Johann Joseph Gassner and the Demons of Eighteenth-Century Germany.* New Haven: Yale University Press, 2005.

Montiel, Luis. "Une révolution manquée: Le magnétisme animal dans la médicine du romantisme allemande." *RH 19* 38 (2009): 61–77.

Morgan, Robert. "A Straussian Question to New Testament Theology." *NTS* 23 (1977): 243–65.
Müller, Gotthold. *Identität und Immanenz: Zur Genese der Theologie von David Friedrich Strauss, eine theologie- und philosophiegeschichtliche Studie mit einem bibliographischen Anhang zur Apokatastasis-Frage.* Zürich: EVZ-Verlag, 1968.
Nast, William. "Recollections of David Friedrich Strauss." *The New Princeton Review* 4 (1887): 343–48.
Neander, August. *The Life of Jesus Christ in Its Historical Connexion and Historical Development.* Translated by John McClintock and Charles Blumenthal. London: Bohn, 1852. Translation of *Das Leben Jesu Christi in seinem geschichtlichen Zummenhange und seiner geschichtlichen Entwickelung.* 4th ed. Hamburg: Perthes, 1837.
Nietzsche, Friedrich. *David Friedrich Strauss, the Confessor and the Writer.* Vol. 1 of *Untimely Meditations.* Edited by Daniel Breazeale. Translated by R. J. Hollingdale. Cambridge: Cambridge University Press, 1997. Translation of *David Friedrich Strauss, der Bekenner und Schriftsteller.* Vol. 1 of *Unzeitgemässe Betrachtungen.* Leipzig: Fritzsch, 1873.
Olshausen, Hermann. *Biblical Commentary on the New Testament.* Translated by A. C. Kendrick. New York: Sheldon, 1857. Translation of *Biblischer Commentar über sämmtliche Schriften des Neuen Testaments zunächst für Prediger und Studirende.* Königsberg: Unzer, 1830.
Overbeck, Franz. *How Christian is Our Present-Day Theology?* Edited by Martin Henry. London: T&T Clark, 2005.
Oyer, John S. *Lutheran Reformers against Anabaptists.* The Hague: Nijhoff, 1964.
Parker, Theodore. "Strauss's Life of Jesus." Pages 248–308 in *The Critical and Miscellaneous Writings of Theodore Parker.* Boston: Munroe, 1843.
Paul, Jean-Marie. *D. F. Strauss et son époque.* Paris: Les Belles Lettres, 1982.
Paulus, Heinrich. *Exegetisches Handbuch über die drei ersten Evangelien.* 3 vols. Heidelberg: Winter, 1830–1833.
———. *Das Leben Jesu als Grundlage einer reinen Geschichte des Urchristentums.* 2 vols. Heidelberg: Winter, 1828.
———. *Memorabilien.* Vol. 5. Leipzig: Crusius, 1793.
Reil, Christian. *Rhapsodieen über die Anwendung der psychischen Curmethode auf Geisteszerrüttungen.* Halle: Curt, 1803.
Reimarus, Hermann Samuel. *Apologie oder Schutzschrift für die vernünftigen Verehrer Gottes.* Edited by Gerhard Alexander. 2 vols. Frankfurt am Main: Insel, 1972.

———. *Reimarus: Fragments*. Translated by Charles H. Talbert and Ralph S. Fraser. Philadelphia: Fortress, 1970. Translation of *Fragmente des Wolfenbüttelschen Ungenannten*. Edited by Gotthold Ephraim Lessing. Berlin: Sanders, 1835.

———. *Von dem Zwecke Jesu und seiner Jünger: Noch ein Fragment des Wolfenbüttelschen Ungenannten*. Edited by Gotthold Ephraim Lessing. Braunschweig: n.p., 1778.

Rogerson, John W. *W. M. L. De Wette: Founder of Modern Biblical Criticism: An Intellectual Biography*. Sheffield: JSOT Press, 1992.

Rosenberg, Jordana. *Critical Enthusiasm: Capital Accumulation and the Transformation of Religious Passion*. Oxford: Oxford University Press, 2011.

Rosenkranz, Karl. *Encyclopädie der theologischen Wissenschaft*. Halle: Schwetschke, 1831.

———. *Kritik der Schleiermacherschen Glaubenslehre*. Königsberg: Gebrüder Bornträger, 1836.

Sandberger, Jörg F. *David Friedrich Strauss als theologischer Hegelianer*. Göttingen: Vandenhoeck & Ruprecht, 1972.

Sawicki, Diethard. *Leben mit den Toten: Geisterglauben und die Entstehung des Spiritismus in Deutschland 1770–1900*. München: Schöningh, 2002.

Schelling, F. W. J. von. *First Outline of a System of the Philosophy of Nature*. Albany: SUNY Press, 2004. Translated by Keith R. Peterson. Translation of *Erster Entwurf eines Systems der Naturphilosophie: Zum behuf seiner Vorlesungen*. Leipzig: Gabler, 1799.

———. *Ideas for a Philosophy of Nature as Introduction to the Study of This Science*. Translated by Errol E. Harris and Peter Heath. Cambridge: Cambridge University Press, 1988. Translation of *Ideen zu einer Philosphie der Natur*. Leipzig: Breitkopf & Hartel, 1797.

———. "Ueber Mythen, historische Sagen, und Philosopheme der ältesten Welt." Pages 43–83 in *Friedrich Wilhelm Joseph von Schellings Werke*. Vol. 1. Stuttgart: Cotta, 1856.

———. *Von der Weltseele: Eine Hypothese der höhern Physik zur Erklärung des allgemeinen Organismus*. Hamburg: Perthes, 1798.

Schleiermacher, Friedrich. *The Christian Faith*. Translated by H. R. Mackintosh and James A. Stewart. Edinburgh: T&T Clark, 1928. Translation of *Der christliche Glaube nach den Grundsäzen der evangelischen Kirche im Zusammenhange dargestellt*. 2nd ed. 2 vols. Berlin: Reimer, 1830–1831.

———. *Das Leben Jesu: Vorlesungen an der Universität zu Berlin im Jahr 1832*. Edited by Karl August Rütenik. Berlin: Reimer, 1864.

———. *On Religion: Speeches to Its Cultured Despisers*. Edited by Richard Crouter. Cambridge: Cambridge University Press, 1996.

Schneider, Robert. *Schellings und Hegels Schwäbische Geistesahnen*. Würzburg-Aumühle: Triltsch, 1938.

Schröter, Jens, "New Testament Science beyond Historicism." Pages 9–21 in *From Jesus to the New Testament: Early Christian Theology and the Origin of the New Testament Canon*. Translated Wayne Coppins. Waco, TX: Baylor University Press, 2013.

Schubert, Gotthilf Heinrich von. *Ansichten von der Nachtseite der Naturwissenschaft*. Dresden: Arnold, 1808.

———. *Die Symbolik des Traumes*. Edited by F. H. Ranke. 4th ed. Leipzig: Brockhaus, 1862.

Schweitzer, Albert. *The Psychiatric Study of Jesus*. Translated by Charles R. Joy. Boston: Beacon, 1948.

———. *The Quest of the Historical Jesus*. Translated by W. Montgomery. Mineola, NY: Dover, 2012.

Semler, Johann Salomo. *Abfertigung der neuen Geister und alten Irrtümer in der Lohmannischen Begeisterung zu Kemberg*. Halle: Gebauer, 1760.

———. *Beantwortung der Fragmente eines Ungenannten insbesondere vom Zweck Jesu und seiner Jünger*. Halle: Erziehungsinstitut, 1779.

———. *Christliche freye Untersuchung über die so genannte Offenbarung Johannis*. Halle: Hendel, 1769.

———. *Commentatio de daemoniacis quorum in N.T. fit mentio*. Magdeburg: Hendel, 1769.

———. *D. Joh. Salomo Semlers Abhandlung von freier Untersuchung des Canon*. 4 vols. Halle: Hemmerde, 1771–1775.

Sered, Susan Starr. *Priestess, Mother, Sacred Sister: Religions Dominated by Women*. Oxford: Oxford University Press, 1994.

Sheehan, Jonathan. *The Enlightenment Bible: Translation, Scholarship, Culture*. Princeton: Princeton University Press, 2005.

Smart, Ninian, John Clayton, Steven Katz, and Patrick Sherry, eds. *Nineteenth Century Religious Thought in the West*. Vol. 1. Cambridge: Cambridge University Press, 1985.

Spinoza, Baruch. *Ethics*. Edited by Seymour Feldman. Translated by Samuel Shirley. Indianapolis: Hackett, 1992.

———. *Tractatus Theologico-Politicus*. London: Trübner, 1862.

Strauss, David Friedrich. *Ausgewählte Briefe.* Edited by Eduard Zeller. Bonn: Strauss, 1895.

———. *Charakteristiken und Kritiken: Eine Sammlung zerstreuter Aufsätze aus den Gebieten der Theologie, Anthropologie und Aesthetik.* Leipzig: Wigand, 1839.

———. *The Christ of Faith and the Jesus of History: A Critique of Schleiermacher's "The Life of Jesus."* Translated by Leander E. Keck. Philadelphia: Fortress, 1977.

———. *Christian Märklin: Ein Lebens- und Charakterbild aus den Gegenwart.* Mannheim: Basserman, 1851.

———. *Die christliche Glaubenslehre in ihrer geschichtlichen Entwicklung und im Kampfe mit der modernen Wissenschaft.* 2 vols. Tübingen: Osiander, 1840–1841.

———. *Hermann Samuel Reimarus und seine Schutzschrift für die vernünftigen Verehrer Gottes.* Leipzig: Brockhaus, 1862.

———. *In Defense of My Life of Jesus against the Hegelians.* Translated and edited by Marilyn Chapin Massey. Hampden, CT: Archon, 1983.

———. *Kleine Schriften.* Berlin: Duncker, 1866.

———. *Das Leben Jesu: Kritisch bearbeitet.* 2 vols. Tübingen: Osiander, 1835–1836. Repr. 4th rev. ed. 2 vols. Tübingen: Osiander, 1839–1840.

———. "Die Lehre von der Wiederbringung Aller Dinge in Ihrer Religionsgeschichtlichen Entwicklung." Pages 50–75 in Gotthold Müller, *Identität und Immanenz: Zur Genese der Theologie von David Friedrich Strauss, eine theologie- und philosophiegeschichtliche Studie mit einem bibliographischen Anhang zur Apokatastasis-Frage.* Zürich: EVZ-Verlag, 1968.

———. *The Life of Jesus Critically Examined.* Translated by George Eliot. New York: Macmillan, 1892. Translation of *Das Leben Jesu: Kritisch bearbeitet.* 2 vols. 4th rev. ed. Tübingen: Osiander, 1839–1840.

———. *A New Life of Jesus.* London: Williams & Norgate, 1865. Translation of *Das Leben Jesu: Für das deutsche Volk bearbeitet.* Leipzig: Brockhaus, 1864.

———. *The Old Faith and the New: A Confession.* Translated by Mathilde Blind. 2 vols. New York: Holt, 1873. Translation of *Der alte und der neue Glaube: Ein Bekenntniss.* 6th edition. Leipzig: Hirzel, 1872.

———. *Streitschriften zur Vertheidigung meiner Schrift über das Leben Jesu und zur Charakteristik der gegenwärtigen Theologie.* 3 vols. Tübingen: Osiander, 1837.

———. *Zwei Friedliche Blätter.* Altona: Hammerich, 1839.

Tholuck, August. *Die Glaubwürdigkeit der evangelischen Geschichte: Zugleich eine Kritik des Lebens Jesu von Strauss: Für theologische und nicht theologische Leser*. Hamburg: Perthes, 1837.

Tindal, Matthew, and Jacob Foster. *Beweis, dass das Christenthum so alt als die Welt sey: Nebst Herrn Jacob Fosters Widerlegung desselben*. Translated by Johann Lorenz Schmidt. Frankfurt: n.p. 1741.

Toews, John Edward. *Hegelianism: The Path toward Dialectical Humanism, 1805-1841*. Cambridge: Cambridge University Press, 1985.

Toscano, Alberto. *Fanaticism: On the Uses of an Idea*. London: Verso, 2010.

Troeltsch, Ernst. "On the Historical and Dogmatic Methods in Theology." Pages 728–53 in vol. 2 of *Gesammelte Schriften*. Translation by Jack Forstman. Tubingen: Mohr Siebeck, 1913.

Vater, Johann Severin. *Commentar über den Pentateuch*. 3 vols. Halle: Waisenhaus, 1802-1805.

Verheyden, Jack C. Introduction to *The Life of Jesus*, by Friedrich Schleiermacher. Edited and translated by Jack C. Verheyden. Mifflintown, PA: Sigler, 1997.

Vischer, Friedrich. "Dr. Strauss und die Wirtemburger." Pages 3–130 in vol. 1 of *Kritische Gänge*. 2 vols. Tübingen: Fues, 1844.

Weber, Max. *From Max Weber: Essays in Sociology*. Translated and edited by Hans Heinrich Gerth and C. Wright Mills. New York: Oxford, 1946.

Wegscheider, Julius August Ludwig. *Institutiones theologiae Christianae dogmaticae*. Halle: Gebauer, 1815.

Weiland, Christoph. *Sammtliche Werke*. Vol. 35. Leipzig: Göschen, 1840.

Wette, W. M. L. de. *Beiträge zur Einleitung in das Alte Testament*. 2 vols. Halle: Schimmelpfenig, 1806-1807.

———. *Biblische Dogmatik: Alten und Neuen Testaments: Oder kritische Darstellung der Religionslehre des Hebraismus, des Judenthums und Urchristenthums*. Berlin: Reimer, 1831.

———. *Theodore: Or the Skeptic's Conversion*. Translated by James F. Clarke. 2 vols. Boston: Munroe, 1856.

———. *Ueber Religion und Theologie: Erläuterungen zu seinem Lehrbuche der Dogmatik*. Berlin: Reimer, 1815.

Williamson, George S. *The Longing for Myth in Germany: Religion and Aesthetic Culture from Romanticism to Nietzsche*. Chicago: University of Chicago Press, 2004.

Wurm, Johann Friedrich. "Extracts from the Life of Luther: Mexico, 2838." Pages 325–44 in *Voices of the Church in Reply to Strauss's "Leben Jesu."* Edited by J. R. Beard. London: Simpkin & Marshall, 1845.

Zachhuber, Johannes. *Theology as Science in Nineteenth-Century Germany: From F. C. Baur to Ernst Troeltsch*. Oxford: Oxford University Press, 2013.

Zeller, Eduard. *David Friedrich Strauss in His Life and Writings*. London: Smith Elder, 1874.

Ziegler, Theobald. *David Friedrich Strauss*. Strassburg: Trübner, 1908.

Ziolkowski, Theodore. *Clio the Romantic Muse: Historicizing the Faculties in Germany*. Ithaca, NY: Cornell University Press, 2004.

BIBLICAL INDEX

Hebrew Bible

Genesis
- 2–3   107
- 6   121

Exodus
- 7   2

Psalms
- 59   128–29

Daniel
- 7:1–14   145

Joel
- 2:28   37

New Testament

Matthew
- 5–7   189
- 7:3   190
- 8:28–34   85, 95–97, 115–17, 120–21
- 8:29   95
- 8:32   116
- 9:20–22   90, 97
- 12:25–30   144
- 12:28   144
- 17:14–21   85, 96–97
- 24   145
- 25   145
- 27:46   77, 147
- 27:64   99

Mark
- 1:21–28   85, 87–88, 95
- 1:24   85
- 3:23–28   144
- 5:1–20   85, 95–97, 115–117, 120–21
- 5:13   116
- 5:24–34   90, 97
- 9:14–29   85, 96–97
- 13   145
- 15:34   77–78, 147

Luke
- 1:11–20   171
- 4:31–37   85, 87–88
- 6   189
- 8:26–39   85, 95–97, 115–17, 120–21
- 8:33   116
- 8:42–48   90, 97
- 9:37–43   85, 96–97
- 10:18–20   144
- 11:17–23   144
- 21   145
- 24:32   172
- 24:45   172

John
- 8:28   152

Acts
- 2:17   37
- 3:21   101
- 9:1–9   170
- 19:13–16   2–3

1 Corinthians
  9:1   170
  15:1–8   170

2 Corinthians
  12:1–4   170

Galatians
  1:11–16   170

Revelation
  10:5–6   151
  12:3   187

Modern Primary Sources Index*

Bahrdt, *Briefe*	99	Herder, *Vom Geist*	35, 105–6
Bauer, B., *Feldzüge*	24	Heyne, *Apollodori Atheniensis Bibliothecae*	105
Bauer, B., *Kritik*	8		
Bauer, B., Review	135		
Bauer, B., *Trumpet*	188	Hume, "On Miracles"	12, 76
Baur, F. C., *Paulus*	94	Kant, *Critique of Judgment*	150–151
		Kant, *Critique of Practical Reason*	150, 152–54
Eichhorn, "Uebrige"	107		
Eichhorn, *Urgeschichte*	107	Kant, *Critique of Pure Reason*	24, 48–49
		Kant, *Metaphysical Foundations*	32
Feuerbach, *Essence*	8, 168	Kant, "Old Question"	154–55
		Kant, "On the End of All Things"	151
Fichte, *Science*	31–32	Kant, "On Exaltation"	149–50
		Kant, "On the Sicknesses"	149–54
Göschel, *Aphorismen*	135	Kant, *Prolegomena*	30–31
		Kant, *Religion*	12, 78, 128–29
Hegel, *Encyclopedia*	6, 131	Kant, "What Does It Mean"	150
Hegel, *Lectures*	13		
Hegel, *Phenomenology*	13, 58, 134, 136, 155–66, 181	Kerner, *Erscheinung*	60–65
		Kerner, *Franz Anton Mesmer*	33
		Kerner, *Seeress of Prevorst*	1, 4–5, 9, 26, 35–36, 41, 46, 50–54, 92–93, 106
Hengstenberg, *Evangelische Kirchen-Zeitung*	73–75		
		Kerner and Eschenmayer, *Accounts of the Modern Possessed*	2, 4–5, 9–10, 23–25, 45–48, 54–60, 64–65, 69, 85–86, 89, 92–93, 113, 125, 179, 181
Herder, *Ideas of a Philosophy*	27		
Herder, *Maran Atha*	106		
Herder, "Philosophei und Schwärmerei"	149		
		Kluge, *Versuch*	34

* See Works Cited for full titles.

Krummacher, *Autobiography* 1–3, 8, 162
Krummacher, "The last Judgment" 145–46

Lessing, *Theological Writings* 12
Lessing, *Fragments* 12, 77–78. See also Reimarus

Lowth, *De sacra poesi Haebrorum* 105

Marx, "Toward the Critique of Hegel's Philosophy of Law" 24, 69–70

Mesmer, "Letter" 33
Mesmer, *Mémoire* 33

Nast, "Recollections" 38–39, 42

Neander, *Life* 42, 84, 88, 99–100, 170

Nietzsche, *Untimely Meditations* 22, 193, 195–97

Olshausen, *Biblical Commentary* 42, 86, 90–91, 94, 95–97, 115, 119–24

Overbeck, "How Christian" 193

Parker, "Strauss's Life of Jesus" 186–87

Paulus, *Exegetisches Handbuch* 82–83, 87–88, 95
Paulus, *Das Leben Jesu* 80, 83, 99
Paulus, *Memorabilien* 109

Reil, *Rhapsodieen* 34

Reimarus, *Apologie* 12
Reimarus, *Von dem Zwecke* 77–78, 99, 147, 153
See also Lessing, *Fragments*

Rosenkranz, *Encyclopädie* 135
Rosenkranz, *Kritik* 135

Schelling, *First Outline* 29–30, 32–33
Schelling, *Ideas* 29–30, 32–33
Schelling, "Ueber Mythen" 35, 109
Schelling, *Von der Weltseele* 29, 32

Schleiermacher, *Christian Faith* 12–13, 40–41, 135
Schleiermacher, *Life of Jesus* 94, 98–100
Schleiermacher, *On Religion* 81

Schubert, *Ansichten* 26–29, 104–5
Schubert, *Symbolik* 29–30, 35

Semler, *Abfertigung* 86
Semler, *Abhandlung* 5, 13–14
Semler, *Christliche freye Untersuchung* 106
Semler, *Commentatio* 86

Spinoza, *Ethics* 31
Spinoza, *Tractatus Theologico-Politicus* 11, 79

Strauss, *Ausgewählte Briefe* 98–99, 101
Strauss, *Christ of Faith* 99–104, 124, 183, 189
Strauss, *Christian Märklin* 48
Strauss, *Die christliche Glaubenslehre* 100–101, 138
Strauss, *De resurrectione carnis* 16, 38, 100–102
Strauss, *Hermann Samuel Reimarus* 11
Strauss, "Justinus Kerner," in *Kleine Schriften* 9, 45
Strauss, "Justinus Kerner," in *Zwei Freidliche Blätter* 9, 38, 40, 45
Strauss, *Das Leben Jesu*, 1st ed. 7–8, 69, 179, 188–89, 190, 192
Strauss, *Das Leben Jesu*, 1st ed., vol. 1 7–8, 11, 19, 42, 44, 46–47, 61, 72, 77, 82, 99, 105, 108–13, 118, 125, 129–30, 136–37, 144–47, 152–53, 158, 161, 165, 190
Strauss, *Das Leben Jesu*, 1st ed., vol. 2 7, 69, 81–82, 84–88, 90–98, 115–17,

121–25, 136, 138, 144–45, 163–64, 167–175, 177–78
Strauss, *Das Leben Jesu*, 2nd ed.   118
Strauss, *Das Leben Jesu*, 3rd ed.   88–90, 93, 100, 170
Strauss, *Das Leben Jesu*, 4th ed.   16, 74, 79–80, 110, 112, 114, 118, 137, 159–61
Strauss, "Die Lehre"   16, 101
Strauss, *Life of Jesus* 7–8, 10–22, 42–44, 46–47, 69–104, 107–39, 141–148, 152–53, 156, 158–76, 177–95, 197–98
Strauss, *New Life of Jesus*   8, 152, 168, 188–92, 194
Strauss, *Old Faith and the New*   8, 101, 188, 192–198
Strauss, "On the Science of the Nocturnal Side of Nature"   9, 23–26, 36, 41, 44–66, 91–93, 101, 112–13, 117–18, 181–82
Strauss, *Streitschriften* 13–14, 43, 73–75, 80–81, 126–27, 130–36, 189
Strauss, "Vergangliches und Bleibendes" 88

Tholuck, *Glaubwürdigkeit*   59, 84

Tindal, *Christianity as Old as Creation* 87

Vater, *Commentar*   109

Vischer, "Dr. Strauss"   39, 75

Wegscheider, *Institutiones*   82

Weiland, "Enthusiasmus und Schwärmerei"   149

Wette, de, *Beiträge*   109
Wette, de, *Biblische Dogmatik*   87, 146–47, 151–52, 158–59
Wette, de, *Theodore* 155–56
Wette, de, *Ueber Religion* 146, 156–58

Wurm, "Extracts" 186–87

Modern Authors Index

Bahrdt, Karl Friedrich 99
Baier, Karl 27, 34
Bauer, Bruno 8, 15, 24, 126, 135, 187–88, 197
Bauer, G.L. 107
Baur, Ferdinand C. 14, 38, 40, 69, 73, 94
Bell, Matthew 27, 36
Blackwell, Jeannine 86
Blanton, Ward 15, 22, 125, 185
Boddy, Janice 64
Bolingbroke, Henry St. John 11
Bourguignon, Erika 64
Brazill, William 15
Brecht, Martin 14
Breckman, Warren 15, 22
Cavanaugh, William 148
Chubb, Thomas 11, 77
Colas, Dominique 148
Crabtree, Adam 33
Derrida, Jacques 154
Eichhorn, Johann Gottfried 82, 107–9, 111, 131, 171
Ellenberger, Henri 4, 5, 34
Esquirol, Etienne 5, 86, 120
Fenves, Peter 18–19, 154
Feuerbach, Ludwig 8, 15, 168, 188
Fichte, Johann Gottlieb 30–32, 130–32, 146
Foucault, Michel 18
Frei, Hans 14, 70–71, 78, 162, 168, 182–183
Gassner, Johann Joseph 4, 20, 46
Goldberg, Ann 18, 65–66, 149
Gregory, Frederick 27
Göschel, Karl 135
Hanegraaff, Wouter 22, 27, 34–35
Hartlich, Christian 14, 197
Harvey, Van A. 14–15, 70, 182
Hegel, Georg Wilhelm Friedrich 5–8, 13–16, 24, 29–32, 36, 39, 41–43, 52, 58, 70, 73, 79–81, 101, 104, 119, 126–27, 130–39, 146, 160, 165–66, 174–75, 178, 181–84, 186–189, 197
Hengstenberg, Ernst Wilhelm 73–75, 182
Herder, Johann Gottfried 14, 26–27, 35, 104–6, 109–11, 131, 148–49
Heyne, C.G. 105
Hodgson, Peter 16–17, 37–38, 182–83
Howard, Thomas 146, 149, 158
Hume, David 12, 30–31, 76, 80, 93
Kant, Immanuel 5, 12, 14, 18, 24, 30–32, 38, 41, 43, 48–50, 52–54, 62, 73, 78–79, 81, 100–101, 126–34, 143, 146, 148–58, 161, 168–69, 177, 182, 183, 185
Keller, Mary 64
Kerner, Justinus 1–10, 15–17, 19, 21, 23–26, 33, 34–37, 38–42, 45–66, 69, 70 71, 83–86, 89–90, 91–93, 95, 96–97, 99, 104, 105–6, 108, 120, 125, 143, 176, 178, 179–82
Kluge, Carl Alexander Ferdinand 34
Knudsen, Jonathan B. 65

Krummacher, Friedrich Wilhelm 1–3, 7, 8, 145–46, 162
Lange, Dietz 14, 183
La Vopa, Anthony 18, 149
Legaspi, Michael 11, 127
Lessing, Gotthold 12, 77–78, 131, 146, 182, 193
Lowth, Robert 105
Magee, Glenn Alexander 36
Marx, Karl 8, 15, 24, 69–70, 126, 187–88, 197
Massey, Marilyn 14–15, 21–22, 43, 126, 185, 187
Mee, Jon 18–19
Mesmer, Franz Anton 4–5, 33–35, 149
Michaelis, Johann David 13, 105, 127, 128–29
Midelfort, H.C. Erik 4, 86
Montiel, Luis 27
Morgan, Robert 14–15, 168, 182–83
Morgan, Thomas 11, 77
Müller, Gotthold 14–16, 38
Müller, Karl Otfried 112–13
Nast, William 38–39, 42, 47, 66, 69, 89, 178
Neander, August 42, 84, 88, 99–100, 162, 170
Nietzsche, Friedrich 8, 22, 193, 195–97
Olshausen, Hermann 14, 42, 86, 90–91, 94, 95–98, 115, 119–23, 124, 132, 144, 162, 171, 180, 182
Overbeck, Franz 193
Oyer, John S. 19
Parker, Theodore 186–87
Paul, Jean-Marie 10, 16, 43
Paulus, Heinrich 13, 18, 71, 79, 80, 82–83, 87, 88, 90, 94–99, 108–10, 116–17, 119–20, 127, 130, 131–32, 142, 162, 165, 171, 185
Reil, Christian 34
Reimarus, Hermann Samuel 11, 12, 77–78, 82, 99, 110, 131, 141, 146–47, 153, 155, 158, 182
Rogerson, John W. 157
Rosenberg, Jordana 18–19

Rosenkranz, Karl 135
Sachs, Walter 14, 197
Sanderger, Jörg F. 14, 70, 182
Sawicki, Diethard 27, 36–37
Schelling, F. W. J. von 1, 5, 14, 26, 29–36, 38, 40, 50, 52–53, 58, 63, 70, 73, 79–81, 99, 104, 105, 109–10, 112, 119, 127, 130–34, 136, 180, 182
Schleiermacher, Freidrich 1, 7, 12–14, 40–45, 50, 71, 73, 79–81, 94, 98–100, 119, 122, 124, 127, 132, 135, 142, 145, 162–66, 183, 185, 189
Schneider, Robert 36
Schröter, Jens 184
Schubert, Gotthilf Heinrich von 9, 26–29, 34–35, 45–46, 58, 63, 70, 104–5, 178–80
Schweitzer, Albert 7, 71, 83, 153, 183
Semler, Johann Salomo 5, 13, 20, 82, 86, 106, 127, 131
Sered, Susan Starr 64
Sheehan, Jonathan 11, 105
Spinoza, Baruch 11, 14, 31–32, 79–80, 119
Tholuck, August 59, 69, 84, 88, 99–100, 119, 162, 180, 186
Tindal, Matthew 87
Toews, John Edward 15, 22, 133, 135, 185
Toland, John 11, 77
Toscano, Alberto 19
Troeltsch, Ernst 70
Vater, Johann Severin 109
Vischer, Friedrich 39, 43, 75–76, 98, 101
Weber, Max 3
Wegscheider, Julius August Ludwig 80, 82, 127
Weiland, Christoph 149
Wette, W. M. L. de 13–14, 80, 87–88, 94, 109–14, 117, 142, 143, 146–49, 151–62, 165, 166, 168–69, 184–85, 189, 191
Williamson, George S. 14, 35
Woolston, Thomas 11, 77
Wurm, Johann Friedrich 186–87

Zachhuber, Johannes   15, 182
Zeller, Eduard   38
Ziegler, Theobald   15, 191
Ziolowski, Theodore   27

www.ingramcontent.com/pod-product-compliance
Lightning Source LLC
Chambersburg PA
CBHW021809220426
43662CB00006B/238